Checks in the Balance

Princeton Studies in American Politics: Historical, International, and Comparative Perspectives

Suzanne Mettler, Eric Schickler,
and Theda Skocpol, *Series Editors*

Ira Katznelson and Martin Shefter, *Founding
Series Editors (Emeritus)*

A list of titles in this series appears at the back of the book

Checks in the Balance

LEGISLATIVE CAPACITY AND THE DYNAMICS
OF EXECUTIVE POWER

ALEXANDER BOLTON

SHARECE THROWER

PRINCETON UNIVERSITY PRESS
PRINCETON & OXFORD

Copyright © 2022 by Princeton University Press

Princeton University Press is committed to the protection of copyright and the intellectual property our authors entrust to us. Copyright promotes the progress and integrity of knowledge. Thank you for supporting free speech and the global exchange of ideas by purchasing an authorized edition of this book. If you wish to reproduce or distribute any part of it in any form, please obtain permission.

Requests for permission to reproduce material from this work should be sent to permissions@press.princeton.edu

Published by Princeton University Press
41 William Street, Princeton, New Jersey 08540
6 Oxford Street, Woodstock, Oxfordshire OX20 1TR

press.princeton.edu

All Rights Reserved

Library of Congress Cataloging-in-Publication Data

Names: Bolton, Alexander, 1988– author. | Thrower, Sharece, 1987– author.
Title: Checks in the balance : legislative capacity and the dynamics of executive power / Alexander Bolton, Sharece Thrower.
Description: Princeton, New Jersey : Princeton University Press, [2022] |
    Series: Princeton studies in American politics: historical, international, and comparative perspectives | Includes bibliographical references and index.
    Identifiers: LCCN 2021011354 (print) | LCCN 2021011355 (ebook) |
    ISBN 9780691224596 (paperback) | ISBN 9780691224619 (hardback) |
    ISBN 9780691224602 (ebook)
Subjects: LCSH: Executive-legislative relations—United States. | Executive
    power—United States. | Separation of powers—United States. |
    United States—Politics and government. | Legislative power—United States. |
    Policy sciences—United States.
Classification: LCC JK585 .B5145 2022 (print) | LCC JK585 (ebook) |
    DDC 328.7307/456–dc23
LC record available at https://lccn.loc.gov/2021011354
LC ebook record available at https://lccn.loc.gov/2021011355

British Library Cataloging-in-Publication Data is available

Editorial: Bridget Flannery-O'Connor and Alena Chekanov
Production Editorial: Kathleen Cioffi
Cover Design: Karl Spurzem
Production: Erin Suydam
Publicity: Kate Hensley and Kathryn Stevens

This book has been composed in Arno

10 9 8 7 6 5 4 3 2 1

To our parents—Jeffrey, Elizabeth, Joseph, and Sharon.

CONTENTS

ACKNOWLEDGMENTS

We first imagined the idea for this book as graduate students in the Department of Politics at Princeton University. The exact location of its origins is disputed between the authors. One of us claims we were working in 126 Corwin Hall when the idea first struck, while the other insists we were idling in the third-floor fishbowl of Robertson Hall. In any case, numerous people helped nurture this idea along the way to whom we are indebted.

We would first like to thank our graduate school mentors, Chuck Cameron, Brandice Canes-Wrone, and Nolan McCarty, for their steady guidance and mentorship in our first experiences with research and publishing. Thank you to our former graduate student and faculty colleagues at Princeton and the University of Pittsburgh for being helpful audiences in workshopping our very early ideas for this book.

We likewise extend our gratitude to the attendees of our book conference, particularly Thad Kousser, George Krause, Doug Kriner, Chuck Shipan, and Gisela Sin. We appreciate their thoughtful engagement with our work, as well as the extensive feedback, assistance, and encouragement we received from them before, during, and after the conference. Thank you to several colleagues at Vanderbilt University for hosting and participating in our book conference and for generously commenting on various drafts of the manuscript over the years.

Sharece would like to give a shout-out to the fantastic graduate students who took her American Presidency course at Vanderbilt in the spring of 2019: Georgia Anderson-Nilsson, Nick Bednar, Rich Hagner, Meredith McLain, Chris Piper, and Mary Catherine Sullivan. They all provided excellent feedback on the manuscript, participated in our book conference, and gave me life with detailed analysis of current reality TV shows. Our book has also greatly benefited from the countless hours of work by several brilliant undergraduate and graduate student research assistants at Vanderbilt and Pitt: Sean Craig, Justin Hutchings, Claire Larson, Jack Millard, Cassie Schwartz, Kelly Shearin,

Darrian Stacy, Channing Thomas, and Matt Zarit. We really could not have done this without them.

Alex would like to thank all his colleagues at Emory University for their support, particularly Tom Clark and John Patty for their feedback and advice in navigating the writing and publishing process. Many Emory graduate and undergraduate students contributed substantially to the project through their fantastic research assistance: Justin Cohen, Anna Gunderson, Michael Hanley, Dahae Lee, and Christopher Thomas. It was a pleasure to work with them over the years, and we are so grateful for their efforts. We would also like to express our gratitude to the College of Arts and Sciences and Laney Graduate School at Emory for financially supporting this project.

Thank you to Linda Fowler, Doug Kriner, Jason MacDonald, and Eric Schickler for generously sharing their data, and for inspiring much of our work. We would also like to express our gratitude to the numerous panelists, audiences, and discussants at various conferences, workshops, and seminars where we have presented this work at over the years. We have learned immensely from their feedback during these invaluable experiences. They enriched our research, and we are better scholars for it.

A very special thanks to our wonderful editor, Bridget Flannery-McCoy, for believing in our project and going above and beyond to ensure its success. Her guidance and encouragement were integral to the development of our project. We cannot imagine a better or more supportive editor, and we are so grateful to have worked with her. We are also indebted to Brigid Ackerman, Alena Chekanov, Kathleen Cioffi, Kate Hensley, Emily Shelton, Karl Spurzem, Kathryn Stephens, and the rest of the PUP team for providing such a positive and seamless publication process. Thank you to the anonymous reviewers who carefully read the manuscript (when it was much longer!) and offered detailed, constructive feedback. We appreciate their time and insights. Our book is all the better for it.

We offer our sincere thanks to Dave Lewis—an incredible colleague, mentor, and friend. Not only did he read multiple drafts of every chapter, but he offered us heartfelt encouragement at the times we needed it most. Special thanks to Alan Wiseman for also devoting substantial time in reading our manuscript. He has constantly provided critical support and mentorship, ever since saving one of us from attending law school as an undergrad. George Krause has given us some of the most spot-on, in-depth, and timely feedback on this book project and too many other papers to name. Words cannot express how grateful we are for his outstanding mentorship and the positive impact he has had on our careers.

We'd like to thank a number of people who have kept us sane. We are grateful to many of our graduate school peers, including Scott Abramson, Carolyn Abott, Matt Barnes, Mike Barber, PJ Gardner, Yanilda Gonzalez, and Erin Lin, for their grounding friendship throughout the years. Thanks to Allison Anoll for being a friend and constant support system as we navigated the writing process together. Thank you to Celine Dion and Alexz Johnson (the Instant Star catalog) for sustaining our friendship as we worked into the late hours of the night at Robertson Hall.

To my (Sharece) dear husband Ben Leven, who is the best thing that's happened to me and my research: I thank him for his constant encouragement when I'm down, his listening ear when I need a sounding board, his infectious humor when I need a distracting laugh, and for being the best hype man I could ever ask for. Thank you to my fantastic friends and family from around the country, in Nashville, Pittsburgh, Ohio, Alabama, Atlanta, Rochester, Chicago, New York, DC, and Boston, for supporting me in more ways than they'll ever know.

I'd (Alex) like to thank all my family and friends for their love and for lifting my spirits every day. Special thanks to my cat Fifi for his welcome interruptions while writing. I hope we were able to catch all the typos he created walking across my keyboard.

And finally, we'd like to express our deepest gratitude to our parents: Jeffrey and Elizabeth Bolton, and Joseph and Sharon Thrower. They are the pillars of who we are, whose unfailing love, support, encouragement, faith, and strength have upheld us while writing this book, throughout our careers, and far beyond. We dedicate this book to you.

ABBREVIATIONS

ABA	American Bar Association
APA	Administrative Procedure Act
APP	American Presidency Project
APSA	American Political Science Association
BOE	Bureau of Efficiency
CAP	Comparative Agendas Project
CBO	Congressional Budget Office
CDC	Centers for Disease Control and Prevention
CIS	Congressional Information Service
CRS	Congressional Research Service
EO	Executive order
EOP	Executive Office of the President
FDA	Food and Drug Administration
FY	Fiscal year
GAO	General Accountability (Accounting) Office
GDP	Gross domestic product
GSA	General Services Administration
ICC	Interstate Commerce Commission
IG	Inspector general
INA	Immigration and Nationality Act
JCOC	Joint Committee on the Organization of Congress
LRA	Legislative Reorganization Act
LRS	Legislative Reference Service
MRA	Members' Representational Allowance

NCSL   National Conference of State Legislatures

OMB   Office of Management and Budget

OTA   Office of Technology Assessment

SDI   Strategic Defense Initiative

USRA   United States Railroad Administration

WIB   War Industries Board

Checks in the Balance

1

Executive Power in the Shadow of Legislative Capacity

It is a core tenet of this Nation's founding that the powers of a monarch must be split between the branches of the government to prevent tyranny . . . Stated simply, the primary takeaway from the past 250 years of recorded American history is that Presidents are not kings.

— COMMITTEE ON THE JUDICIARY, UNITED STATES HOUSE OF REPRESENTATIVES V. DONALD F. MCGAHN

In ruling against the Trump administration's claims of "absolute testimonial immunity" to ignore congressional subpoenas, the DC District Court (quoted above) reminded the parties involved that the US separation of powers system was created to preclude the concentration of power in the hands of any one individual or institution, not least among them the president.[1] Informed by their experiences with colonial rule, the Constitution's framers indeed designed a system of competition to ensure no one branch of government mastered the others.

Though many at the time feared Congress and state legislatures would come to dominate governments, others predicted the executive branch would eventually pose the greatest threat. In a letter to his colleague James Madison, Thomas Jefferson wrote, "The tyranny of the legislature is really the danger most to be feared and will continue to be for many years to come. The tyranny of the executive power will come in its turn, but at a more distant period."[2] Madison, however, believed separation of powers would preclude that scenario. Writing in defense of this system, he argued functional governments required a "necessary partition of power among the several departments" with proper checks and balances, so that the branches would keep "each other in their proper places." In his now-famous dictum, "Ambition must be made to counteract ambition" (Hamilton, Madison, and Jay 2009).

In this book, we argue ambition is not enough to prevent the aggrandizement of executive power, even in a system where shared responsibilities impel institutional rivalries. Instead, legislatures must possess the political will *and the institutional capacity* to assert their authority and effectively constrain the executive branch. Capacity is central for understanding when executive power will flourish in a separated system and when it will be more equitably distributed across the branches.

Whether balance is actually maintained in US separation of powers systems is a critical debate in public and academic discourses. The specter of unbridled executive power looms large in the American political imagination, and presidents have not been reluctant to articulate sweeping visions of their authority. As the first wave of the COVID-19 pandemic raged in spring of 2020, President Donald Trump found himself at odds with governors who imposed myriad stay-at-home orders and business closures. Speaking from the White House, he presented a muscular view of his ability to override gubernatorial edicts: "When somebody's the president of the United States, the authority is total." Though he claimed this statement was validated by "numerous provisions" of the Constitution, it was quickly rebuked by many constitutional scholars and politicians, even those from his own party.[3]

Trump is hardly the first president to offer forceful claims of authority for his office. Confronting congressional gridlock, Barack Obama declared his intention to bypass legislative opponents in pursuit of his policy agenda, asserting, "I've got a pen to take executive actions where Congress won't and I've got a telephone to rally folks around the country on this mission."[4] George W. Bush embraced expansive presidential prerogatives to justify signing statements designed to negate parts of the law and controversial national security powers, such as expansive wiretapping, enhanced interrogation, and indefinite detention. Decades earlier, Richard Nixon defended his actions during the Watergate scandal by virtue of merely being president, declaring in a 1977 interview with journalist David Frost, "When the president does it that means it is not illegal."[5]

Many argue this "imperial" view of presidential power has grown increasingly common over time (Healy 2008; Rudalevige 2008; Schlesinger 1973).

As one political observer recently noted, "Trump per se isn't the problem. Power is the problem, and years and the chickens we have so carefully raised by weakening constraints on the executive branch are finally coming home to roost."[6]

Some academics, too, believe such expansions of executive power have undermined the US separation of powers system. Law professor Neal Devins, for example, calls checks and balances in the contemporary era "an abject failure."[7] Professor Peter Shane contends we are currently living in "Madison's nightmare," as the separation of powers system grows "increasingly battered" by the "gathering concentration of power in the hands of the federal executive" (2009, 3). Pessimism reigns regarding legislatures' ability to redress encroaching executive power. Posner and Vermeule (2010, 14) write, "The administrative state does indeed feature an imperial executive; the critics are wrong only in thinking that anything can be done about this fact."

Fears of executive overreach likewise pervade state governments, where gubernatorial power comes under the microscope. Like presidents, governors also advance capacious views of their executive prerogatives. In 2015, New York Governor Andrew Cuomo remarked: "I am the executive and therefore I use executive power. . . . I have many powers beyond those which the Legislature passes . . . the executive, whether it's the President, the mayor or the governor, you run the government. . . . And you have a whole host of powers that are apart and aside from the Legislature."[8]

The COVID-19 pandemic alerted many to the broad powers governors wield, as decisions to issue stay-at-home orders and mandate health requirements for businesses became subjects of national controversy. While most applauded gubernatorial actions to quell the deadly pandemic, others decried executive abuses. In a letter to the Oregon Legislature, Jackson County commissioners demanded limitations on Governor Kate Brown's puissant emergency powers, pleading: "While this level of authority may be appropriate for a short-term state of emergency caused by a fire, earthquake, or other natural disaster, as applied to an emergency like the novel coronavirus, the Governor has essentially unchecked authority to issue orders for an unlimited amount of time which dramatically impact the lives of everyday Oregonians."[9]

In this book, we ask a series of questions related to these lamentations: Is there a balance of power between the branches of government, in line with Madison's vision? Or are legislatures dominated by overpowered executives, as many fear? What resources and policymaking opportunities do legislatures need to constrain executives? Do American legislatures possess them? What are the implications for executive power and its limits? How do these dynamics vary across time and contexts? The answers to these questions have profound consequences for the distribution of institutional power in the United States. These concerns are not just academic. They are also the subject of ongoing policy debates.

Members of Congress and policy experts alike attribute at least part of what they see as ebbing legislative power to their declining institutional resources. A new wave of reformers has emerged intent on bolstering congressional capacity. For example, the Legislative Branch Capacity Working Group was founded in 2016 to "assess the capacity of Congress to perform its duties" and "to collaborate on ideas for improving the legislative branch's performance in our separation of powers system."[10] These efforts are complemented by the House Select Committee on the Modernization of Congress, created in 2019 to study issues regarding legislative capacity. Broadly, this reform movement advances proposals to enhance staff size, salaries, expertise, and other resources. However, the questions of whether these remedies would effectively restrain presidential action, and the degree to which legislative power has actually diminished, have received less scrutiny.

We agree that whether a separation of powers system fails or succeeds depends on legislatures' capacity to challenge the executive branch. We develop a theory specifying a new understanding of what legislative capacity is as well as how and when it matters for legislatures *and* executives. When their capacity is lacking, legislatures struggle to check executive power. We further delineate the direct and indirect effects of capacity on executives' incentives for unilateralism. Presidents and governors can act alone to shift policies, potentially in ways that make legislative majorities worse off relative to the status quo. When legislative capacity is high, however, executives will hew closer to the legislature's preferences. Under these circumstances, they will forbear from using their relatively diminished discretion to act against highly capable legislative majorities for fear of retribution. Whether executive power is thwarted or thrives thus depends on legislatures' capacity for constraint, not just their will. We leverage rich variation in legislative capacity at the federal and state levels to provide empirical support for these new conceptual and theoretical arguments, demonstrating its effects on discretion, oversight, and executive unilateralism. Across time and contexts, our results reveal that legislative constraint over presidential or gubernatorial prerogatives is far from constant. Separation of powers does not guarantee executive restraint.

Overall, our argument and its accompanying evidence demonstrate legislative capacity is at the heart of separation of powers politics in the United States and affirms the importance of legislatures in checking executive power. Yet scholarly and public attention has traditionally focused elsewhere.

Separation of Powers Politics and Policymaking

Since World War II, US politics has experienced a surge in interparty polarization and incidences of divided partisan control between the presidency and Congress. Unsurprisingly, executive-legislative conflicts are often at the forefront of public and academic discourse regarding public policy. Research in this area clearly demonstrates these interbranch dynamics have strong effects on policymaking outcomes, particularly with respect to lawmaking, appropriations, and appointments (e.g., Binder 1999; Cameron 2000; Howell et al. 2000; Jones 2001; Kirkland and Phillips 2018; Krehbiel 1998; McCarty 2015).

Such findings are perhaps unsurprising given the assent of *both* legislatures and executives is generally required for these activities in systems of separate, but shared powers. But are legislative preferences still influential in policymaking where only action by the executive is necessary? Can legislatures constrain the exercise of executive unilateral power? And, if so, why? After all, presidents and governors can seemingly pursue policies unilaterally that Congress and state legislatures cannot amend, given the debilitating gridlock and perpetual delay inherent to lawmaking. Despite provocative presidential rhetoric, many empirical studies of unilateralism do not reveal an executive unbound. Instead, the literature largely finds that legislatures confine executive power, even when they have divergent political and policy goals.

Many studies, for instance, demonstrate interbranch divisions motivate legislative activities, such as oversight, discretion, budgets, and appointments, to restrain the executive branch (e.g., Epstein and O'Halloran 1999; Kriner and Schickler 2016; Lewis 2004; McGrath 2013). Other research shows executives alter their policymaking actions in the face of partisan opposition in Congress, issuing fewer unilateral actions, such as executive orders, proclamations, and memoranda (e.g., Belco and Rottinghaus 2017; Howell 2003; Lowande 2014; Mayer 2002), relying less on other administrative activities like rulemaking (Potter and Shipan 2019; Yackee and Yackee 2009; Acs 2019), and even reducing the use of military force internationally (e.g., Howell and Pevehouse 2007). The fact that executives adjust their behavior in this way implies they face constraints from legislative actors, even for ostensibly independent powers like unilateral actions.[11]

The juxtaposition of the expansive views of executive power described at the outset of the chapter with these findings presents numerous unresolved puzzles about separation of powers systems in the United States: Why are there high levels of executive restraint, particularly since the rising prevalence of divided government and gridlock should increase incentives for unilateral action? What mechanisms underlie these patterns? Do such findings manifest across time and space, or are there contexts where we observe less legislative constraint and thus greater executive ambition? Answering these questions requires a deeper examination of the institutional capacities of legislatures. Specifically, we highlight their opportunities for challenging executive power and the resources available to act upon those opportunities.

What Is Legislative Capacity?

In general, institutional capacity is the ability of an institution to execute the core functions of its mission. In the case of legislatures, these functions encompass, but are not limited to, representation, constituent services, and legislation. Here, we highlight activities most implicated in constraining executive actors, including executive branch oversight, crafting legislation to limit bureaucratic discretion (i.e., the leeway given to executive actors when implementing the law) or to undermine executive policy actions, and generating policy information required for all of these endeavors.

We depart substantially from previous conceptualizations of legislative capacity, by arguing it can be divided into two distinct domains: *resource capacity* and *policymaking capacity*. We define the former as the tangible materials and human capital legislatures can acquire, usually through financial means, to carry out their core tasks. For example, legislators require a sufficient number of qualified, expert, and experienced staff to manage their legislative and oversight duties. Staffers research policy alternatives, draft legislation, maintain contact with executive agencies, and prepare questions for oversight hearings.

We additionally spotlight policymaking capacity, which we define as the opportunities afforded to legislatures to influence the development and implementation of public policy. These opportunities are typically conferred through the institutional rules that define legislative power. Policymaking capacity is largely missing from contemporary discussions of congressional capacity but plays a somewhat larger role in research on state legislatures, where scholars sometimes consider factors like session length. The opportunities for legislatures to influence policy, however, are much broader and encompass an array of statutory and nonstatutory tools. Oversight hearings, agenda power, legislative vetoes, appointment and confirmation powers all offer mechanisms for legislatures to impose costs on executives for acting against their interests and may deter such actions in the first place. Importantly, many of these tools do not require supermajorities to execute, which allows legislatures to employ them as ex post checks on the executive even under circumstances of gridlock.

Our conceptualization of legislative capacity is not merely a taxonomic enterprise. Instead, we argue these distinct domains interact to determine the degree to which legislatures can advance their interests in the policymaking process. *Both* policymaking and resource capacities are necessary conditions for legislatures to be high-capacity institutions in our conceptual framework. Lacking either leaves them illequipped to constrict executive power.

Legislative capacity is by no means a fixed or predetermined entity. It has varied substantially in both historical and contemporary eras, across Congress and state legislatures. These changes, which we explain and leverage throughout the book, have produced significant consequences for the distribution of policymaking power in the United States and for the question of whether executive power is constrained in different contexts.

Transformations in Legislative Capacity across Time and Context

Writing in 1888, British statesman Lord Bryce observed, "Congress . . . has succeeded in occupying most of the ground which the Constitution left debatable between the president and itself" (Bryce 1995 [1888], 203). Presidents in the nineteenth century, particularly after the Civil War, are frequently described as forgotten clerks who left little imprint on the institution (Neustadt 1990 [1960]). Given its constitutional powers and the limited functions of the government in the early republic, Congress naturally became the center of US governance and dominated federal policymaking during this era.

Yet, by the turn of the twentieth century, Congress found itself outmatched by the growing technological, social, and economic challenges facing the country and an energetic executive branch seemingly better positioned to manage these dramatic developments (Cooper 2017). The federal government undertook unprecedented economic and social interventions that continued through the New Deal and World War II.

Presidents responded to this shift in the locus of policymaking power by seizing greater control over executive branch agencies, typically with congressional acquiescence. During the first four decades of the twentieth century, Congress responded little in terms of institutional change to the extraordinary policy developments it was itself creating. As the federal government expanded, Congress stayed the same and consequently became relatively less powerful. Legislative staff sizes barely increased, spending on the institution stagnated, and the public showed little appetite for augmenting congressional resources and power. As shown in figure 1.1, Congress spent $229 million (in 2009 dollars) on itself and employed 225 committee staffers in 1905.[12] But by 1935, these figures grew little in real terms, to only $248 million and 294 staffers. While some improvements did occur during this period (e.g., the creation of the Legislative Research Service and the Government Accounting Office), by and large Congress's capacity lagged behind the quickly changing nature of American governance.

Motivated by the desire to equalize power between the two branches, this institutional disparity belatedly led to numerous legislative reforms. Prodded by legislative entrepreneurs like Senator Robert LaFollette, and outside groups such as the American Bar Association and the American Political Science Association, Congress assembled broad, bipartisan coalitions to enact major reforms augmenting its capacity, including the Legislative Reorganization Acts of 1946 and 1970. New legislative support institutions, such as the Congressional Budget Office (CBO) and the Office of Technology Assessment, promised to afford legislators access to unbiased, policy-relevant information independent of the executive branch.

Indeed, the need for self-sufficiency was a commonly cited rationale for these reforms. When creating the CBO in 1974, for example, the reporting committee noted, "Compared to the president, Congress is in a disadvantaged position for making budgetary decisions. Congress does not have its own budget staff and it must rely upon the President for information, judgments, and evaluations. . . . All this makes Congress painfully dependent upon Presidential agencies. . . . It gets only what the executive gives, and only when the executive gives it" (H. Rpt. 93-579, 7).

Accordingly, congressional resource capacity rapidly increased following these mid-twentieth century reforms, as depicted in figure 1.1. Legislative expenditures surged dramatically, reaching a peak of $5.8 billion in 2010, and

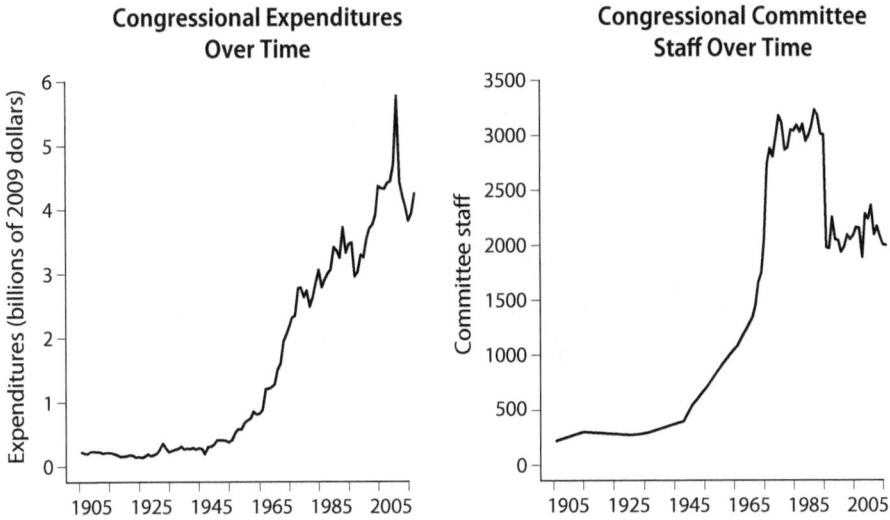

FIGURE 1.1. Congressional expenditures, in billions of 2009 dollars (left), and the number of congressional committee staff (right), between 1905 and 2015.

hovered between $4 billion and $5 billion throughout most of the twenty-first century. At the same time, committee staffing also rose dramatically, but crested earlier in the late 1980s and early 1990s (3,231 staffers in 1991). Importantly, resources have also *decreased* at times. New Republican majorities in the 1990s, for instance, reduced staffing to fulfill their Contract with America's central tenet of curtailing congressional spending.

Legislative capacity in US states has likewise ebbed and flowed. State constitutional framers too were scarred by their colonial origins, initially designing constitutions featuring robust legislative power and weak governors. Chief executives gradually acquired additional powers, such as qualified vetoes and appointments, to better counterbalance once omnipotent legislatures (e.g., Squire 2012). Yet states today still differ considerably in the relative balance of executive and legislative power. Some states' governments, for instance, only require a simple majority to override a gubernatorial veto, while others mandate a two-thirds supermajority. Other legislative powers, like the amount of time legislators spend in session, have likewise fluctuated historically within and across states, which has implications for the manifestation of gubernatorial authority (Bolton and Thrower forthcoming).

State legislative resources also vary, featuring periods of expanding resource capacity and decline. For instance, the top panel of figure 1.2 illustrates

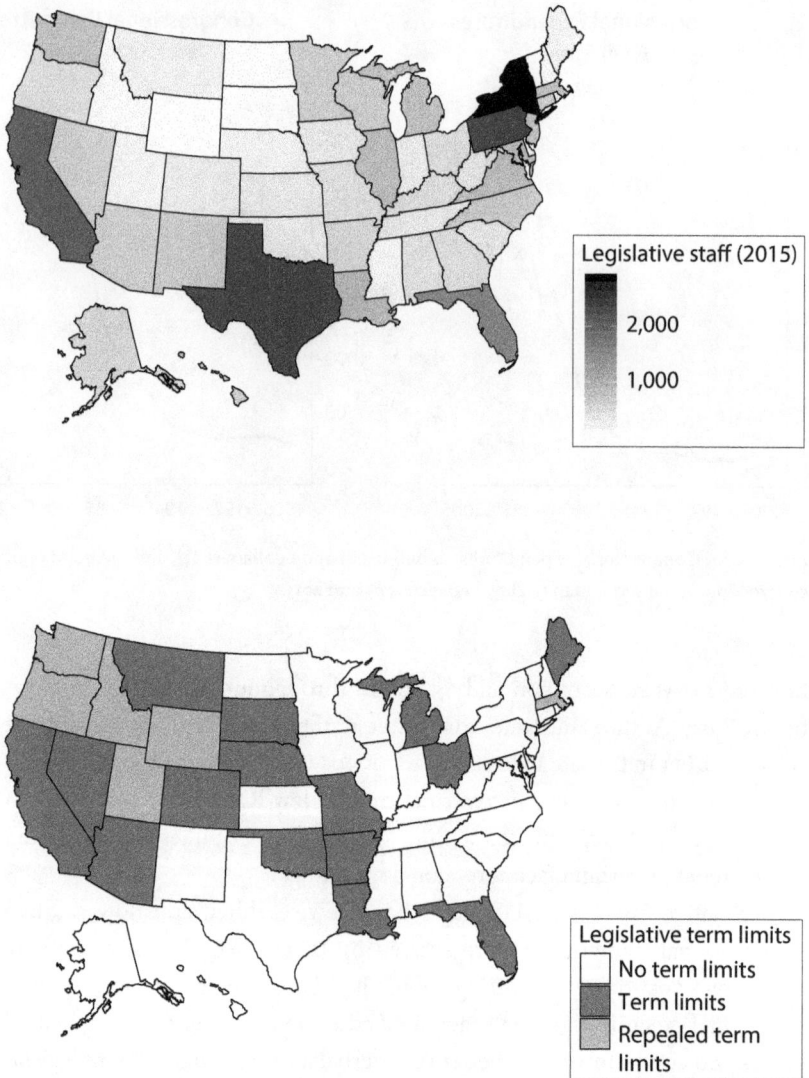

FIGURE 1.2. Staffing numbers and the incidence of term limits across the US states in 2015.

differences in total staff available for each state legislature in 2015. States like New York, California, and Texas employed the most legislative staff with each exceeding two thousand total individuals, while others such as Delaware, Idaho, and Vermont all maintained less than two hundred staffers. Additionally, the 1980s and 1990s ushered in a wave of new term limit reforms that restricted the time legislators could hold office. These reforms have been the subject of much scholarly research, due to their implications for legislators' turnover and human capital (e.g., Kousser 2005). As the bottom panel of figure 1.2 demonstrates, many states have implemented (e.g., Ohio, Florida, Nevada) and in some cases subsequently removed (e.g., Washington, Massachusetts, Oregon) these restrictions, while others never imposed them in the first place (e.g., Tennessee, Wisconsin, and Pennsylvania). Overall, just like Congress, there is substantial variation in state legislative capacity, which has profound consequences for separation of power politics.

Executive Power through the Lens of Legislative Capacity

Accordingly, we develop a new understanding of interbranch policymaking and executive power that brings legislative capacity to the fore to answer two central questions. First, how does a legislature's capacity influence its ability to constrain the executive branch in pursuit of its policy and political goals? Second, how does legislative capacity shape executive incentives to exercise power, particularly through unilateral actions?

Theoretical Argument and Contributions

Briefly, we argue that a legislature's capacity has a direct impact on its production of ex ante and ex post constraints on the executive. Legislative capacity, furthermore, can moderate the effects of executive-legislative disagreement on such policymaking activities. While legislatures might want to check executives in different circumstances, they can only do so when endowed with sufficient resources and opportunities to make policies. In this way, their ability to act according to their ideological and other motivations is limited by their institutional capacity. When capacity is plentiful, legislative majorities can constrict executive branch discretion. They can likewise deploy, or threaten, ex post sanctions for executives using discretion in ways they find unfavorable. These ex ante and ex post control mechanisms act in concert to restrain executives and are not perfectly substitutable.

Of course, we are not the first to posit legislative capacity as important for legislative outputs. Similar to previous scholars (e.g., Huber and Shipan 2002; McGrath 2013), we argue capacity should moderate the relationship between interbranch policy disagreement and legislative actions limiting executive power, like oversight and laws restricting discretion. Differing from these studies, we jointly analyze ex post and ex ante activities, asserting both are necessary for executive constraint. Further, we contend capacity can influence these activities under divided or unified government, though to a greater extent for the former.

Although legislative capacity has more or less straightforward consequences for legislative outputs, a key contribution of this book is to unite disparate literatures to understand its incentive effects for executives' behavior— even for *unilateral* actions that do not ostensibly implicate legislatures. The prospect of unfettered unilateral power poses stark challenges to separation of powers systems, seemingly allowing executives to "evade" adversarial legislatures to obtain more favorable outcomes than what they might achieve from the legislative process. We argue, however, such an evasion strategy is premised on the idea that executives do not expect retribution if they use their discretion against legislative interests. This assumption might be true when legislatures lack either the resources or the opportunities to impose such constraints. Yet, when legislatures maintain the opportunities and means for confronting executive power, executives must tread more carefully. If they use their discretion to unilaterally shift policies in opposition to legislative preferences, chief executives may face costly punishment, either directly or indirectly related to the policy. Whether executives can expect such sanctions of course, depends on legislative capacity. In the face of interbranch conflict, executive power prospers under diminished legislative capacity, but recedes when encountering legislatures properly equipped with resources and opportunities. Importantly, both domains of legislative capacity are necessary, but not alone sufficient, conditions for executive constraint.

Our argument has important implications for assessing the nature of executive power and resolves a central tension in the study of American politics. While political observers view executives as being able to freely brandish unilateral actions to bypass unfriendly legislatures, political scientists repeatedly find modern presidents decrease their reliance on unilateralism in the face of congressional opposition. Yet few explore the theoretical and empirical underpinnings of this counterintuitive result. By highlighting legislative capacity, our theory identifies what legislatures need to constrain executives. In doing so, we can identify conditions under which presidents and governors should forbear from unilateralism or when executive power will flourish. In relating capacity to unilateral action, moreover, we acknowledge the centrality of legislative power for executive constraint.

While our theoretical account might appear obvious to some readers, it runs counter to recent scholarship questioning whether legislatures—or any other institution, for that matter—perform a meaningful role in tempering executive power. Much of this literature instead promotes the public, and threats of its disapproval, as the most effective check. According to Posner and Vermeule (2010, 4), "The major constraints on the executive do not arise from law or from the separation-of-powers framework . . . but from politics and public opinion." Christenson and Kriner (2020, 26) reinforce this view: "Because the institutional checks exercised by Congress and the courts are so weak, public opinion may be the last and most important check on the unilateral president."

We recognize the serious institutional constraints legislatures encounter when passing laws, highlighted by these and other scholars. However, the consistent findings of executive responsiveness to *congressional* preferences indicate it may be premature to jettison legislative explanations of executive constraint. By acknowledging that legislatures' powers go well beyond passing laws and further exploring how policymaking opportunities, resources, and interbranch division interact, we gain important insights into what they need to curb executive power.

We do not reject the idea that the public informs executive action. Indeed, our account reinforces some of these dynamics. For instance, Christenson and Kriner (2020) show how congressional "fire alarms" can raise controversy over presidential actions and diminish public support. We posit Congress needs capacity to actually pull the alarm, an activity that requires information, along with other resources, to investigate and publicize executive violations. These same capacities endow legislatures with the means to impose ex ante and ex post constraints that curtail unilateralism in other ways. In sum, our argument affirms the centrality of legislatures, and by extension separation of powers politics, to executive constraint through a variety of mechanisms.

Empirical Findings and Contributions

We use numerous original datasets to empirically evaluate these claims. First, we collect new historical data on congressional capacity, beginning in the early twentieth century. In the aggregate, we employ data on overall committee staffers and legislative expenditures. At the committee and subcommittee levels, we rely upon congressional directories dating back to the 1950s to develop annual measures of staff sizes, along with staffer and member experience to characterize human capital. Unlike previous congressional studies that mostly examine one of these resources at a time, we use multiple measures of capacity in various legislative contexts to provide validation of our theory.

Second, we offer comprehensive qualitative and quantitative analyses of the historical origins and political dynamics underlying both congressional and state legislative capacity (chapters 3 and 7, respectively). Previous research considering capacity typically assumes it to be exogenous. By studying the evolution of legislative capacity, we can not only better understand its political development, but also improve the quality of our empirical inferences about its effects on legislative and executive behavior.

Third, we analyze the consequences of legislative capacity and partisan division for ex ante and ex post mechanisms of control over the executive branch. With respect to the former, we use a measure of discretion based on the federal appropriations process (chapter 4), which yields a consistent and comparable characterization of discretionary authority for more than three hundred agencies from fiscal years 1960–2012. We likewise explore a variety of measures capturing the frequency and intensity of congressional oversight activities, at both the chamber and committee levels (chapter 5). With our combined data, we offer the most comprehensive study of congressional discretion and oversight to date, clarifying a literature conflicted about when, and even if, capacity matters. We uncover strong overall support for our hypotheses, demonstrating that Congress's ability to limit discretion and engage in oversight to achieve its goals depends fundamentally on its resources. While capacity is typically ignored in legislative research (especially at the federal level), our analyses demonstrate its importance for producing familiar empirical findings in the literature on the consequences of interbranch division.

Next, we leverage annual variation in congressional capacity to examine its impact on executive unilateralism. By compiling a dataset of presidential executive orders issued between 1905 and 2019 (chapter 6), we show patterns of evasion or constraint depend centrally on congressional capacity. Prominent scholarly findings of constraint in the modern era are not inevitable, but the product of a series of mid-twentieth-century reforms enacted by Congress to invigorate its capacity. Moreover, we link data on executive orders by issue area to our measure of discretion developed in chapter 4, illustrating the way presidents rely more extensively on unilateralism when they retain greater perceived leeway from Congress in a particular policy area. This empirical test provides direct support for the mechanisms underlying our theory by confirming one key way capacity connects legislative and executive action.

We further evaluate our theory in the US states, which feature many structural similarities to the federal separated system. Importantly, though, there are vast differences between and within states over time, in *both* policymaking and resource capacities. The former has remained sufficiently elevated in Congress (see chapter 3), thus precluding a full assessment of our theoretical claims in the federal context. Variation in the US states, however, facilitates the testing of our predictions about how both domains of capacity interact to affect executive power. We do not examine state governments hoping to merely replicate the findings of the federal analysis. *Instead, the states provide the key test for the sum of our theoretical claims.*

There are few studies of executive unilateralism in the states, most of which consider a limited time frame or a single issue area. Here, we assemble the most exhaustive dataset of over twenty-five thousand state executive orders, spanning all fifty states between 1993 and 2013 (chapter 7). Unlike existing state politics studies that either focus on a singular aspect of legislative capacity or aggregate multiple domains into one additive index (e.g., legislative professionalism), we offer several measures of our two dimensions of capacity. Similar to our federal analyses, we capture resource capacity using staffing, as well as factors like legislative expenditures and term limits. We operationalize policymaking capacity through numerous legislative powers that vary across and within states over time, such as veto override thresholds, majority party agenda-setting power, and regulatory review. In doing so, we engage seriously with the two distinct concepts of legislative capacity to understand their individual and interactive effects on executive unilateralism.

We believe the sum of these conceptual, theoretical, and empirical contributions advances the study of legislative-executive interactions in the United States. By bringing legislative capacity to the fore of our analysis and examining executive power through its lens, we gain new insights into the conditions necessary for constraint in separation of powers systems. These insights have important implications for understanding the dynamics of institutional power in both the federal and subnational contexts.

Summary and Conclusion

The first article in the inaugural issue of the *American Political Science Review*, "The Usurped Powers of the Senate," by A. Maurice Low, studied whether the balance of power between the House, Senate, and the president had strayed from constitutional intent. Since its publication more than a century ago, political scientists remain intrigued by the political dynamics of executive-legislative conflict and the degree to which one branch may overpower the other. Scholars have extensively probed these interactions, yielding deep insights about how the branches of government interact in the policymaking process, how different institutional features influence their bargaining, and how the actions of one branch affect the incentives and strategies of the other.

Recognizing this long line of outstanding research, we offer a different understanding of interbranch relations by examining executive power through the lens of legislatures. We do so by bringing legislative capacity to the vanguard of study. Previous literature on separation of powers mostly centers on how partisan and ideological division between these two branches drives public policy choices. We argue, however, that many of those relationships—on both the legislative *and* executive sides—are contingent to an unacknowledged degree of legislative capacity.

In the process, we offer an important conceptual distinction between two domains of legislative capacity: policymaking and resource capacities. Both work in concert to forge the incentives of executives engaging in unilateralism. Centering the narrative on legislative capacity sheds light on the puzzle of why executives are restrained in some contexts, but not others. In this way, we directly link legislative capacity, legislative activities, and executive behavior in a way that has not been previously done, emphasizing the centrality of legislatures for executive constraint.

Consequently, we can better discern whether and when our democratic system of separation of powers operates truly as the constitutional framers intended. Though Madison seemed confident the "ambitions" of one individual or branch of government would be properly checked by the others, we illuminate conditions under which this principle fails. Legislators, and any other political actors for that matter, require not only the *will* but also the *ability* to check other branches of government and prevent the aggrandizement of any one institution. As such, capacity is crucial for understanding the distribution of power in American governance.

2

Legislative Capacity, Executive Action, and Separation of Powers

Amid public controversies surrounding Facebook's role in propagating misinformation from Russian intelligence during the 2016 election, US senators convened a 2018 joint hearing of the Judiciary and the Commerce, Science, and Transportation Committees to probe the company's data policies and practices. While Facebook CEO Mark Zuckerberg certainly received his fair share of ridicule after the hearing, reports did not cast senators in a particularly flattering light either. Exchanges between Zuckerberg and the committee members illuminated the lawmakers' widespread technical illiteracies and limited knowledge of how complex corporations operate.

The senators posed uninformed, and at times comical, questions during the hearing. Senator Orrin Hatch (R-UT) asked, "How do you sustain a business model in which users do not pay for your service?"—a strange question given that advertising, Facebook's key source of revenue, was at the center of the hearing. Senator Brian Schatz (D-HI) inquired about the popular encrypted messaging (non-email) application, WhatsApp: "If I'm email . . . if I'm mailing . . . emailing within WhatsApp, does that ever inform your advertisers?" Senator Lindsey Graham's (R-SC) ill-informed question "Is Twitter the same as what you do?" led to further pillorying.[1] As Trevor Noah, host of *The Daily Show*, colorfully described, "Zuckerberg has already experienced the worst punishment of all: he had to spend four hours explaining Facebook to senior citizens."[2]

Of course, one can hardly expect all senators to be engaged with the details of every digital platform. However, if they have so little understanding of how social media functions at a basic level, how can lawmakers develop public policies that will effectively regulate it? More generally, if Congress lacks the expertise on these issues, who steps into the void? We argue that if Congress cannot muster the expertise within the institution, other actors in the political system, notably presidents and executive branch agencies, can capitalize on such power vacuums to forge policies in potentially self-serving ways. The implications of legislative capacity do not simply affect congressional outputs, but ripple throughout a government predicated on separate but shared powers. Our book's central contention is legislative capacity fundamentally underlies the distribution of power in a separated system.

But what exactly constitutes a legislature's "capacity"? In this chapter, we advance a new understanding of the concept, consisting of two major domains: policymaking capacity and resource capacity. In brief, "policy-making capacity" refers to legislatures' opportunities to influence policy, often through the institutional rules and practices that confer power upon them. "Resource capacity" is the tangible materials, institutions, and human capital that aid legislatures in generating policy-related information and executing various tasks. Though previous studies on capacity almost exclusively consider the latter, we argue the former is equally important for legislatures' ability to carry out the essential tasks of policymaking and executive constraint.

Uniquely, we contend policymaking and resource capacities are each necessary, but not alone sufficient, for legislatures to influence the development and implementation of policy. Legislative resources are meaningless without the opportunity to employ them. At the same time, legislatures cannot capitalize on opportunities for action without the requisite resources. Though some scholars do consider legislative capacity, they either narrowly fixate on one particular resource like staff or aggregate various components of resource and policymaking capacities into a single measure. Both approaches mischaracterize capacity, providing an incomplete picture of the broader concepts of resource and policymaking capacities and how they interact to influence policymaking.

To this end, we develop a theory addressing two central questions. First, how do legislatures' capacity influence their ability to constrain the executive branch, in pursuit of their policy and political goals? Second, how does legislative capacity shape executive incentives to exercise power, particularly through unilateral actions?

Here, we investigate unilateralism as a tough case for observing the effects of capacity because it does not require direct legislative assent. Low-capacity legislatures, which we define as those lacking either policymaking or resource capacity, face difficulties curtailing unilateralism through ex ante limitations on discretion and ex post retaliatory actions such as oversight that affect executives' calculations about how they use their discretion. The absence of capacity provides more opportunities for executives to use unilateral actions to further their policy goals, potentially at the expense of legislatures. As legislative capacity increases, however, legislators are better able to cabin executive branch behavior through a combination of diminished discretion and more credible threats of punishment for using it in ways majorities dislike. Executives are consequently deterred from employing unilateralism to evade legislatures. In this way, legislative capacity is key to preventing the undue accumulation of executive power and the operation of an effective separated system as envisioned by Madison.

While the preponderance of studies spotlight partisan or ideological discord when explaining interbranch politics, we illuminate the central role of legislative capacity in underlying the distribution of power in separated systems. Though a handful of scholars argue legislative capacity—primarily resources—moderates the effect of interbranch conflict on legislative constraints (e.g., Huber and Shipan 2002; Kousser 2005; McGrath 2013), we contend both resources and policymaking opportunities are necessary conditions for these constraints. We moreover consider the influence of legislative capacity during unified and divided government, whereas previous work largely discounts its role in the former.

Our study is also unique in linking legislative capacity to the behavior of executives, not just legislatures. Most existing studies on legislative capacity offer no concrete predictions (or empirical tests) about its effects on executive behavior. They tend to extrapolate that if legislative outputs decrease as capacity recedes, executives will evade. However, without theoretically specifying how executives' behavior manifests under circumstances of evasion or how their incentives are specifically affected by capacity, these claims about the balance of power cannot be falsified empirically. This task is especially important given the puzzling discrepancy between the grievances of many political observers that contemporary congresses lack capacity to check executive power and scholarly findings of presidential responsiveness to congressional preferences discussed in chapter 1. Theoretically connecting capacity and unilateral action directly facilitates the empirical assessment of whether, when, and to what degree executives can exploit legislatures. It also reveals new insights into what legislatures need to cabin executive power and how their various ex ante and ex post mechanisms of constraint interact. Lastly, our argument is applicable to the US federal level and across the fifty states, in contrast to most interbranch policymaking theories developed for a specific context.

Altogether, our theoretical account helps to resolve a long-standing puzzle as to why presidents and other chief executives sometimes restrain their unilateral actions during divided government, when they seemingly have the greatest desire to circumvent legislatures. Our theory also identifies circumstances in which we would expect presidents and governors to evade legislative rivals. Thus, separation of powers does not guarantee executive constraint, even under interbranch ideological and political conflict. The executive restraint commonly documented in existing work is the product of particular institutional arrangements and is far from inevitable. Whether patterns of executive constraint or evasion emerge depends on the opportunities and resources legislatures maintain to alter executive incentives.

Conceptualizing Legislative Capacity

Fundamentally, legislative capacity refers to the ability of legislatures to carry out their core responsibilities, which include, but are not limited to, policymaking, representation, and institutional maintenance (Jacob 1966; Keefe 1966). We are primarily interested in those activities that implicate separation of powers concerns, notably executive constraint. To begin, legislative policymaking crucially depends on access to reliable information for understanding the status quo and the range of available policy options. Such information should be independent of the executive branch if legislatures hope to meaningfully influence public policy to constrain executive actors. They do not have to disregard information from the executive branch, but rather must have the means to assess it through their own information-generating and analytic capabilities.

Legislatures must also convert their policy preferences into legislation and other nonstatutory instruments, such as legislative vetoes or committee reports, that restrict executives implementing the law. Doing so requires expertise about translating policy goals into instruments that can direct bureaucratic implementation in ways the legislature desires. After a law is passed, regularized monitoring of executive branch activities, through formal oversight mechanisms like hearings or less formal contact with agencies, can ensure the law is being implemented consistent with legislative intent. Oversight often compels bureaucrats to change course or deters them from selecting policies opposed to legislatures' preferences in the first place (see, e.g., McCubbins and Schwartz 1984).

Though these tasks are vital for the effective functioning of any legislative body, they are not automatic. Legislatures must possess institutional capacity—that is, the ability to carry them out. Capacity, we posit, consists of two equally important factors—the *opportunities* to engage in the policymaking process (which we term "policymaking capacity") and the *means* to take advantage of these opportunities (which we term "resource capacity"). Legislatures lacking opportunity, resources, or both are lower in capacity and less able to perform the previously described activities to the same degree. In short, we contend that *both policymaking and resource capacities are necessary conditions for legislatures to be high-capacity institutions.*

The conceptualization we advance here is substantially different from previous ones. Existing studies typically focus on resources and take opportunities as fixed, or they combine the two concepts as one. Scholars commonly examine one indicator of capacity at a time, such as salaries, session lengths, or legislative vetoes, or, alternatively, analyze multiple indicators without considering their interactions. Others combine disparate components of capacity, typically in additive scales. For instance, Squire (2007, 211) conceives of legislative professionalism as "the capacity of both individual members and the organization as a whole to generate and digest information in the policymaking process" and couples aspects of opportunities, such as session length, with resources like salaries and staff into a single index. Aggregating these indicators of professionalism may be inappropriate, since it does not account for important differences and interdependencies among the constituent parts of legislative capacity.

To be clear, our conceptualization of capacity concentrates on the *ability* of legislatures to carry out the above tasks and is not related to their will to do so. Arter (2006) argues that many studies conflate "can" and "do," thus confusing discussions of legislative capacity on the one hand, and legislative performance on the other. We agree. For instance, the absence of activity by an oversight committee is not sufficient to diagnose it as low-capacity. Similarly, it may be in the interest of a high-capacity legislature to delegate broad power to the executive branch in some cases. Rather, we need to distinguish between a legislature's will to act and its ability to act on those impulses. While the former is obviously of theoretical interest, only the latter is included in our definition of capacity. With these important distinctions in mind, we now discuss policymaking and resource capacities in detail.

Policymaking Capacity

The first domain of legislative capacity that we identify is policymaking capacity. We define this broadly as the opportunities afforded to the legislature to influence policy in a political system. Such opportunities allow legislatures to claim a meaningful role in the development and implementation of new policy, which has implications for restraining the executive branch through statutory *and* nonstatutory means.[3] Specifically, we argue policymaking capacity is composed of the institutional rules and norms developed over time that bind legislative power in a political system.

Perhaps the clearest source of a legislature's policymaking capacity is the constitution that structures political activity in a given system. For instance, the US Constitution endows Congress specific powers in Article I: the power to appropriate funds, declare war, issue letters of marque and reprisal, and regulate interstate commerce, as well as senatorial advice and consent, among others. These and other enumerated powers offer relatively clear understandings of the types of activities in which Congress will engage and its role in the policymaking process relative to the other branches of government.

Statutory enactments likewise confer policymaking capacity to legislatures. The Budget and Accounting Act of 1921, for example, delineates the now familiar process through which the president's budget is developed and submitted to Congress. The Congressional Budget and Impoundment Control Act of 1974 details how Congress passes its annual budget resolution and procedures to reconcile it with existing laws. These statutes regularize congressional participation in policymaking, creating expectations about its proper role in the annual budget and appropriations processes.

The time legislatures spend in session, which varies substantially across the US states, is another important component of policymaking capacity. When legislative bodies hold regular sessions throughout the year, they have greater opportunities to influence policymaking. The opportunity costs of remaining in session are high, however, if legislators have other jobs and sources of income; this may compel them to have shorter sessions and therefore fewer opportunities to alter policy (Kousser and Phillips 2012). Accordingly, state politics scholars argue session length is important for legislative professionalism and can seriously impact legislative outputs (e.g., Bowen and Greene 2014; Rosenthal 1996).

The rules of the legislature itself also influence its policymaking capacity. For instance, the cloture rule in the US Senate has important implications for its deliberations and ability to pass legislation. The Senate long lacked a formal way to end debate, but the addition of Rule XXII allowed super-majorities to invoke cloture and end filibusters, thus ostensibly increasing their policymaking capacity.

Of course, not all legislative powers are clearly defined by written rules, statutes, or constitutional stipulation. Established practices within a political system might also confer legitimacy on legislative actions. For example, scholars of the federal appropriations process note the degree to which agencies pay attention to and act in accordance with the pronouncements of congressional committee reports accompanying legislation (e.g., Fenno 1966; Schick 2008). Though these reports are not binding law, agencies have incentives to adhere to the instructions of their subcommittee for fear of future sanctions. Thus, repeated legislative-executive interactions in the appropriations process undergird this informal tool empowering Congress, despite the absence of any official sanction from the Constitution or a statute.

Other sources of informal power include intracameral precedents. For instance, the decision of Democratic and Republican majorities in 2013 and 2017, respectively, to establish new precedents related to cloture requirements for executive branch and judicial nominees empowered legislative majorities in their advice and consent power. Similarly, the right of first recognition is a precedent that makes majority leaders in the Senate first among equals, giving them the ability to set the agenda for the body. Both powers are simply norms and precedents, rather than formal rules, but still have important consequences for the ability of majorities to advance their interests.

While formal rules and informal routines are important for defining legislative power, whether they are binding on legislatures' behavior may depend on other external factors. For instance, ideological polarization between the Democratic and Republican parties can certainly frustrate legislative action. While we do not consider polarization itself a part of policymaking capacity, it can interact meaningfully with certain features that limit legislatures' ability to check executive power. Polarization might exacerbate the effects of supermajority requirements in Congress, complicating efforts to pass a law needing cross-party consensus. Importantly, however, Congress also has many nonstatutory tools to constrain executive power that may serve as substitutes for statutory powers. These nonstatutory powers, which do not face the same supermajoritarian hurdles, buttress congressional policymaking capacity even when polarization makes lawmaking difficult. Thus, we must examine legislatures' full complement of powers, both statutory and non-statutory, when considering whether they are high or low in policymaking capacity. In this sense, legislatures can be high in policymaking capacity even if passing a law is difficult. However, opportunity alone is not sufficient for a legislature to be high in capacity.[4]

Resource Capacity

The second domain of legislative capacity is resource capacity. Here, we are referring to tangible resources and capital legislatures can acquire, typically through financial means, to carry out their central legislative tasks. It is in this sense of financial acquisition that resource capacity is distinct from policy-making capacity. The components of resource capacity are varied but likely familiar to students of legislative politics.

First, legislatures require physical meeting and office space. While a seemingly trivial concern today, scholarship consistently associates physical capital resources with a legislature's ability to attract members and maintain its standing within a political culture (Squire 2012). By increasing the relative value of legislative work, the trappings of physical space can incentivize legislators to invest personal time and resources for policymaking, while also increasing the outward prestige of the job. Most important, such space facilitates legislative functioning independent of the executive branch. As one former Tennessee state senator recounted, "The construction of Legislative Plaza was a great step forward in cementing and crystallizing the independence of the legislature."[5]

Second, professional legislative staff often serve an important role in increasing the overall capacity of legislatures by managing their time-consuming, labor-intensive, and often competing tasks. Legislators are engaged in myriad activities, such as meeting with interest groups; coordinating with other legislators; formulating testimony, statements, and speeches; and writing briefs and reports. As legislatures increase the number of individuals they employ, their capacity with respect to most tasks increases as well (see, e.g., Fox and Hammond 1977). Such undertakings are critical for learning about existing policies and gauging how proposed policy alternatives might translate into actual outcomes. Staff likewise facilitate the load of legislating and are often responsible for identifying important issues; formulating strategies; researching policy; assembling drafts of bills and amendments; reading and analyzing other bills being considered; composing floor statements; and briefing members on matters relevant to their policy and representational work. Committee staff members in the legislature can also assist in these functions by aiding in initial research, data collection, briefings, and legislative drafts.

Legislative staff, furthermore, are critical for overseeing the executive branch, keeping in close and constant contact with agencies under a committee's jurisdiction. High-level committee staffers maintain well-developed, intensive networks of contacts with executive branch officials both in leadership positions and scattered more widely throughout an agency (Aberbach 1990). Staffers are also imperative in legislators' attempts to employ more formal tactics of oversight, such as hearings and investigations, through information collection and analysis.

All staffers are not created equal when impacting policy production, and their influence on the capacity to check executive power may depend on their function and purpose. Press aides, information technology specialists, and documents clerks may have less influence on policy outcomes than policy advisers, lawyers, and other professional staffers. Staff serving at the pleasure of the majority party might prove to be more relevant for policymaking than those aiding the minority, particularly if the parties have starkly different preferences and there is strong partisan control over the levers of legislative power. In circumstances with close collaboration between members of the majority and minority parties, however, both types of staff can influence policy outcomes. We focus primarily on majority staffers in this book given the persistent conflicts between the two major US parties, as well as evidence of the majority leadership's control over the agenda and other policymaking opportunities.[6]

In highly centralized legislatures where rank-and-file members give substantial procedural or policy determination power to their leaders, leadership staff may be another relevant indicator of capacity, as compared to decentralized systems where committee and personal staff might be more crucial. Taken together, all three types of staff—personal, committee, and leadership—can play an essential role in achieving the policy goals of the majority party vis-à-vis the executive branch (Curry 2015; Dodd and Schott 1979; Fox and Hammond 1977). The locus of capacity at any given time or in any given legislature, however, may depend to some degree on the centralization or decentralization of power within the party caucuses. Whether some element of the legislative majority is able to leverage any of these resources on behalf of the institution is the critical question for resource capacity.

Legislators are also served by institutions of their own design. As Fox and Hammond (1977) note, personal office staff often do not conduct original research, but gather information collected by interest groups and executive branch agencies. It can be difficult to constrain executives if legislatures rely on them for policy information without the independent ability to interpret and verify it. High-capacity legislatures, however, frequently maintain alternative in-house sources of information, acting as vital repositories for expertise in legislative policymaking. Examples include the Government Accountability Office, the Congressional Budget Office, the Library of Congress, and the Congressional Research Service.

The expert staff of these institutions assist legislators in numerous duties including oversight, understanding the policy and economic effects of proposed legislation, as well as generating and interpreting policy-relevant information. They produce in-depth studies of policy proposals, economic analyses, and audits of executive branch policy implementation that guide legislative action. Importantly, these types of organizations are fundamentally legislative agencies not subject to executive control, thereby allowing legislatures to develop independent policy information.

Legislative support organizations (LSOs)—legislative caucuses or groups of legislators organized around any number of shared concerns—can also enhance resource capacity. They offer staff support and deliberative forums for individual legislators outside of their personal offices and committees. Clarke (2020), for example, shows that the abolition of resources for these organizations following the 1995 Republican takeover of Congress negatively impacted legislative effectiveness for members.

Legislative budgets are another key indicator of resource capacity, serving as the lifeblood for these institutions and the other resources enumerated above. Increased funding permits legislatures to create well-staffed independent support agencies or organizations to collect and disseminate information vital for policymaking. Financial resources likewise facilitate the hiring of more high quality staff, affording legislators additional time, experience, and expertise to adequately perform their jobs (see, e.g., Squire 2012).

Indeed, human capital has long been acknowledged to be a valuable input for organizational performance and effectiveness in a variety of contexts.[7]

It is thus imperative that legislative staff maintain human capital, which is rooted in previous experiences, training, expertise, and "on-the-job" knowledge acquisition. The longer staffers remain employed by the legislature, the more they learn about different policy issues and processes to benefit their legislative principals. The keys to attracting and retaining high-quality staff include generous salaries and benefits, professional development, and the legislatures' prestige, as well as opportunities to meaningfully shape policy and actualize public service motivations (Perry and Wise 1990).

Legislators, who bring diverse experiences and skills, must also acquire sufficient human capital to effectively execute their duties. They too can invest in expertise by learning about policies within their jurisdictions. Long-serving members bring important institutional knowledge and experience to legislative debates. Repeated interactions among legislators may facilitate cooperation. The prestige associated with being a legislator as well as the attendant salary and benefits are important for incentivizing individuals with appropriate experiences and expertise to run for office. When individuals do not perceive the work of the legislature to be of great importance, they are less likely to commit to it as a viable career option or to perceive it as anything but a transitory step on a political career ladder. Once again, financial resources can attract and retain both high-quality staff and legislators.

Institutional features and the rules of legislatures, both formal and informal, can likewise facilitate or inhibit the development of human capital among legislators. For instance, term limits can discourage members from investing time in learning policy, while also degrading institutional memory. They can empower executives, at the expense of legislatures, and have deleterious effects on various legislative outcomes (Carey et al. 2006). Term limits might also stunt the development of expertise, further exacerbating executive advantages (Kousser 2005).

In sum, legislatures' resource capacity is a key determinant of their ability to undertake important tasks related to confronting executive power. Information is the currency of the policymaking process, and legislatures need access to high-quality, policy-relevant information that is independent of the executive branch if they hope to entrench their preferences into policies. They must also possess the capacity to transform this information into statutory and non-statutory activities to serve their interests. Legislative support institutions, efficacious oversight designs, and information-generation procedures can all help mitigate these institutional disadvantages vis-à-vis the executive. And, finally, robust legislative budgets are instrumental in enhancing many of these elements of resource capacity.

Interactions between Opportunities and Resources

How might policymaking and resource capacities relate to one another? To begin, legislatures must possess policymaking capacity to assert power over policy determination. If the political environment admits no role for independent legislative power, then there is not much for legislatures to do to affect policy. Hence, policymaking capacity is a necessary condition for elevated legislative capacity. Its presence, consequently, determines whether resources will impact legislatures' performance. In other words, a legislature may retain ample experienced staff, long sessions, or a beautiful building, but these resources will not meaningfully translate into relative political power if they are not accompanied by the opportunities to influence policy.

Policymaking capacity, however, is not a sufficient condition for a legislature to be high in capacity. Even if a legislature has opportunities to influence policy, it cannot act upon those opportunities without the requisite resources. In other words, policymaking capacity provides the opportunities but not the means for legislatures to play an authoritative role in the political system. The elements of resource capacity form the basis for the "means" aspects of legislative capacity. These elements are critical for transforming the opportunities offered by policymaking capacity into actual legislative action.

Taken together, *both* policymaking capacity and resource capacity are necessary conditions for a legislature to be high capacity. If either or both are absent, legislatures will be foiled in pursuing their goals. In this sense, the distinction between policymaking and resource capacities is not merely taxonomic; rather, it has substantial implications for theory and empirics. With this novel understanding of legislative capacity in hand, we now consider how and when it influences legislative activities and executive constraint.

Legislative Capacity, Executive Action and Separation of Powers Politics

Scholars and observers of politics predominantly spotlight policy disagreements between the legislative and executive branches of government as the primary impetus for policymaking, or the lack thereof, in the United States. Such conflict manifests most palpably under divided government, when the executive office and at least one chamber of the legislature are controlled by different parties. Conventional wisdom and media lore widely view these as times when executives flex the most power to evade legislative desires. Yet the opposite appears to be true. Political scientists repeatedly find that executive actors are constrained in their use of unilateral and other administrative actions (e.g., Acs 2019; Howell 2003; Yackee and Yackee 2009). So, why are executives not using their powerful unilateral toolkit to sidestep hostile legislatures, especially in a polarized era where legislative action is more arduous than ever? This question is a central puzzle in US separation of powers politics.

We argue the answer lies in legislative capacity, which is a necessary condition for legislatures to limit executive power. Restrictions in discretion, ex ante, and threats of ex post sanctions from high-capacity legislatures deter chief executives from unilaterally shifting policies in ways legislative majorities find disagreeable. This argument has clear empirical implications for both legislative and executive strategies. Thus, the ability of the US separated system to deliver the constraint Madison promised is contingent on the opportunities *and* the resources legislatures possess to challenge executive ambitions. Our theoretical framework, outlined below, applies to such systems across federal and state governments in the United States.

Underlying Assumptions

We begin by identifying the key assumptions upon which our argument rests. First, executives and legislatures have distinct preferences about public policy, and their actions are primarily driven by their desire to achieve policy outcomes as close to their preferred ones as possible (see, e.g., Krehbiel 1998). Both branches can be well represented by the preferences of key individuals, based on political features such as chamber rules isolating some legislative actors as pivotal (see, e.g., Cox and McCubbins 2005; Krehbiel 1998) and a mélange of presidential strategies to ensure bureaucratic compliance (Moe 1985b). While pursuing their policy preferences is a central imperative for political actors, executives and legislators may also possess other motivations that drive their activities.

Legislators, for instance, notoriously hold strong reelection incentives that underlie a variety of their activities (Mayhew 1974). Achieving any of their other goals, after all, requires them to be officeholders in the first place. Legislators likewise want to preserve the standing of the institutions in which they reside, which is important for securing their desired policies and main-taining their job's prestige (Schickler 2001). Members of Congress often cite institutional loyalty as a forceful motivation for opposing executive actions, as did Senator Thom Tillis (R-NC) in 2019 when voicing concern over President Trump's—a partisan ally—national emergency declaration to construct a wall on the southern border: "I have grave concerns when our institution looks the other way at the expense of weakening Congress's power. It is my responsibility to be a steward of the Article I branch, to preserve the separation of powers and to curb the kind of executive overreach that Congress has allowed to fester for the better part of the past century. . . . As a U.S. senator, I cannot justify providing the executive with more ways to bypass Congress."[8] These sentiments exemplify an institutional spirit that impels legislators to protect their power in the face of executive encroachments, perhaps to the detriment of policies they might otherwise support.

Next, we assume the executive branch has informational and resource advantages over their legislative counterparts (see, e.g., Epstein and O'Halloran 1999). Legislatures are generalist institutions, grappling with all issues that affect a society. Agencies, on the other hand, work in specific policy areas and employ numerous staffers with specialized training and experience. As head of the administrative state, chief executives can channel the deep informational advantages of the executive branch, and transform them into policy tools that advance their own interests.

Our argument centers on the use of unilateral actions to further executive policy preferences. Unilateral actions, which do not require legislative assent, are a tough case for examining the consequences of legislative capacity. Of these actions, executive orders are the most prominent and are used by both presidents and governors to instruct, interpret, and implement the law (Cooper 2002; Ferguson and Bowling 2008). We contend executives have sufficient institutional capacity to pursue their preferences through these and other unilateral directives. Although such directives may be costly to write, in terms of time, policy expertise, and coordination among various agencies, we argue executives maintain enough resources to overcome these internal costs.

Even before the rapid institutional developments of the presidency and executive branch during the 1930s and 1940s, including the birth of the Executive Office of the President in 1939, presidents have long demonstrated their ability to exercise unilateral powers. Notably, Theodore Roosevelt, whose presidency predated the modern White House staffing structure, issued an average of 145 executive orders per year while Barack Obama averaged 35 per year. Clearly, then, a robust and institutionalized White House executive office is not a requirement for using unilateral policy tools. Instead, presidents have apparently maintained the necessary resources during our examined time periods to issue executive orders. In the modern state-level contexts we study (i.e., 1993–2013), it is likewise relatively uncontroversial to assume that state bureaucracies retain expertise advantages over their legislative counterparts, while gubernatorial offices are generally highly professionalized.

Of course, this is not to say that chief executives themselves have the knowledge and wherewithal to develop and write directives. Instead, they draw upon the broader expertise of their offices and agencies. As heads of their respective executive branches, presidents and governors in the United States can invoke this expertise to craft directives that change policies in beneficial ways (Moe and Howell 1999). Executive office staffs assist in coordinating these functions. Indeed, Rudalevige (2012) finds that even in the modern era, where presidents ostensibly have access to White House staff and expertise, 65.2 percent of executive orders were drafted by agencies from 1947 to 1987.

As such, we do not anticipate the strategic dynamics we delineate here will be greatly affected by indicators of executive capacity, such as executive office budget size or staffing levels. Of course, this is merely an assumption at this point. We examine whether executive office capacity dictates presidential and gubernatorial unilateralism in chapters 6 and 7. To preview, we find little evidence that accounting for executive capacity materially impacts the empirical evaluations of our theory. Consequently, we do not focus on how executive capacity shapes actions in our theoretical framework, though we acknowledge its potential utility in contexts outside the United States.

At the same time, we do assume legislative efforts to constrain executive power are associated with binding costs. Generating and interpreting information to write detailed legislation and conducting oversight require time and resources (Aberbach 1990; Squire 2012). More fundamentally, legislatures must possess the opportunities to intervene in the policymaking process in the first place (Barber, Bolton, and Thrower 2019). While expertise and resources may be plentiful for executives, they are generally a far more limiting constraint for legislatures. With these assumptions in mind, we first present our theory of how legislative capacity influences legislative outputs, and then we consider executive incentives to act unilaterally.

Legislative Capacity and Mechanisms of Constraint

We begin by considering high-capacity legislatures, which possess the means and opportunities to constrain the executive branch. We are hardly the first to highlight how legislatures use various tools to curb executive powers. Since the introduction of the new economics of organization literature into the discipline of political science, scholars have often conceived of legislative-executive interactions in the form of a principal-agent problem (e.g., Hall and Taylor 1996; Moe 1984). Here, legislatures are taken to be the principals and executive branch actors are the agents. The latter hold superior information, relative to the former, about the link between policy choices and outcomes. This advantage provides legislatures a rationale for delegating some degree of policymaking authority to executive branch actors, as they hope to leverage this expertise in policy implementation (e.g., Bendor and Meirowitz 2004; Gailmard and Patty 2012; Moe 1985a; Weingast and Moran 1983). While executives could employ such delegated authority to craft policies closely reflecting their preferences, capacity-rich legislatures enjoy opportunities to constrain this behavior through ex ante and ex post mechanisms.

With respect to the former, these legislatures can reduce statutory discretion—that is, the leeway afforded to the executive branch in implementing the law. By writing specific laws narrowing available policy choices, legislatures may exploit executive expertise while simultaneously mitigating bureaucratic drift, wherein implementing agencies create policies that differ from legislative intent (see, e.g., Bawn 1995; Epstein and O'Halloran 1999; Miller 2005). They can likewise impose ex post constraints on the executive branch for using discretion in ways that run counter to legislative preferences. Oversight allows them to generate information relevant for understanding policy implementation and to signal their preferences to bureaucratic actors who may then adjust course. It further provides opportunities to publicly expose administrative actions in ways that are costly to the executive (Kriner and Schickler 2016). Administrative procedures likewise inform legislatures about executive policy choices and incentivize bureaucratic actors to select policies more in line with legislative priorities (McCubbins, Noll, and Weingast 1987). Furthermore, legislatures can pass new statutes to correct executive actions that make majorities worse off relative to the status quo. Beyond directly overturning an order, legislatures can respond with other statutory and nonstatutory mechanisms that impose costs onto the executive. Such retaliatory measures include defunding specific programs, slow-walking executive priorities not salient to the legislature, or rejecting executive branch nominees.

These and other tools work in concert to stave off executive evasion. Ex ante constraints are needed to limit the degree of executives' policy movement, while ex post ones are necessary to guarantee executives use this authority as statutorily intended and in ways that simultaneously promote the interests of legislative majorities. In this way, the ex ante and ex post mechanisms of control reinforce one another to ensure executive power is constrained.

To execute these constraints, legislatures require sufficiently high degrees of *both* policymaking and resource capacities. Limitations on when a legislature can meet or consider legislation can inhibit its responses. Low thresholds for lawmaking facilitate the passage of statutes overturning administrative actions or inflicting sanctions over the objections of the chief executive. Nonstatutory powers, such as regulatory review, the confirmation of executives' nominees, oversight hearings and investigations, and the appropriation of funds, provide opportunities for legislatures to damage executive actors that promulgate policies counter to the majority's interests. Many of these powers only require a simple majority, or in some cases just the consent of a small committee or its chair, to effect. The absence of these tools makes legislative restraint of the executive branch nearly impossible.

A lack of resources similarly hinders legislatures' capacity to act, even if they have the opportunities to do so. For example, their ability to manipulate discretionary levels will depend on their success at recruiting numerous expert staff and legislators (Huber and Shipan 2002). Writing specific laws necessitates time and expertise to gather and translate information into statutory language that will meaningfully bind executive policymaking. Oversight similarly demands competent staff to organize hearings, prepare for witnesses, pore over policy-related documents, and generally work to understand the activities of the executive branch. Finally, passing legislation after a program has been implemented also requires substantial resources to aid legislators in understanding the policy environment and how legislation must be forged to change it.

Whether legislatures' capacity is consequential for policymaking in a separated system, however, depends also on their incentives to use these opportunities and resources to restrain other actors. Previous studies mainly contend legislatures only engage in constraining activities when they do not share the policy goals of the executive. Consequently, we have little indication as to whether or why legislatures curb executive power when they ostensibly share these goals, notably during unified government. Prominent theories that directly connect capacity to legislative constraints likewise propose a null relationship outside periods of interbranch partisan or ideological division. For example, as Huber, Shipan, and Pfahler (2001, 334) posit, "If there is no conflict of interest, then there is no need to draw upon legislative capacity."

As our previous discussion of legislators' institutional and reelection incentives implies, however, they may invoke their capacity even when partisan conflicts are relatively muted. Reelection-seeking members of Congress crave activities to publicize their value to constituents. Executive branch oversight may offer them the opportunity to garner favorable publicity in their districts or states, even if they mostly share the executive's policy goals. It is an easily "traceable" activity, allowing constituents to clearly link representative's actions to public policy outcomes (Arnold 1990). Indeed, many of the most important and high-profile oversight hearings in American history transpired during unified government, including the Teapot Dome investigation during the Harding administration; Senator Harry Truman's investigations into World War II defense contracting; Senator Joseph McCarthy's hearings into alleged communist infiltration of the bureaucracy; hearings into the Whitewater scandal during the first years of the Clinton administration; and the investigations into the abuses at Abu Ghraib prison during the Iraq War (Kriner and Schickler 2016; Mayhew 1991).

Legislators may likewise use capacity to accomplish less traceable tasks that can aid their reelections. For instance, they might insert specific instructions into legislation directing resources to their districts. Though it limits executive branch discretion, legislators may pursue this strategy nonetheless for electoral purposes. Given these activities do not garner publicity as extensively, we might expect a stronger direct effect of capacity for more public acts like oversight.[9]

In addition to reelection incentives, legislators are motivated by a desire to protect the interests, position, and power of their institutions in the political system. Many scholars have dismissed these incentives for members of Congress. Levinson and Pildes (2006), for example, reject the Madisonian idea that separate powers would prompt Congress and the president to actively confront each other under all circumstances, arguing the US political system is best characterized as "separation of parties, not powers." Other scholars, however, identify institutionally-based incentives as the impetus behind major developments in Congress throughout American history (e.g., Schickler 2001), a question we return to in the next chapter.

Taken together, even during periods of relative ideological harmony, activities that constrain the executive branch should be increasing with legislative capacity. This relationship, if true, would seemingly be consistent with a Madisonian vision of branches checking one another irrespective of partisan commitments. Still, we agree with previous accounts asserting the effects of capacity are *even more* consequential when legislatures also possess clear ideological incentives to curtail executive power. Specifically, when they expect executive actors to implement policies counter to their preferences, legislatures will place more constraints on executive action to prevent bureaucratic drift. On the other hand, legislatures can trust executives who share their ideological views to implement policy in a mutually agreeable way. Consequently, high-capacity legislatures facing friendly executives place fewer limitations on their power.

For the reasons outlined earlier, however, low-capacity legislatures (i.e., those lacking either resource or policymaking capacity) are unable to differentiate based on partisan or ideological alignment. When facing an executive ally, there are few incentives to impose constraints. Conversely, when confronting an executive opposed to its policy and political goals, legislatures have the motivation to impose constraints, but lack the opportunities or means to do so. Regardless of their relationship to the executive, capacity-deficient legislatures falter in combating their rival branch of government.

This discussion leads to our first two hypotheses regarding the role of capacity in shaping legislatures' ability to deploy tools of executive constraint:

Hypothesis 1: When legislatures have high levels of both policy-making *and* resource capacities, they place more overall constraints on the executive branch relative to when either is lacking.

Hypothesis 2: When legislatures have high levels of both policy-making *and* resource capacities, they place more constraints on the executive branch as interbranch preference divergence increases. Interbranch disagreement does not impact the level of constraints legislatures place on the executive when they lack either policymaking or resource capacity.

Legislative Capacity and the Dynamics of Executive Power

While the foregoing discussion emphasized the substantial role of legislative capacity in determining *legislative* outcomes, we argue its effects are not simply confined to this branch of government. Instead, capacity influences executive incentives to shift policy toward their own preferences through unilateral actions, potentially at the expense of legislative majorities. Indeed, the apparent allure of unilateral action for executives is the possibility of achieving their will alone and unencumbered by legislative majorities with which they disagree (Moe and Howell 1999). In this way, executives might "evade" legislatures by short-circuiting the statutory process to obtain their preferred policy outcomes (Martin 2000).

Of course, chief executives do not have completely free rein in deploying unilateral actions. They must rely on discretion from the constitution or a statute to justify their policy. These sources of authority limit the degree to which unilateral actions can be used to advance executive policy interests. In particular, legislatures can curtail policymaking discretion when delegating authority, which places restrictions on the magnitude of policy movement executives can actuate through unilateral tools (Cooper 2002).

Further, unilateralism is not completely free. First, considerable transaction and bargaining costs are associated with developing directives such as executive orders, given the frequent consultation with experts in the bureaucracy to craft them (Rudalevige 2012). Additionally, chief executives must exert time and effort monitoring executive branch implementation to minimize drift (Kennedy 2015). Finally, policymaking through unilateralism rather than legislating is associated with public costs, though to varying degrees (see, e.g., Christenson and Kriner 2017; Reeves and Rogowski 2015).

Consequently, presidents and governors will be disinclined to employ unilateral directives that do not yield substantial policy benefits. Such benefits are, at least in part, determined by whether executives can unilaterally obtain more favorable policy outcomes than what they might otherwise achieve through the legislative process. This determination depends, of course, on the amount of discretion they hold to shift policy unilaterally and the preferences of the legislative majorities they would be bargaining with to pass a law. Statutory outcomes should, on average, be more palatable to chief executives when they share the partisan or ideological goals of legislatures than when their preferences diverge, as under conditions of unified government.[10] Seemingly, then, executives should have the greatest incentives to pursue unilateral strategies during divided government, given the larger marginal policy gains. Accordingly, the "evasion" view of unilateralism contends that chief executives can impose their will on legislative foes with more unilateral actions during these times.

Despite its intuitive appeal, scholars have found little empirical support for this prediction. Why? The answer, we argue, lies in executives' perceived discretion and threats of ex post legislative constraints, both of which depend on legislative capacity. Typically, formal theories of unilateralism assume executives cannot use their discretion to unilaterally shift policy in ways that legislative majorities find disagreeable (Chiou and Rothenberg 2017; Howell 2003).[11] When legislatures and executives have convergent preferences, many policies can be changed in mutually beneficial ways. When their preferences are misaligned, executives are less able to draft a unilateral directive that they, along with the legislature, prefer to the status quo. This leads to patterns of constraint wherein executives issue more directives when they share the preferences of the legislative majority.

This dynamic, of course, raises an interesting question: What might constrain executives to use their supposedly puissant unilateral powers only in ways that do not conflict with the legislative majority's preferences? The existing literature offers few indications. We argue the most likely explanations emanate from the legislature itself, since its interests are most implicated in the question of whether executives can use their discretion unfavorably. Some may point to the courts as another source of constraint. The judiciary, however, is unlikely to retaliate against unilateral actions, given its challenges and disincentives to strike at the heart of executive power (Moe and Howell 1999). Furthermore, since the *Chevron* decision, courts ostensibly give some measure of deference to an agency's reading of its own statute, and thus its discretion. As discussed in the previous chapter, others view the public as the primary fount of executive restraint. Yet even those studies note congressional opposition to a directive can mobilize public opinion (Christenson and Kriner 2020). Instead, we argue that constraint arises from legislatures' powers and resources to restrict discretion for opposed executive actors and to inflict costly retaliatory measures against unilateral actions they find distasteful. The former limits the policy benefits from an order, while the latter deters it in the first place.

What types of actions can legislatures employ to apply these costs? Most intuitively, they might overturn an executive order through statute (Bailey and Rottinghaus 2014). While this act might discourage unilateralism, executives can prevent such reversals if they place the new unilateral policy in the gridlock interval—that is, a set of (relatively moderate) policies where legislatures are unable to change the status quo due to preference disagreement (Moe and Howell 1999). In this way, executives can take advantage of supermajoritarian institutions in Congress, like cloture or veto override requirements, to strategically locate policies where sufficient legislative coalitions cannot block their alteration.

Given the difficulties in responding to unilateralism statutorily, legislatures may be better suited to retaliate through nonstatutory measures that do not necessitate a supermajority (Chiou and Rothenberg 2017). They can engage in hearings and investigations, calling executive branch officials to testify about a directive and its implementation. Such oversight activates public concerns about executive overreach and harms the administration's public standing (see, e.g., Kriner and Schickler 2014). Oversight also has important policy effects, signaling to agencies the policy directions legislatures prefer, with an eye toward reducing bureaucratic drift. These activities are appealing because they do not require supermajority or even majority support, but often only committee chair approval. Some legislatures have other retaliatory tools at their disposal, like legislative vetoes that invalidate bureaucratic actions without executive assent. Given many executive orders are used to initiate regulatory processes, such invalidations are a powerful way for legislatures to combat adverse executives. All of these ex post actions are costly to executives, and their threat may prevent the promulgation of evasive policies.

Yet these aforementioned measures demand legislatures maintain sufficient resource and policymaking capacities. If legislatures lack opportunities to influence policy, then executives can reasonably be assured they will face few ex post costs to unilateralism. Without proper resources for understanding the policy effects of unilateral orders and crafting appropriate constraints, legislatures are unable to seize whatever opportunities to confront executives they may encounter. Facing little ex ante or ex post constraint on their actions, executives will employ unilateral action more freely, both on average, and particularly in periods of interbranch conflict, when the marginal benefits of unilateralism are the highest relative to possible legislative outcomes.

Altogether, it is now relatively clear how legislative capacity affects unilateralism. If legislative majorities possess both the opportunities and resources for ex ante *and* ex post sanctions (whether they be statutory or nonstatutory), then executives will be reluctant to pursue policies that evade legislative majorities with divergent preferences. At the same time, when the executive and legislature share policy goals (e.g., unified government), many possible unilateral actions can be mutually beneficial. When legislative capacity is high, we thus expect patterns consistent with constraint—that is, greater unilateralism during unified government relative to divided. When legislative capacity is lower, however, executives have less fear of reprisal for unilaterally circumventing the statutory process. Because there are substantially more policy gains relative to the costs of developing directives in divided government, we expect evasive unilateral behavior to prevail.

This discussion yields two hypotheses about how executive incentives for unilateralism are shaped by legislative capacity. First, there should be a direct relationship between capacity and unilateralism. Low-capacity legislatures are less capable of constraining unilateral directives through restrictive discretion or retaliatory measures, providing increased marginal policy benefits for executive unilateralism. Second, whether executives turn to unilateralism more or less in the face of an opposed legislative majority depends on its capacity. When legislatures possess sufficient resource and policymaking capacities, they can limit discretion and sanction executives for actions they oppose, thereby deterring unilateral action. On the other hand, chief executives are freer to pursue evasive strategies to sidestep low-capacity legislative foes powerless to impose constraints. These arguments are summarized in our third and fourth hypotheses:

Hypothesis 3: When legislatures have high levels of both policymaking *and* resource capacities, executives issue fewer overall unilateral actions as legislatures increase their resources.

Hypothesis 4: When legislatures have high levels of both policymaking *and* resource capacities, executives issue fewer unilateral actions during interbranch ideological conflict, but more unilateral actions during interbranch ideological conflict when either type of capacity is low.

Together, our hypotheses offer a clear theoretical framework for assessing the effects of capacity on both legislative and executive action in a separated system. Of course, we are not the first to study legislative capacity and interbranch policymaking. The studies that do examine these topics, however, typically only spotlight the impact of capacity on either legislative or executive behavior. Our argument considers both simultaneously. Doing so has multiple benefits. Most notably, we can link legislative capacity directly to executives' incentives for unilateralism, thus specifying precisely why evasion and constraint should occur, under what circumstances, and how it manifests "in the real world."

A related theory to ours is the seminal work by Huber and Shipan (2002). They include legislatures and executives in their model, though they only derive empirical predictions for the former. As in most models of discretion, the executive moves after the legislature in their account, deciding whether to adhere to legislatively determined discretionary boundaries or exceed them. Examining unilateralism, as we do here, has somewhat different implications. In our account, executive actions are intermediary—that is, they occur after discretion is granted but in the shadow of possible retaliation from the legislature (thus, the legislature is the last mover). Moreover, the key question for us is whether executives elect to issue directives at all, given the political environment they face. The decision to forbear or act is central to unilateralism. Finally, we argue capacity affects executive calculations not only through its impact on discretion but also in how executives *use* discretion, particularly when deciding whether to pursue policies legislative majorities oppose.[12] Discretionary limits alone are not sufficient to ensure the executive will adhere to legislative desires. Instead, legislatures must retain the opportunities (statutory and nonstatutory) and resources to impose costs on the executive if discretion is used in ways that make majorities worse off. We thus contend ex ante and ex post mechanisms of control are not perfectly substitutable, at least in the case of unilateralism. Legislatures must enjoy the capacity to pursue both avenues of constraint to prevent executive evasion.

Summary and Conclusion

In this chapter, we explored the conceptual foundations of legislative capacity and its impact on the distribution of power in a separated system. Legislative capacity is separable into two distinct but interrelated domains: policymaking capacity and resource capacity. The former refers to the institutional rules that bind legislatures' power to influence policy and the political assets that facilitate it. Though necessary, policymaking capacity alone is insufficient to empower legislatures. They must also possess adequate resources to carry out their functions and policy goals. Likewise, resources are not enough for the exercise of legislative power, but require sufficient opportunities for use. Previous conceptualizations of legislative capacity are incomplete given their narrow attention to one particular aspect or the erroneous aggregation of both domains, while also not considering the interrelationships between the two.

With this novel understanding of legislative capacity in mind, we addressed a central question in the study of American politics: Do executives take actions to bypass a legislature with divergent policy and political goals or are they effectively constrained by their legislative opponents? Our argument contends these questions cannot be answered by a simple yes or no, but rather "it depends." More specifically, the constraint and exercise of executive power, particularly when the branches have distinct preferences, is contingent on legislative capacity. This insight has implications for where the balance of power tips between these branches of government and how well they are each able to pursue their own political goals. We offer the only theory to date that considers the implications of legislative capacity on both legislative and executive behavior in the context of unilateralism.

Overall, when legislatures lack sufficient capacity, executive actors are empowered to act in ways that may make legislative majorities worse off. Once their capacity increases, legislators can constrain executive activities through ex ante and ex post means, both of which are necessary for inducing executive restraint in unilateralism. Correspondingly, executives' power to bypass legislatures should be weakened overall and even more so when facing high-capacity ideologically-opposed majorities. Executives are better able to pursue their policy goals when legislative capacity is low, while legislatures can more easily institute constraints with greater capacity. Once more, both types of capacity are necessary conditions for these relationships to hold. Legislatures need the policymaking opportunities and the resources to work within these policy windows to temper executive action.

While scholars and political observers alike have noted the importance of divided government for governance in separated systems, we argue the capacity of these institutions to act is also crucial in influencing policymaking. Political actors require not only the will but also the ability to act in pursuing their goals. Understanding this relationship helps resolve the enduring puzzle of why presidents today appear so constrained even when Congress seems too gridlocked to do anything about executive actions. By recognizing that legislative powers extend beyond passing laws and that Congress has substantial resources at its disposal in the modern era, it is clear why presidents and agencies might defer to congressional interests. Our argument, however, also implies there are contexts under which evasion may thrive in a separated system. Indeed, we provide a general framework for analyzing the conditional relationship between capacity and interbranch conflict that can be applied to both federal and subnational contexts in the United States, unlike previous separation of powers theories developed for one or the other.

In the chapters to follow, we empirically evaluate the theory presented here. We test the hypotheses related to legislative constraints by examining statutory discretion and oversight. We then consider executive power by reviewing both presidential and gubernatorial executive orders in separate chapters. All throughout, we provide distinct measures of resource and policymaking capacities to test the interactive relationships posited in this theory. But, first, we begin our empirical expedition by examining the political dynamics driving the development of Congress's capacity throughout the twentieth century.

3

"Outmanned and Outgunned"

THE HISTORICAL DEVELOPMENT
OF CONGRESSIONAL CAPACITY

We firmly believe that investing in the legislative branch—which has suffered from a funding deficit and significant loss of institutional capacity in recent decades—is of key importance to the health of our democracy.... While the Framers envisioned Congress as the first among three co-equal branches, Congress's capacity has declined to the point where it cannot fully meet its constitutional duties.

—LETTER TO THE HOUSE AND SENATE APPROPRIATIONS
COMMITTEES, MARCH 21, 2019

In the above-quoted letter, ten former legislators and other prominent policy reformers urge the Appropriations Committees in both chambers to augment congressional capacity, citing its centrality for legislative power.[1] Indeed, contemporary political observers frequently attribute perceptions of encroaching executive power to deficits in congressional resources. Yet, as one reformer asserted, "Congress can act alone to fix this ... the policy vacuums filled by executive actions only exist because Congress creates them."[2] Through the power of the purse, the choice to be a low- or high-capacity institution ostensibly resides with Congress itself.

If revitalizing legislative capacity is the obvious solution to fixing the United States' purportedly ailing democracy, why doesn't Congress simply do it? Instead, its capacity has often stagnated, or even waned, in the shadow of growing executive power. Perhaps most notably, retrenchment occurred in the wake of newly elected Republican majorities fulfilling their

1994 campaign promises to eliminate "wasteful" government spending—regardless of the fact that they were confronting a Democratic opponent in the White House. Yet, at other times, Congress has also passed extensive reforms bolstering its capacity. Major legislation, including the Federal Register Act of 1935, the Legislative Reorganization Acts of 1946 and 1970, and the Administrative Procedure Act of 1946, increased staff and created independent sources of information through support institutions like the Legislative Reference Service (later to become the Congressional Research Service) and the General Accounting Office (known today as the Government Accountability Office). Thus, congressional capacity has neither steadily diminished nor relentlessly surged throughout history, but instead has ebbed and flowed.

Such fluctuations imply that legislators might face substantial barriers in developing their own capacity. What, then, ultimately led to changes in congressional capacity? This chapter endeavors to provide a survey of Congress's capacity development from the early twentieth century to the present. We focus in particular on modifications to resource capacity, since—as we will show—Congress has maintained enough policymaking opportunities to exercise executive constraint. Later in chapter 7, we detail the assorted, and often analogous, developments in US state legislatures creating variation in their policymaking and resource capacities across time.

Here, we consider two competing explanations about what drives congressional reforms. Scholars subscribing to the *partisan* explanation posit members of Congress enhance their capacity to challenge presidents who might advance policies they ideologically oppose (e.g., McCubbins, Noll, and Weingast 1999). In this account, enhancements will primarily occur during interbranch conflict and legislators' votes on these measures should consequently fall along party lines. Under the *institutional* explanation, capacity-enhancing reforms are motivated by Congress's desire to increase its institutional power vis-à-vis the executive (see, e.g., Schickler 2001). If true, we should observe bipartisan agreement on proposed developments, near-universal voting coalitions, and no relationship between interbranch disagreement and legislative reform.

Our historical evidence suggests changes in congressional resource capacity are best understood through the lens of institutional incentives. The scope and magnitude of government activity expanded considerably during the early twentieth century, complicating the task of governance for Congress. Newly created agencies and programs exercised increasing power over American social and economic life, while Congress and its resources largely stayed the same. Congressional resource capacity eventually strengthened, albeit in a piecemeal nature with false starts along the way, as both individual and institutional incentives militated against a desire to buttress capacity.

Successful reforms reflected broad-based consensus, often motivated by the shared desire to keep pace with expanding executive power, whereas politicized ones failed to pass or endure (e.g., the Office of Technology Assessment and the recommendations of the 1993 Joint Committee on the Organization of Congress). Our narrative likewise highlights the multifaceted incentives and constraints that stymie legislative reform, such as presidential opposition, public distaste for congressional self-spending, and reelection concerns. Understanding these dynamics provides insights into why Congress does not simply increase its capacity whenever it wants to curb the executive, even if its power would so plainly be enhanced by doing so.

Furthermore, the qualitative accounts we provide on the institutional motivations of reform serve to substantiate the claims underlying our theory. Congressional capacity is not simply epiphenomenal to underlying interbranch ideological or partisan conflicts, but has independent effects on policy outcomes. We likewise affirm these arguments with quantitative analyses confirming the null effects of partisan disagreement on congressional resources. Taken together, the evidence in this chapter affords greater confidence that the empirical results presented in subsequent chapters on the interactive effects of interbranch conflict and capacity are not subject to concerns about post-treatment bias.

More generally, we offer a comprehensive and in-depth account of the historical development in congressional policymaking and resource capacities. The few studies examining the effects of legislative capacity tend to take this concept as exogenous, without contemplating its origins. Though Squire (2012) offers a detailed chronicle of the institutional evolution of state legislatures, no such sweeping narrative exists for Congress. Other research explores major reforms in isolation and mostly does not consider when they fail, yielding an incomplete story of Congress's transformation as an institution. Taken together, the rich qualitative and quantitative evidence provided in this chapter offers important validation for the dynamics underlying our theoretical arguments and informs our empirical investigations throughout the remainder of the book.

Two Accounts of Capacity Reform

What drives changes in congressional capacity? We highlight two possible accounts: a partisan and an institutional explanation. The former posits that institutional developments are induced by Congress's desire to confront, counter, and deter presidents with divergent goals. This model has two straightforward empirical implications. First, increases in capacity should occur during periods of interbranch ideological or partisan conflict, when the desire to constrain the executive is seemingly the highest. Second, capacity-enhancing reforms should be primarily driven and supported by members of the party opposed to the president.

The institutional explanation, on the other hand, attributes developments in Congress's capacity to concerns about protecting its own institutional prestige, power, and standing. Deficits in capacity correspond to the decreased importance and influence of Congress, which may trigger broad-based legislative incentives to strengthen the institution. While the policy benefits of capacity may redound primarily to the majority, increased institutional prestige is beneficial to all members. If these incentives predominate, there should be little relationship between interbranch preference divergence and capacity development. Reform coalitions should be sizable and bipartisan. Finally, congressional capacity should trail expansions in the size and scope of federal activity rather than respond to contemporary or anticipated preference divergence between majorities and the executive branch.

External constraints can also impel Congress toward bipartisan reforms. Bills designed to disadvantage the executive branch will certainly face a presidential veto, which almost always requires a cross-party coalition to override. Such alliances must transcend political motivations and appeal to the wider-ranging desires of legislators to preserve their relative institutional power. Furthermore, augmenting congressional capacity could be perceived as electorally risky, possibly priming public concerns of legislative excess, aggrandizement, and overall government waste. Near-universal coalitions, however, can mitigate these concerns by eliminating the partisan dimensions of potential criticisms.

So, which motivation best explains changes in congressional capacity? The answer to that question has profound implications for validating our arguments and empirical analyses throughout the remainder of the book. Our theory contends legislative capacity moderates the effects of interbranch policy disagreement on executive constraint. If the partisan explanation of reform is true, however, these conditional effects between divided government and congressional capacity might be called into question, since the latter would be a consequence of the former. Yet, if legislatures face substantial barriers to altering their own capacity to confront executive actors at will (as the institutional explanation suggests), then we can more confidently assess the independent impact of capacity. The remainder of this chapter delineates the major changes in congressional capacity, while revealing the institutional motivations underlying these reforms.

An Era of Federal Government Expansion

For much of early American history, executive branch activities were relatively limited. The country emerged from the Revolutionary War with a deep distrust of state power. The Articles of Confederation made no real provision for an executive branch with any meaningful authority, which in part led to its collapse, as the system proved incapable of addressing the significant issues facing a nascent nation. The Constitution subsequently sought to address these maladies. Article II provides for a president vested with executive power. Though it delineates the process for appointing executive officers, the Constitution provides little structure for a bureaucracy. Instead, the broader executive branch materialized from the early practices of the first congresses and presidencies.

The nascent federal government was fairly limited in size and scope and was largely subsumed by state and local governments responsible for regulating most policy areas during much of the nineteenth century. By some accounts, courts and political parties dominated national level governance relative to presidents (Skowronek 1982).[3]

Following the Civil War, a broader administrative state began to emerge. New federal programs administered benefits to Civil War veterans and their families (Skocpol 1992). Economic and social changes in the ensuing decades spurred further demands for federal activity. Telegraphs and railroads connected people and markets in the United States in new ways. Such social and economic integration, combined with increasing industrialization and urbanization, had enormous consequences for the US political economy. As firms merged and trusts formed to compete on a national scale, economic power became more concentrated. Many feared that political power would follow suit, stimulating calls for federal economic regulation (Eisner 2000).

Nowhere was the consolidation of economic and political power more pronounced than the railroad industry, which formed the backbone of the economy's transportation and supply system. After the Supreme Court ruled state regulation of railroads inhibited interstate commerce (*Wabash v. Illinois*, 1886), a policy window for federal management emerged ushering the passage of the Interstate Commerce Act of 1887 (Cushman 1941; Gailmard and Patty 2013). In creating the Interstate Commerce Commission (ICC), Congress established the first major economic regulatory commission in US history.

The Progressive Era brought even further enlargements of governmental interventions in the economic and social spheres. Between 1891 and 1915, the number of paid civilian federal executive branch employees grew from 157,442 to 387,294 (US Census Bureau 1976). The major legislative enactments of the early twentieth century (as determined by Stathis 2014) represent a significant expansion of the federal government's role: the creation of the Department of Commerce and Labor (1903); the Elkins and Hepburn Acts, which supplemented the authority of the ICC to regulate railroads; the Mann-Elkins Act (1910), which empowered the agency to regulate communications; the Federal Reserve Act (1913); the Federal Trade Commission Act (1914); and the Clayton Antitrust Act (1914).

The executive branch assumed ever-greater responsibility for policy formulation and implementation (Eisner 2000; Sklar 1988). It began to insert itself into intrafirm affairs, particularly management-labor relations. The creation of the Department of Labor, along with mandates for eight-hour workdays for federal contractors' employees, reflected the growing dissatisfaction with working conditions and the new political power of labor unions. The newly constructed Federal Reserve System represented an important shift in federal control over the macroeconomy. The Meat Inspection and Pure Food and Drug Acts of 1906 reflected concerns with the public health consequences and potentially harmful by-products of competitive production processes.

On the international front, executive actors sought to increase US land holdings overseas and administer them to advance their policy goals, even in the face of fairly entrenched congressional opposition to these policies. As Moore (2107, 6) demonstrates, presidents and colonial administrators, fearing backlash from Congress, pursued strategies centered on "private finance, secrecy, and extraconstitutional action" to skirt congressional preferences. US involvement in World War I only intensified these trends, as the size of the federal government and the complexity of governing surged.

During the war, more than 20 percent of the nation's economic resources were directed toward the nation's mobilization effort, mainly through the direction and coordination of the executive branch. The War Industries Board (WIB), in particular, represented a major assertion of federal power over the economy and society. WIB was responsible for ensuring the armed forces maintained sufficient supplies. It set production targets and prices, while also inducing industries to pay higher wages to quash employee unrest. The federal government likewise nationalized the railroad system, placing it under the control of the United States Railroad Administration (USRA). Once again, this marked an incredible departure from previous federal involvement with railroads that primarily focused on promoting competition (Rockoff 2004).

As the exigencies of war subsided, the federal government ceded much of the power it had seized—for example, by abolishing the WIB and USRA. However, these experiences played a significant role in shaping governmental expansion during the New Deal Era. Just as economic changes spurred government intervention during the Progressive Era, the Great Depression proved an important impetus for further growth. By 1939, federal employment was nearly one million—almost triple the 1915 levels (Census 1975). Government expenditures reached nearly $9 billion (10 percent of GDP), increasing more than nine times its 1915 amount ($746 million or 2.72 percent of GDP). New agencies were created, including the Securities and Exchange Commission, the Federal Communications Commission, the Federal Deposit Insurance Commission, the National Labor Relations Board, and the Civil Aeronautics Board.

US entry into World War II only cemented the augmentation of government activity. Federal expenditures multiplied tenfold between 1939 and 1945, a remarkable increase from 10 to 48 percent in spending as a percent of GDP. Even with the post–World War II drawdown, it was clear that the experience of five decades, the Great Depression, and two world wars had expanded the size and scope of the federal government in a nonreversible way, touching more aspects of economic and social relations than ever before.

Indeed, these trends continued, as regulation in the decades after the war shifted away from economic management to new areas of worker safety, the environment, and consumer protection in the 1960s and 1970s. Government expenditures continued to steadily build throughout the twentieth and twenty-first centuries. The relative stability and prosperity of the macroeconomy in this postwar era led to fresh regulatory attention on topics such as water and air pollution as well as product safety. Public mobilization, including the civil rights, environmental, and consumer movements propelled these trends (see, e.g., Eisner 2000; Harris and Milkis 1989; Jones, Theriault, and Whyman 2019; Nader 1965). The social regulatory advancements of these decades led to additional government roles and organizations in these areas, with the creation of the Environmental Protection Agency, the Occupational Safety and Health Administration, and the Consumer Product Safety Commission, among others.

Beginning in the 1970s and 1980s, a considerable movement for deregulation led to the abolition of some agencies—such as the ICC and the Civil Aeronautics Board—as well as the emergence of new regulatory oversight processes, notably centralized review by the Office of Management and Budget (Derthick and Quirk 1985; Jones, Theriault, and Whyman 2019; Rudalevige 2018). These reforms had important policy consequences for executive branch policies and in some areas eliminated them altogether. Nevertheless, they did not radically address the legitimacy of most government activities that arose during the twentieth century.

In sum, the size and scope of federal government expanded significantly over the course of the twentieth century, with particularly large upticks occurring during the Progressive Era, the Great Depression, and World War II. This growth created tremendous challenges for elected officials tasked with overseeing administration. Presidents responded in several ways, like increasing presidential staff, reorganizing the Executive Office of the President, transferring the Bureau of the Budget into the White House, as well as creating new budgetary, legislative, and regulatory clearance procedures. All of these developments enhanced presidents' power over agencies in accordance with presidential policy programs (Moe 1985b). Congress, however, lagged behind.

The Roots of Congressional Policymaking Capacity

Indeed, the Congress of 1940 was not much different from the one of 1900, at least with respect to capacity. Such torpidity had profound implications for its policymaking role and power (Cooper 2017). As the tasks of governing grew, Congress became increasingly reliant on the executive branch for policy information and ideas. We argue this dependence was primarily a function of stagnant legislative resource capacity.

Throughout the twentieth century and into the twenty-first, Congress's policymaking capacity has been high enough to maintain opportunities for executive constraint. Even when encountering intense polarization that frustrates lawmaking, Congress has still retained the ability to influence policy and confront executive power through nonstatutory mechanisms that require lower thresholds for action. This is not to say policymaking capacity has gone unaltered. Rather, it has never receded to a point where Congress lacks the opportunities or legitimacy to challenge the executive. Instead, resources have been the more binding constraint on its power. Nonetheless, we begin by surveying congressional policymaking capacity.

Article I of the Constitution is the fount of formal congressional power. Section 1 grants Congress plenary legislative authority ("All legislative Powers herein granted shall be vested in a Congress of the United States"). The Elastic (Article I, Section 8: "The Congress shall have the power to . . . make all Laws which shall be necessary and proper for carrying into Execution the foregoing Powers") and the Commerce Clauses (Article I, Section 8: "to regulate Commerce with foreign Nations, and among the several States, and with Indian Tribes") give it the ability to exercise this legislative power broadly. Judicial interpretations of these provisions have not always taken an expansive view, particularly before and at the beginning of the New Deal. However, these interpretations did not affect Congress alone, but instead limited the entire federal government.

"The power of the purse" (Article I, Section 9: "No Money shall be drawn from the Treasury, but in Consequence of Appropriations made by Law") ensures Congress can continuously oversee the implementation of its legislation. The Constitution also grants it nonstatutory authorities, further enhancing its power. Congress alone can declare war and raise an army. A supermajority in the Senate is necessary for ratifying treaties. The advice and consent power granted to the Senate also gives Congress influence over personnel decisions. Through its ability to veto nominees, Congress shapes how agencies and courts treat its legislative mandates. It can likewise oust or censure executive officials through the impeachment and removal processes.

Extraconstitutional practices further entrenched the policymaking capacity of Congress during the twentieth century. For instance, the insertion of legislative vetoes into statutes was a frequent practice prior to the 1980s. These tools allowed Congress to pass resolutions nullifying certain executive branch actions. First used in an appropriations bill in the 1930s, they quickly became a common method for controlling executive branch policy implementation.

However, these types of legislative vetoes were ruled unconstitutional by the Supreme Court in the 1983 case *INS v. Chadha*.

Though ostensibly a weakening of its policymaking capacity, Congress quickly acted to preserve its ex post veto power (Fisher 2005). For instance, some vetoes were changed to require congressional approval through a joint resolution with the president's signature before an agency action went into effect. This requirement was the case for executive branch reorganizations, which previously had been subject to congressional approval. Other effective vetoes, particularly provisions requiring executive actors to report and wait on decisions so Congress could muster the resources to block them if necessary, were unaffected by the *Chadha* decision (Korn 1996).

Legislative vetoes also gained renewed life post-*Chadha* through committee reports accompanying appropriations legislation. By tradition, the appropriations subcommittees include reams of instructions for agencies about how they should spend their appropriated funds (Fenno 1966; Schick 2008). Though these committee reports do not have the force of law and are not approved by the president, agencies nonetheless show considerable deference to them because of their regularized, repeated interactions with their overseeing appropriations subcommittees. The history of legislative vetoes demonstrates how informal powers, and norms about their use, may serve as (perhaps imperfect) substitutes when formal powers are unavailable or difficult to exercise (Bolton 2021).

Executive branch oversight is another important avenue of congressional power outside the statutory realm. Though not in the Constitution, the power to investigate executive branch activities has long been recognized (Kriner and Schickler 2016). Both the House and Senate endow committees with the authority to subpoena witnesses and evidence in the course of oversight. The courts have likewise acknowledged this power, though with some limits (e.g., *Eastland v. United States Serviceman's Fund*, 421 US 491 [1975]; *Trump v. Mazars USA, LLP*, 520 US [2020]).[4]

Finally, Congress controls its agenda. It is not required to take up any particular issue, in contrast to many parliamentary systems where executive actors have formal agenda-setting powers in the legislature. Only legislators may introduce a bill for consideration, and each chamber independently structures its agenda. This agenda-setting power is a key way Congress can regulate the federal policymaking process. It also gives legislators leverage against presidents eager to pass a legislative program. Presidential priorities can be killed with no effort by Congress, particularly if those priorities are unimportant or antithetical to the majority party's preferences in either chamber.

Of course, other factors may deplete congressional policymaking capacity. For instance, supermajority rules often necessitate bipartisan support for lawmaking. The filibuster effectively mandates a three-fifths coalition to pass most legislation in the Senate. Presidents' power to veto laws requires either accommodating their preferences or obtaining two-thirds majorities in both chambers for an override. These supermajoritarian institutions, combined with relatively marginal majority party sizes and high polarization at various times, place real limitations on Congress's ability to pass legislation.

Despite these challenges, congressional majorities can leverage other formal and informal powers to dissuade executives poised to act against their interests. Our conception of policymaking capacity encompasses more than statutes. Nonstatutory powers facilitate Congress's position in the policymaking process, even when it cannot muster supermajorities to act. For instance, Kriner and Schickler (2016) document the important ways policymaking and presidential approval are influenced by oversight, an activity that does not entail the same collective action problems inherent in lawmaking. Typically, committee chairs have almost complete oversight agenda control and only simple majorities are needed to issue subpoenas.

The appropriations process provides other examples of how collective action problems might be avoided in this particular, but important, policy area. The must-pass status of appropriation legislation and the prospect of a government shutdown bolster the bargaining leverage of majorities. Accompanying committee reports, moreover, are not subject to approval beyond the committee (Bolton 2021).

Congress can likewise leverage many of its formal powers to impose costs on presidents who advance unfavorable policies. For instance, the Senate's advice and consent power requires a majority to approve presidential nominees. The possibility of confirmation can be dangled in exchange for policy concessions from the president, even without passing legislation.

Overall, we argue Congress possesses considerable informal and formal powers to qualify as high in policymaking capacity throughout the entire period of our study. The Constitution and norms that emerge through historical practice have ensured it has enough opportunities to pursue its policy preferences. Some conditions that vary over time—for example, polarization and majority sizes, or interpretations of constitutional provisions—may limit its ability to exert its will through *statute*. Congress, however, has still retained numerous nonstatutory powers allowing it to constrain executive branch behavior.

Yet, as discussed in chapter 2, policymaking opportunities are necessary, but not sufficient, for legislatures to be high-capacity institutions. They also need adequate resources to capitalize on these opportunities. On this dimension, congressional capacity has lagged substantially at various moments in time. Several developments during the twentieth century, however, eventually boosted Congress's resource capacity and transformed it into one of the most professionalized legislatures in the world.

The Evolution of Congressional Resource Capacity

The growth of the federal government posed a significant challenge to Congress's power. While it had once been able to micromanage the details of administration, this became infeasible as governmental responsibilities expanded. Ultimately, Congress enacted a series of institutional reforms that increased its resource capacity, most notably providing itself sources of unbiased, policy-information and the requisite staff to use that information. Its ability to effectively constrain an energetic executive branch was thereby enhanced. Table 3.1 summarizes the major developments we review in this chapter and their broad effects on congressional resource capacity. We highlight both successful and failed attempts at legislative reform to fully understand their underlying political dynamics, particularly whether partisan or institutional motivations were ultimately the impetus for advancing capacity. Overall, we find support for the latter, and supplement this qualitative evidence with systematic quantitative analyses at the end of the chapter.

The Legislative Reference Service/Congressional Research Service

Information is an essential feature of resource capacity. Congress faced informational disadvantages vis-à-vis the executive in the early 1900s, often relying on agencies for information when formulating policies. To address these disparities, Congress developed its own institutions that could independently generate information, as was the case with the 1914 creation of the Legislative Reference Service (LRS), housed within the Library of Congress.

Inspired by the rise of legislative reference bureaus across the states in the late nineteenth century, the LRS was designed to provide legislators

TABLE 3.1. Summary of Congressional Resource Capacity Developments, 1900-present

Year	Action	Effect on Capacity
1914	First appropriation for Legislative Reference Service	Legislative information
1921	Budget and Accounting Act	Creation of GAO Administrative information
1935	Federal Register Act	Administrative information
1946	Administrative Procedure Act	Administrative information
1946	Legislative Reorganization Act	Increased staffing Additional funding for support agencies Codified oversight responsibilities
1970	Legislative Reorganization Act	Increased staffing for committees New resources and mandate for CRS
1972	Technology Assessment Act	Creation of OTA Legislative information
1974	Congressional Budget and Impoundment Control Act	Creation of CBO Legislative information
1978	Inspector General Act	Created IG positions in agencies Administrative information
1993	Joint Committee on the Organization of Congress	None
1995	Contract with America	Abolition of OTA Reduced staffing

with information from a bill's conception to its passage (Brudnick 2011; Rothstein 1990). Though similar bills were considered throughout the early 1900s by Progressives such as Robert LaFollette, they did not advance beyond committee.[5] After several failed attempts, the FY 1915 appropriations bill for legislative, executive, and judicial expenses (PL 63-125) appropriated $25,000 "to enable the Librarian of Congress to employ competent persons to prepare such indexes, digests, and compilations of law as may be required for Congress." These funds led to the creation of the LRS.

Its functions were initially limited. Though the LRS was intended to engage in "bill drafting," this provision was removed after members feared it would consequently become a biased "bill factory" (Putnam 1915). Instead, the agency originally only supplied members of Congress relevant federal and state laws, eschewing the example of more active units like those in Wisconsin at the time (Graves 1947; Rothstein 1990). Its mission broadened considerably in 1946, however, after the passage of the Legislative Reorganization Act (LRA). This law created a permanent authorization for the LRS and expanded its activities related to information generation and interpretation, while also permitting staffing increases to accommodate these new tasks. Specifically, Section 203 of the law authorizes the LRS to "advise and assist" committees considering legislation; "gather, classify, analyze, and make available data" relevant to legislation; and create summaries of hearings and legislation for members.

In 1970, Congress further expanded the duties of the newly renamed Congressional Research Service (CRS) to include creating a list of expired authorizations; naming potential policy changes committees might "profitably analyze;" preparing reports to help members "in their legislative and representative functions;" and providing prehearing memoranda about legislative measures under consideration. The 1970 act likewise empowered the CRS to hire any personnel necessary for its mission, while also giving it authority to contract out services. Following passage, CRS's staff enlarged by 150 percent between 1971 and 1977 (Robinson 1992). Overall, the law deepened the active role of the CRS at multiple stages of the policymaking process (Brudnick 2011). Today, the agency annually responds to more than sixty-five thousand information requests and holds hundreds of briefings on specific policy issues and legislation. By providing expert and neutral analysis, independent of interest groups and executive branch agencies angling for their own policy desires, the CRS ultimately strengthened legislative resource capacity in crucial ways.

The history of the LRS/CRS certainly appears to support the institutional explanation of capacity building. While spurred by Progressive entrepreneurs, its consideration and passage on the floor engendered broad congressional support. The debates over its enactment were not geared toward advancing the causes of the majority party at the expense of the president, but rather recognized the institutional imperatives of information required for policymaking. The decision to remove bill-drafting powers exemplifies the concern members had in creating an institution that would be nonpartisan and serve all members.

The General Accounting Office

As federal spending flourished, budget management became a key locus of policy conflict for Congress and the executive branch. To this end, the General Accounting Office (GAO) marks another important milestone for the development of resource capacity. Created by the Budget and Accounting

Act of 1921 (PL 67-13), the GAO assumes a vital role in assessing the use of appropriated funds by agencies, thereby aiding oversight. Prior to the GAO, the Department of the Treasury was responsible for auditing spending. Several developments led Congress to create a budget watchdog under its control (Schick 1983; Trask 2001; White 1948; Wilmerding 1943).

In particular, the surge in governmental activity occurring in the early twentieth century led to mounting demand for rationalization of the budget process. Fiscal reforms were first implemented in the states, requiring governors to prepare and propose budgets on behalf of the entire executive branch to be considered by the legislature (Trask 2001). Concomitantly, Theodore Roosevelt's Keep Commission and William Howard Taft's Commission on Economy and Efficiency, both of which centered on rationalizing the executive branch, paved the way for an early forerunner of the GAO—the Bureau of Efficiency (BOE). This new agency provided numerous services to Congress, ranging from information about executive branch programs to evaluations of policy and management practices.[6] Finally, expenditures ballooned during World War I and "normalized" the idea of spending by a more intrusive government (Rockoff 2004). This growth created new management, information, and coordination problems for Congress, tasked with allocating and overseeing governmental funds.

These developments impelled Congress toward reforming the budgetary process to reduce fragmentation and aid in oversight of federal expenditures. In 1920, it passed a bill allowing for an executive-based budgeting system, whereby presidents, through the Bureau of the Budget, would have centralized control over agency budget requests. In this way, it empowered presidential control over the executive branch. This centralization likewise benefited Congress, helping it overcome the fragmentation in the appropriations process, wherein each agency separately developed and submitted a budget to legislators. The law also created the GAO, which would be responsible for auditing executive expenditures and reporting to Congress—a clearer win for congressional capacity.

The GAO was designed to be responsive to Congress. The original proposed bill mandated the comptroller general—who would head the GAO—be appointed by the president and confirmed by the Senate. The comptroller general was to serve a fixed term and could only be removed through a resolution in Congress, requiring the approval of both chambers but not the president. Objecting to these removal procedures, President Wilson vetoed the bill and instead argued removal should be the prerogative of the president (Trask 2001). In a revised bill that ultimately became law, the provision in question was altered to require a joint resolution that mandated presidential input for removal. The bill passed in 1921 with near-unanimous majorities in both the House and Senate, earning President Harding's signature.

This legislative history provides insights into the constraints legislators face in increasing their own capacity. The bargaining over the GAO comptroller appointment and removal provisions demonstrates how widespread capacity reforms require broad support because presidents will not simply assent to new laws they perceive as encroaching on their power. The need to overcome vetoes or veto threats necessitates tempering ambitions and building large, usually bipartisan coalitions for reform or accommodating presidential preferences. In doing so, majority parties are unable to only pursue policies that advance their political interests. Instead, the perceived consequences of reform must benefit the institution broadly and not disadvantage the minority party, whose votes are imperative for passage.

Since its creation, the GAO has monitored executive branch expenditures and operations, in the service of Congress. Yet the exact method of operations has shifted over time. Before World War II, the GAO was concerned almost solely with agency spending. After the war, however, its mandate expanded to oversee issues related to governmental management and policy, policy analysis, and program investigations with recommendations for agencies and Congress. Renamed the Government Accountability Office in 2004, the GAO currently describes its mission as follows: "To support the Congress in meeting its constitutional responsibilities and to help improve the performance and ensure the accountability of the federal government for the benefit of the American people. We provide Congress with timely information that is objective, fact-based, nonpartisan, nonideological, fair, and balanced." Since the 1970s, its primary "clients" have been congressional committees, which typically request a GAO program investigation and recommendations for improvement. In this way, it differs from the CRS, which often initiates its own studies. According to the GAO's budget justification, it produced reports in response to 95 percent of the standing committees of Congress for FY 2016.[7]

Overall, the GAO's mission has broadened greatly from its envisioned role as an independent auditor of expenditures in the 1920s. While still focused on the sound expenditure of funds, it now also strives to understand executive branch policy and management issues that lead to inefficiencies. In this sense, the GAO has become an indispensable arm of Congress in overseeing executive activities. By providing information to legislators in these areas, it has served to greatly augment congressional resource capacity.

The Federal Register Act of 1935

While the GAO aided congressional oversight of spending, Congress still encountered substantial barriers in monitoring the implementation of its non-appropriation policies in the early twentieth century. New Deal legislation granted executive branch agencies enormous authority, but Congress often lacked the means to track how this authority was used. Unless agencies directly publicized their actions, there was no consistent way for Congress to understand or even know about regulations until they were enforced. The 1934 report of the American Bar Association's (ABA) Special Committee on Administrative Law summarized the confusion:

> Practically every agency to which legislative power has been delegated (or sub-delegated) has exercised it, and has published its enactments, sometimes in the form of official printed pamphlets, sometimes in mimeograph form, sometimes in privately owned publications, and sometimes in press releases. Sometimes they exist only in sort of unwritten law. Rules and regulations, upon compliance with which important privileges and freedom from heavy penalties may depend, are amended and interpreted as formally or informally as they were originally adopted. (ABA 1970 [1934], 228)

Presidents' unilateral directives were similarly opaque (Mayer 2002). The same ABA panel wrote regarding executive orders in the 1930s: "Some orders are retained or buried in the files of the government departments, some are confidential and not published, and the practice as to printing and publication of orders is not uniform" (ABA 1970 [1934], 229).

How can Congress check the executive branch if it does not know it has acted? These concerns were the backdrop for the introduction of the Federal Register bill in 1935 (H.R. 6323), which tasked the Government Printing Office and the National Archives with publishing a serial called the *Federal Register*. The bill required the printing of executive branch documents ("any Presidential proclamation or Executive order and any order, regulation, rule, certificate, code of fair competition, license, notice, or similar instrument issued, prescribed, or promulgated by a Federal agency") in the *Federal*

Register before it could have the force of law. This provision substantially enhanced the transparency of executive policymaking.

Congressional debate of the bill was limited. Interestingly, the primary concerns related to the size of the budget and salaries for officials, highlighting the anticipated costs of appearing spendthrift to constituents. No doubt, these concerns were heightened by the ongoing economic crisis. The bill passed on voice vote with no recorded opposition in the House (Congressional Record, House, April 1, 1935, 4785–91) and unanimously in the Senate (Congressional Record, Senate, June 10, 1935, 8663–64). Overall, then, the enactment of the Federal Register Act was a fairly noncontroversial affair with universal support across both chambers and parties, consistent with the institutional explanation of capacity development.

The Administrative Procedure Act of 1946

As the New Deal progressed, the ABA's Special Committee on Administrative Law repeatedly decried the chaotic state of administrative procedures in the United States, which lacked coherent standards for agency regulation or adjudication applicable across the whole government (Shepherd 1996). In 1941, an Attorney General's ad hoc Committee on Administrative Procedure concluded its study of agency processes, writing, "Laymen and lawyers alike . . . are baffled by a lack of published information to which they can turn when confronted with an administrative problem" (Committee on Administrative Procedure, 77 S. Doc. 8, 25). These conclusions led an array of actors to support administrative procedure reform by the early 1940s.

Administrative procedures, however, are not policy neutral. Disputes about their policy effects inhibited legislative action on the matter for much of the 1930s. Early ABA reports promoted diminishing agencies' authority through enhanced judicial review, proposing specialized judicial tribunals to review administrative actions (Shepherd 1996). Skeptical of New Deal legislation, Republicans and some conservative Democrats in Congress were receptive to these proposals in the mid-1930s. A Republican-dominated judiciary appeared their best hope of limiting the New Deal (McCubbins, Noll, and Weingast 1999).

Increased conservatism in the 76th Congress (1939–40) set the stage for consideration of the Walter-Logan Bill (H.R. 6324), the first attempt at administrative procedure reform. The bill passed both chambers, largely based on the votes of Republicans and Southern Democrats. Though ostensibly centered on procedures, the bill would also likely dismantle the New Deal. Notable provisions required that all regulations be passed only after public hearings, retrospective review of regulations, and expanded judicial review (Kerwin and Furlong 2011; McCubbins, Noll, and Weingast 1999).

The law's application to agencies was fairly selective. The new burdens predominately fell on New Deal agencies and exempted many created before the Roosevelt presidency. Conservative votes were wooed by exempting their favored agencies, including all military agencies, the Department of State, and the Patent Office (Shepherd 1996, 1618–1619). Unsurprisingly, Roosevelt objected to the Walter-Logan bill, raising concerns about onerous administrative procedures and their effects on his economic program. In the end, he vetoed the bill on December 8, 1940. This episode again indicates presidents will not accept reforms that disadvantage their administration. Thus, congressional coalitions require broad support if reforms are to succeed in the shadow of presidential opposition.

Although the demands of World War II pushed administrative procedures off the agenda, a renewed appetite for reform emerged by the war's end. The bill that would eventually become the Administrative Procedure Act (S. 7) was introduced in January 1945. It passed almost unanimously with little formal debate and was signed by President Truman (Public Law 79-404) on June 11, 1946. The APA, like the Walter-Logan bill, required greater transparency in administrative operations. Agencies were now required to publish information in the *Federal Register* about their organization and procedures, in addition to continuous information on their regulatory actions. Why did the APA receive such high levels of support, especially given the doomed fate of the Walter-Logan bill?

The short answer is the content of these two bills differed markedly. While the Walter-Logan bill mandated public hearings for every proposed regulation, the APA—in delineating the now-familiar procedures for federal rulemaking—only required these hearings if explicitly mandated by statute. Instead, the new law outlined an "informal" rulemaking process, whereby agencies publish notice of proposed rules in the *Federal Register* to receive public comment. Additionally, the APA clearly sketched the basis for judicial review of agency actions. Federal courts were empowered to overturn agency actions they found arbitrary or capricious, unconstitutional, outside the discretion granted to the agency in statutory law, or unsupported by the facts. While certainly a new burden, these procedures were nowhere near as cumbersome as those in the Walter-Logan bill, which likely explains the ability of the APA to attract more liberal congressional support and President Truman's signature.

These three features of the APA—publication of information, notice and comment, and judicial review—all increased congressional capacity to oversee the bureaucracy through the additional information provided by way of procedures. By forcing agencies to publicly declare their intent to regulate, Congress and relevant interest groups would have forewarning of agency actions (McCubbins, Noll, and Weingast 1987). Administrative procedures can also induce agency compliance with congressional preferences. Since promulgating regulations is costly in terms of time and resources, the threat of being overturned by the courts or Congress can motivate agency responsiveness to these actors.

Beyond institutional concerns, McCubbins, Noll, and Weingast (1999) contend Democrats had partisan motives for supporting the APA, hoping it would prevent the dismantling of New Deal programs. Democrats, they argue, feared losing control of Congress in the 1946 election (which they did) and the presidency in the 1948 election (which they did not). Because the judiciary was dominated by Roosevelt appointees at the time, the New Dealers sought to "lock in" their policies by making agency policymaking more onerous and subject to judicial review.

However, there are reasons to doubt this partisan-based account. As Schwartz (1999) notes, it is not clear why Republicans would also support an arrangement to solidify New Deal programs. Assuming they too expected to win, why would Republicans assent to procedures that would tie their own hands and prevent them from actualizing key parts of their ideological agenda? Moreover, Republicans supported the APA and advocated for even more strenuous review procedures during the limited floor debate (Shepherd 1996). It is true Northern Democrats in Congress now backed the 1946 administrative procedure reforms, which they eschewed in the 1930s. But again the content of the Walter-Logan bill and the APA were starkly different. We believe these distinctions explain the failure of the former and the success of the latter, based on the composition of their supporting coalitions.

Indeed, few dispute the APA yielded significant benefits for congressional resource capacity. As even McCubbins, Noll, and Weingast (1999) acknowledge, "The common factor influencing all members of Congress was that the APA strengthened Congress at the expense of the president." This idea is consistent with the unanimity of support for final passage and highlights the institutional, rather than ideological, incentives for reforms that strengthen congressional capacity.

Taken together, the LRS/CRS, GAO, Federal Register Act, and APA represented advances in congressional resource capacity to develop policy and oversee the executive branch. All endowed Congress with access to information necessary to execute its functions. Yet, if legislators wanted to meaningfully utilize this information, they required additional resources that were eventually acquired through the Legislative Reorganization Act of 1946.

The Legislative Reorganization Act of 1946

Beyond its informational needs, Congress also lacked staff personnel and expertise. Legislative branch expenditures were relatively stagnant in the first decades of the twentieth century. Without sufficient funding, offices and committees could not be adequately staffed as workload increased. Between 1891 and 1935, the number of committee staffers grew from 103 to 294. At the same time, federal outlays multiplied by 710 percent in real terms.[8] While other reforms enhanced information, Congress needed skilled and experienced staffers to use this information productively in legislating and overseeing the executive branch.

In general, Congress struggled to author legislation that could meaningfully temper executive action. Statutory discretion given to executive actors expanded as legislative tasks grew in complexity and number (LaFollette 1943; Schick 1983). During the 79th Congress, a Joint Committee on the Organization of Congress (JCOC) was created to examine congressional effectiveness and offer recommendations for improvement. Its final report heavily criticized Congress's failures and their consequences for democratic governance (79th Congress, 2nd session, Senate Report 1400). Acknowledging these resource deficits prompted the passage of the Legislative Reorganization Act of 1946 (LRA), which spurred congressional modernization. In introducing the bill, Senator LaFollette remarked, "It has been evident to all those interested in and concerned about efficient Government, that because of the separation of powers in our Constitution the gap between the executive and the legislative arms of the Government has been growing and widening throughout the years" (Congressional Record, June 5, 1946, 6344).

Importantly, support for the LRA was bipartisan. Only 16 senators voted against it, 9 of whom were Southern Democrats against the provision reducing the number of committees that would eliminate their chair positions. Republicans and non-Southern Senate Democrats voted 23–3 and 17–4, respectively, in favor of the LRA. Individual votes were not recorded in the House on initial acceptance, but the final bill passed 229–61. Indeed, Schickler (2001, 150) declared the passage of the 1946 LRA a "broad, bipartisan affair."

The new act had several important implications for resource capacity.[9] It significantly restructured committees in both chambers, reducing their numbers to nineteen in the House and fifteen in the Senate. It likewise endowed them with a new statutory responsibility to oversee the executive branch. Section 136 of the act mandated "each standing committee of the Senate and the House of Representatives shall exercise continuous watchfulness of the execution by the administrative agencies concerned of any laws, the subject matter of which is within the jurisdiction of such committee."

The LRA also made new provisions for funding staff resources, allowing each committee to hire up to four professional staffers with subject area expertise and additional clerical staff. The House and Senate Appropriations Committees were authorized to employ as many staff as they might require, subject to funding limitations. While slow to start, the number of committee staffers increased dramatically over time (see fig. 1.1), as chairs began to avail themselves of the newly available resources (Galloway 1955; Kammerer 1951). The LRA also removed staffing caps for the LRS.

Furthermore, the new law raised the annual salaries for members of Congress from $10,000 to $12,500 and allowed them to collect federal pension payments after six years of service. These changes were notable in light of an earlier debacle over legislative pensions. Indeed, a similar 1942 provision was quickly repealed, following an outpouring of public opposition over what was called a "pension grab." This episode cemented constituents' resistance to perceived government excess in legislators' minds. By 1946, however, the political winds had seemingly shifted following a public relations campaign led by George Galloway (Byrd 1989; Galloway 1951).

Overall, the LRA proved to be one of the most consequential congressional reforms in US history. Consistent with the institutional explanation, it passed with sizeable bipartisan support in an effort to improve the overall capabilities of Congress. Its effects on human capital are perhaps its most vital, producing increases in professional staff sizes across congressional committees. These changes were crucial to the development of congressional resource capacity in the mid-twentieth century and undoubtedly set the stage for US separation of powers politics in the post–World War II era.

Post-1940s Developments in Congressional Resources

Advancements in resource capacity did not halt in the 1940s. New changes to capacity trailed a continued expansion in the scope and size of the administrative state after World War II (Jones, Theriault, and Whyman 2019). However, unlike the changes we have reviewed thus far, the postwar period featured the passage of some less durable reforms, the failure to produce legislation at times, and a 1990s retrenchment in legislative resources. Understanding these "failures" of capacity-building alongside the successes yields important insights into the constraints legislatures face when trying to bolster their institutional capacities.

The Legislative Reorganization Act of 1970

To begin, a new bipartisan Joint Committee on the Organization of Congress (JCOC) formed during the 89th Congress (1965–66). As in the 1940s, perceptions of stunted capacity were the primary impetus for its creation (Schickler 2001; Sundquist 1981). In the words of the JCOC's report, "Many contend that Congress no longer is capable of exercising initiative in the solution of modern problems. . . . Under the pressure of modern circumstances, Congress has tended to delegate authority to the executive branch of the government" (Final Report of the JCOC, 89 S. Rpt. 1414, 1).

Although the JCOC's recommendations were not immediately implemented, they are clearly reflected in the Legislative Reorganization Act (LRA) of 1970. Like previous institutional reforms, the 1970 LRA was a widely bipartisan initiative, receiving strong support from liberal Democrats and Republicans. The bill initially passed with only nineteen "no" votes in the House and five in the Senate. Dissent throughout the debate was mostly confined to committee chairs, who would stand to lose individual power within their chamber. On the whole, though, legislators were largely motivated by institutional, not partisan, concerns when passing this reform.

One key provision was the previously discussed CRS reforms that increased staff resources, while also adding new oversight and committee responsibilities. The JCOC's staffing proposals were likewise implemented. In particular, Section 301 of the law authorized committees to hire six professional staff members and an additional six clerical staffers. The law also guaranteed staff resources for the minority on each committee (P.L. 91-510, Sections 301-302). Furthermore, the LRA allowed committees to contract out staff on an as-needed basis.

Beyond increasing overall staff in Congress, the 1970 LRA also shifted the distribution of employee types within the chamber. Whereas majority party staff dominated committees in 1970 (comprising over 90 percent of committee staff), minority staffers composed increasing shares of the total committee staff. By 1980, 16.7 percent of staffers were designated as minority professional staffers. By 2000, this figure was 25 percent, where it has since hovered. Thus, the LRA simultaneously broadened the capacity of both majority and minority legislators.[10]

Another widespread change in staff composition occurred in the proportion of administrative support staff. In 1970, 32.6 percent of committee staffers held primarily "administrative," rather than policy-oriented, positions. These nonpolicy, administrative roles included stenographers, typists, information technology professionals, documents clerks, printing clerks, and secretaries. By 1980, this number dropped to 22.4 percent. With little change since 1990, the percentage of staff in administrative roles has stabilized around 15 percent. This pattern may in large part be attributed to changes in technology that increased staff efficiency and led to decreases in occupations such as secretaries and typists. Not all nonpolicy jobs declined, however. Communications staff, in particular, have spiked in recent decades. In 1970, just 0.2 percent of committee staff contained "press" or "communications" in their job title. By 2012, 5.6 percent of all committee staffers did.

These changes occurred in a context of increasingly centralized majority party leadership power within Congress. From 1970 to 2010, Senate leadership staff grew more than fourfold, while House leadership staff enlarged more than threefold. In 1970, the House Speaker's staff consisted of nine individuals, for example. But by 2010, Speaker Pelosi's staff numbered fifty-seven. Increases in committee and leadership staff likely facilitated and also reflected trends toward centralizing power away from rank-and-file members, documented in recent studies on Congress (e.g., Curry 2015; Hanson 2014; Sinclair 2016). This book is less concerned about that distribution of power *within* chambers, but rather whether some element of congressional majorities have the capacity to carry out the institution's functions. While these intrachamber power shifts are important, their causes are outside the scope of our argument and left as fruitful avenues for future exploration. But whether viewed through the lens of committees or organizational changes empowering the party leadership, congressional staff capacity surged beginning in the 1970s in ways that enabled majorities to better carry out the institutional prerogatives of Congress.

The Politics of Budgeting in the 1970s and the Congressional Budget Office

Legislative-executive conflict reached new heights in the 1970s as Nixon battled a Democratically controlled Congress, most notably over spending. Presidents beginning with Thomas Jefferson have acted to "impound" appropriated funds—that is, not spend up to the levels of budget authority granted by Congress. This practice weakens the ability of Congress to use appropriations to influence executive actors. Impoundments prior to the 1970s were relatively limited. Nixon, however, wielded them to an unprecedented degree, impounding between 17 and 20 percent of appropriated funds in his first five years in office (Stanton 1974).

Further aggravating the interbranch dispute, Nixon pressured Congress to impose a $250 billion spending ceiling for FY 1973, claiming expenditures would otherwise soar billions of dollars above planned levels. When Congress declined and the administration's predictions did not materialize, the need for budget-related information independent of the executive became heightened (Schick 1975). Indeed, in the first half of 1973, legislators had submitted more than 250 bills addressing the budgetary process (S. Rpt. 93-579).

The budget crisis led to the appointment of a Joint Study Committee on Budget Control. It recommended the creation of House and Senate budget committees, assisted by a nonpartisan staff of budgetary experts, to oversee a congressional budgetary process to rival that of the president (Joyce 2011). Committees in both chambers accordingly crafted legislation that would ultimately become the Congressional Budget and Impoundment Control Act of 1974 (PL 93-344).

In reporting its 1973 bill (S. 1541), the Senate Committee on Government Affairs detailed legislative deficiencies in administering the budget and appropriations process in the 1970s. In the words of the Committee, "Congress does not have its own budget staff and it must rely upon the President for information, judgments, and evaluations.... All this makes Congress painfully dependent upon Presidential agencies.... It gets only what the executive gives, and only when the executive gives it" (S. Rpt. 93-579, 7).

The Congressional Budget and Impoundment Control Act of 1974 was signed into law by Nixon on July 12, 1974. Support for the act was broad and bipartisan, with votes of 401–6 in the House and 75–0 in the Senate. Once again, this episode confirms the institutional explanation for capacity reforms. The Budget Act was not simply the tool of Democratic majorities to rein in a Republican administration. Instead, Republicans in Congress also valued the need to fortify their institution in the budgetary process.

While the law made several consequential changes, a key development was the creation of the Congressional Budget Office (CBO). At its core, the CBO was designed to remedy the informational deficits in budgetary information. Unlike the GAO, the CBO Director is chosen by consensus between the Speaker of the House and the president pro tempore of the Senate. The director can be removed by resolution of either chamber, ensuring a leader acting against the institution's interests (however they are conceived) could be expeditiously ejected.

The job of the CBO is to support Congress, and in particular the budget committees. To do so, it offers economic analyses in evaluating legislative proposals, including baseline budget and economic projections, long-term budget projections, and cost estimates of most laws. Additionally, it produces "scores" as to whether legislation is consistent with the budget resolution's goals and an annual "reestimate" of the president's budget to provide an alternative to the presidentially-managed Office of Management and Budget (OMB) analysis (CBO 2016).

The Congressional Budget and Impoundment Control Act likewise authorized the CBO to hire as much staff "as may be necessary" for these purposes. During its existence, CBO staffing has consistently hovered in the range of 200 to 250 full-time equivalents. The law further mandates staff be appointed "without regard to political affiliation and solely on the basis of their fitness to perform their duties." From its inception, the directors of the CBO have attempted to keep the agency above partisan squabbles—a difficult task when its work implicates almost every piece of legislation Congress considers. Alice Rivlin, the first CBO director, was adamant that the agency deal not with policy prescription, but with policy questions. The agency would never take a position for or against a bill (Blum 1992). While systematic evidence on the

CBO's efficacy is relatively lacking, several studies find it does provide distinct information that sometimes contradicts OMB's reports and forecasts on the same matters (Engstrom and Kernell 2004; Joyce 2011).

The Inspector General Act of 1978

Several scandals involving waste, fraud, and abuse in federal programs in the 1960s and 1970s prompted heightened congressional scrutiny of agency activities. Examples include the General Services Administration (GSA) paying out millions of dollars for services never performed in exchange for kickbacks to its employees; high rates of default on improperly granted federal loans costing the government around $500 million; and fraudulent spending of up to $25 billion in any given year, as estimated by the GAO (S. Rpt. 95-1071). Existing agency spending controls and audit procedures were fragmented, underresourced, and ineffective at best or nonexistent at worst (Naughton 1998).

After a series of stand-alone laws created inspectors general (IG) in specific agencies throughout the 1970s, Congress passed the 1978 Inspector General Act to establish an IG in every Cabinet department and several large independent agencies.[11] The law endowed IGs with expansive authority to investigate their agencies. While the IGs were technically under the authority of agency heads, the law mandated "such head shall prevent or prohibit the Inspector General from initiating, carrying out, or completing any audit or investigation, or from issuing any subpena during the course of any audit or investigation." Congress further mandated a semiannual report on IG activities and findings (P.L. 95-452). It is through this information valve that IGs enhance congressional resource capacity.

Numerous agencies opposed the act on the record, arguing it was unnecessary since IGs could be established administratively and their independence would create contention within agency leadership (H. Rpt. 95-584). Congress overwhelmingly supported it over these objections, however, by a vote of 388–6 in the House and unanimously in the Senate.

The Short-Lived Office of Technology Assessment

Finally, we discuss the establishment of the Office of Technology Assessment (OTA). This office was created and operated in a much more politically acrimonious environment than the other previously discussed reforms, which prevented it from truly enriching congressional capacity and ultimately led to its abolition. The case of the OTA thus serves to reiterate the importance of bipartisanship and separation of powers motivations for capacity-enhancing reforms—in support of the institutional explanation.

The OTA was established to help Congress cope with policy issues arising from the proliferation of new technologies in the 1960s and 1970s. As technology advanced, Congress found itself falling behind the evolution of policy and governance. Beginning in the 1960s, the executive branch commenced quantitative analyses to support its programs, using new computing power Congress lacked. Legislative staffers were not up to the task of interpreting and incorporating such information into policy (Carson 1992). To remedy this problem, a new congressional support institution was envisioned to understand the technological and scientific dimensions of contemporary policy debates. The technology assessment movement outside of government also no doubt influenced the mission of the organization and the timing of its creation (Bimber 1996).

Ultimately, Congress passed the Technology Assessment Act (TAA) in October of 1972, and the OTA was born. Though the vote was unanimous in the Senate, it passed by only 256–118 in the House. Of the legislative support institutions we examine in this chapter, the OTA was the most contentious at its creation. The majority of Republicans voting were opposed (79–76), while Democrats were widely supportive (180–39).

Arguments in favor of the agency revolved around the increasingly complex technological issues on which Congress was required to legislate. Several representatives touted its prospective separation of powers benefits, claiming the lack of staffing and specialization inhibited congressional power. As Representative Charles Mosher (R-OH) poignantly remarked in his speech supporting the OTA, "We in the Congress are constantly outmanned and outgunned by the expertise of the executive agencies. We desperately need a stronger source of professional advice and information, more immediately and entirely responsible to us and responsive to the demands of our own committees."'

Opponents, on the other hand, thought the proposed agency would not be worth the costs and advised bolstering existing committees with additional resources instead. This concern was particularly salient given the OTA was to be responsible for introducing external facts and policy ideas to

Congress. Such a mandate appeared dangerously similar to prescribing policy recommendations, which the CBO, CRS, and other support institutions avoided (Kunkle 1995).

Despite this partisan opposition, the OTA was designed to be bipartisan in nature to preserve the neutrality of its work. It would be led by a Technology Assessment Board (TAB) consisting of six congressional members from each party and a nonvoting director to oversee its day-to-day management (Bimber 1996). The TAB was originally led by Senator Edward Kennedy (D-MA), even then a liberal bête noire. After he relinquished the TAB leadership position, the OTA was still recognized as very much beholden to Kennedy, exacerbating Republican concerns that the agency was biased against their policy desires. The choice of directors, primarily individuals who identified as liberal or in one case a Republican that endorsed Jimmy Carter for president, only heightened conservative suspicion (Sadowski 2015).

The agency's actions also drew conservative ire. The OTA's report on the Reagan administration's Strategic Defense Initiative (SDI) asserted that Reagan's goal of rendering enemy nuclear capabilities obsolete through SDI "should not serve as the basis of public expectation or national policy about ballistic missile defense" (quoted in Mooney 2005). Subsequent reports doubled down on this position.

Overall, the OTA may seem like an anomaly to the institutional explanation for capacity development, given the partisan nature of its creation and perceptions of bias in its operation. Indeed, these factors contributed heavily to its abolition in 1995, after Republicans assumed control of Congress. In this way, the rise and demise of the OTA actually lends itself to the institutional story, by illustrating the inability of politicized institutional reform to meaningfully enhance congressional capacity in the long run. We further detail OTA's collapse in the following section, along with other 1990s developments that ushered in an era of capacity retrenchment.

The 1990s: An Era of Retrenchment?

The 1990s featured several important capacity-related developments that, unlike the previously described reforms, led to a *decline* in congressional resources. The impetus for these changes were not related to interbranch policy developments, but rather scandal within Congress itself. In 1992, revelations emerged that members of the House were knowingly overdrawing their checking accounts at the public's expense and without penalty. Unsurprisingly, this discovery generated a public outcry that soon led to a newly assembled JCOC and helped catalyze a total Republican takeover of Congress for the first time in decades.

The Joint Committee on the Organization of Congress of 1993

Amid the fallout and public outrage from the House Banking scandal, a new JCOC convened in January 1993 (Saint-Martin 2014). The JCOC was commissioned to study the operations of Congress and provide recommendations on "strengthening the effectiveness of the Congress, simplifying its operations, improving its relationships with and oversight of other branches of the United States Government, and improving the orderly consideration of legislation."[12]

The committee, however, missed the mark in providing coherent, consensual proposals to Congress. Instead, House and Senate contingents on the JCOC produced different recommendations. There was little buy-in from leadership. Most notably, Speaker Tom Foley halted a markup of legislation based on the JCOC's recommendations due to opposition in his caucus from committee chairs. Ultimately, no legislation advanced to the floor, though some of the recommendations (e.g., that federal civil rights and employment laws be applicable in Congress) were subsequently enacted by congressional Republicans following the 1994 midterm elections (Bloch Rubin 2020; Wolfensberger 2013). Yet the 1993 JCOC clearly had nothing approaching the accomplishments of its predecessors in terms of strengthening the capacity of Congress vis-à-vis the executive (Strand and Lang 2019).

After examining the successful JCOC cases earlier in this chapter, it is relatively easy to see why. Previous committees operated under widespread consensus for reform in the face of a real threat to institutional power. The 1993 iteration, however, was birthed from the need for crisis management, while lacking cross- and intrachamber consensus about what changes to make or even if any were needed. The fact that powerful House members were resistant to the reforms and could not be persuaded by their fellow members or public campaigns only further doomed the JCOC. Ultimately, the committee failed to serve the goals of Democratic leadership. It did not immediately produce reforms they could tout, nor did it manage the public appearance of congressional corruption, providing an opening for the Republican ascension to power in 1995.

The Contract with America

On September 27, 1994, nearly four hundred Republican congressional candidates signed the "Contract with America," which detailed ten bills they would introduce and pass if they claimed the majority. The contract reflected the party's pledge to revitalize conservative governance, and chief on their agenda was reducing the size of government. Many of its proposed reforms were directed at Congress itself to eliminate alleged "waste, fraud, or abuse." Six weeks later, Republicans were given the opportunity to fulfill that promise after gaining fifty-four seats in the House and nine seats in the Senate, securing majorities in both chambers against Democratic president Bill Clinton. Newly empowered Republicans made good on their word to slash congressional spending, their primary targets being the OTA and committee staffers. These reforms reflect the single greatest decline in congressional resources in the twentieth century.

Given the conditions of its founding and its subsequent operations, there is little surprise the OTA was at the top of the Republicans' hit list. Its Reagan-era reports on SDI and the perception of its liberal disposition provided reason to doubt its pronouncements and informational value. Consequently, the organization simply did not advance the goal of congressional capacity from the Republican perspective. In Speaker Gingrich's words, "We constantly found scientists who thought what [OTA] was saying was incorrect." His spokesman, Rick Tyler, was more blunt about their problems with the OTA: "In some cases, it was politicized work" (both quoted in Mooney 2005, 45–46). Thus, the association of the OTA with the Democratic Party led Republicans to view the institution and its information as useless for their purposes. This perception coupled with the possible electoral benefits associated with cutting spending in Congress, led Republicans to abolish the OTA.

With respect to staffing, Republicans explicitly promised to curtail committee staff sizes by one-third. And, as figure 1.1 displays, their promise was realized. Such a contraction could ostensibly mean a Republican-led Congress was unilaterally disarming its capacity in the face of a Democratic president, but it also demonstrates the enduring political appeal of appearing more economical in the eyes of the public. This tension between institutional capacity and reelection interests are familiar from other reform debates we recounted earlier, such as those over the LRS, the Federal Register Act, and congressional pensions. The OTA abolition and staffing cuts were deemed a political winner by Republican majorities, even at the expense of its own institutional capacity. Perhaps softening the blow to capacity, contractions in staff were not uniformly distributed across Congress. Instead they were concentrated among subcommittees and minority party staffers, with the OTA's elimination also providing a sizable portion (Congressional Quarterly 2012). In this sense, Republican-initiated staffing reductions were not quite as damaging to congressional majority power as might be anticipated from raw numbers alone.

Overall, then, this seeming Republican "disarmament" in the face of a Democratic president can be explained by two factors. First, Republican-led cutbacks were not completely party neutral and disproportionately impacted Democrats in terms of staff, information, and therefore capacity. Second, legislators' perceptions that the public views investments in the institution as largesse, or, worse, corruption, provide an additional incentive against expansion and, in this case, in favor of retrenchment.

Quantitatively Evaluating the Dynamics of Capacity

While the foregoing qualitative analysis emphasized the importance of bipartisan, broad coalitions for the passage of major capacity reforms, it is possible that the politics of these adoptions do not accurately capture the year-to-year dynamics of capacity. That is, the allocation of resources after reform adoptions may more clearly reflect partisan concerns.

To tackle this question, we employ a series of regression analyses examining the correlation between interbranch division and two measures of capacity: logged aggregate congressional spending ($Ln[Leg.\ Staff]$) and logged committee staff sizes ($Ln[Leg.\ Staff]$). Both measures are plausible indicators for Congress's resources to carry out its core functions, but each has some disadvantages. Aggregate spending includes some irrelevant line items from the perspective of congressional capacity, like funding for the Botanical Garden. Committee staffing represents just one indicator of capacity, albeit an important one. Thus, we use both measures to ameliorate their respective shortcomings.

Table 3.2 displays the results of first-differenced Ordinary Least Squares (OLS) regression models.[13] In models 1–3, our dependent variable is first-differenced logged legislative branch spending from 1905–2016, using data collected from the *Statistical Abstracts of the United States*. In models 4–6, our dependent variable is first-differenced logged congressional committee staff

TABLE 3.2. The Effects of Interbranch Division on Congressional Capacity

	Model 1	Model 2	Model 3	Model 4	Model 5	Model 6
Δ D(Pres, Congress)	−0.068			−0.138		
	(0.088)			(0.108)		
Δ Divided		−0.011			−0.064	
		(0.034)			(0.036)	
Δ Opp. Seat Share			−0.085			−0.157
			(0.178)			(0.186)
Δ Dem. President	0.014	0.014	0.014	−0.055*	−0.072**	−0.046
	(0.031)	(0.032)	(0.032)	(0.032)	(0.035)	(0.034)
Δ Dem. Senate	−0.053	−0.054	−0.054	0.027	0.020	0.024
	(0.041)	(0.041)	(0.041)	(0.022)	(0.022)	(0.023)
Δ Dem. House	0.076	0.076	0.076	0.051	0.056	0.048
	(0.056)	(0.055)	(0.056)	(0.040)	(0.040)	(0.046)
Δ Spending as % GDP	−0.007	−0.007	−0.007	0.001	0.001	0.001
	(0.004)	(0.004)	(0.004)	(0.002)	(0.002)	(0.001)
Δ Ln(Exec. Exp.)	0.087*	0.089*	0.089*	0.030	0.043*	0.034
	(0.047)	(0.048)	(0.047)	(0.020)	(0.026)	(0.024)
Δ Ln(EOP Exp.)	0.020**	0.019**	0.019**	0.010*	0.011*	0.007*
	(0.009)	(0.009)	(0.009)	(0.005)	(0.006)	(0.004)
Δ War	−0.021	−0.020	−0.020	−0.006	−0.009	−0.002
	(0.029)	(0.030)	(0.029)	(0.016)	(0.018)	(0.014)
Δ Inflation	−0.006**	−0.006**	−0.006**	0.001	0.002	0.001
	(0.003)	(0.003)	(0.003)	(0.002)	(0.002)	(0.002)
Δ Ln(Leg. Exp.)$_{t-1}$	−0.131	−0.126	−0.129			
	(0.135)	(0.131)	(0.134)			
Δ Ln(Leg. Staff)$_{t-1}$				0.143	0.142	0.169
				(0.121)	(0.112)	(0.106)
N	110	110	110	109	109	109
Years	1905–2016	1905–2016	1905–2016	1905–2015	1905–2015	1905–2015
President FEs	✓	✓	✓	✓	✓	✓

OLS regression coefficients reported, with standard errors clustered by Congress in parentheses. All variables in Models 1-3 are lagged by one year to account for when fiscal decisions are made about overall legislative branch spending. Presidential fixed effects and constant not shown. Significance codes: *$p < 0.10$, **$p < 0.05$, ***$p < 0.01$, two-tailed tests.

from 1905 to 2015, collected from the Brookings Institution's *Vital Statistics on Congress*.[14]

We employ three plausible indicators of interbranch preference divergence: the absolute distance between the ideal points of the president and the chamber-averaged median of Congress, measured by DW-NOMINATE scores (D [*Pres, Congress*]) in models 1 and 4;[15] an indicator for divided government (*Divided*), coded as "1" if either congressional chamber is controlled by the party opposite the president and "0" otherwise (models 2 and 5); and the share of seats the party opposite the president holds in Congress (*Opp. Seat Share*) in models 3 and 6.[16] If capacity is allocated to combat opposition presidents, we would expect the estimated coefficients for these variables to be positive and statistically significant.

To account for whether there are partisan differences in preferences for either capacity or the size of government, we also include variables capturing if the presidency, House, and Senate are controlled by Democrats. We likewise track the overall size of the executive branch and federal spending by including spending as a percentage of GDP (*Spending as % GDP*) and logged executive branch expenditures (*Ln[Exec. Exp.]*), both collected from the *Statistical Abstracts of the United States*. These measures may be too coarse, however, to capture the institutional story of interest. Therefore, we also include EOP spending (*Ln[EOP Exp.]*), gathered from the *Statistical Abstracts of the United States*.[17] We expect these variables to be positively correlated with legislative spending and staff sizes, since our qualitative evidence illustrates congressional growth trails executive expansions.

We further control for economic factors using the *Inflation* rate, given congressional reticence to appear spendthrift during poor economic conditions.[18] Additionally, we include an indicator for years in which the United States is engaged in large-scale armed conflicts.[19] Finally, all of the models incorporate a lagged dependent variable and presidential fixed effects, with standard errors clustered by Congress.[20]

The results of our analyses overwhelmingly align with the narrative provided throughout this chapter. There is little correlation between ideological or partisan divergence and changes in legislative resources. In all six models, the estimated coefficients for these variables are actually *negative*, implying congressional capacity *decreases* in the face of presidential opposition. Moreover, none of the estimated coefficients is statistically significant at anywhere near conventional levels. These findings are not at all what we would be expected if Congress were able to bolster its capacity without constraint to challenge administrative foes.

There is some evidence, particularly when examining the expenditures measure, that congressional spending is responsive to changes in the executive branch and presidential office growth. We estimate positive and sometimes statistically significant coefficients for these two variables. The coefficients are far from one, however, suggesting a lack of parity in spending shifts across branches and that Congress only responds partially to executive augmentation, which is consistent with the reform narratives in the chapter.

Summary and Conclusion

Today, the US Congress is among the best-resourced and highest-capacity legislatures in the world. Its position was not an inevitability. Instead, congressional capacity increased in a punctuated fashion, while at times retreating.

Late nineteenth-century federal government growth threatened to sideline Congress's power in the policymaking process. Indeed, for several decades, its role in the constitutional system became progressively diminished. Eventually, Congress evolved. It created new legislative support institutions to generate and interpret policy relevant information. New procedures imposed on the executive branch supplemented Congress's own information generation and likewise enhanced oversight. Legislative staff sizes enlarged to utilize this new information. Armed with resources, congressional power surged throughout the twentieth century.

Successful reforms to its capacity emerged due to broad-based bipartisan support within Congress. Witnessing their institution in decline, members acted to preserve their relative power. Thus, congressional reforms reflected legislators' larger institutional concerns, rather than resulting from partisan duels. Such widespread support is likewise critical for overcoming supermajoritarian legislative hurdles, presidential vetoes, and the public skepticism inherent to instituting congressional self-spending.

Altogether, this chapter provides important insights into our broader theoretical argument. Our narratives and quantitative analyses offer a clear view of the institutionally based concerns underlying variation in congressional resources. Such capacity is not epiphenomenal to underlying policy and political disagreements across the branches. Congress does not simply increase its capacity at will whenever it needs to challenge the executive branch, as political observers might hope. These findings will aid in validating and interpreting our statistical analyses in the coming chapters, while dispelling some questions of endogeniety.

Finally, we provide evidence for enduring congressional policymaking capacity. Throughout the period considered, Congress has maintained sufficient levels of opportunities to challenge the president and executive branch. While there have certainly been some fluctuations in policymaking capacity over time, its total complement of statutory and nonstatutory powers have provided Congress with abundant opportunities to influence policy, at least when it retained the requisite resources. As we will explore in chapter 7, policymaking capacity cannot be taken for granted in other contexts. State legislatures have varied substantially in the opportunities to confront governors and the resources available to them to do so over time. With this understanding in hand, chapters 4–7 examine capacity's consequences for imposing constraints onto the executive branch and shaping chief executives' incentives for unilateralism.

4

Pulling the Purse Strings

LEGISLATIVE CAPACITY AND DISCRETION

In an administration characterized by persistent political conflict, one of President Trump's most controversial policy actions was restricting the travel of individuals from Chad, Iran, Libya, North Korea, Syria, Venezuela, and Yemen to the United States. Infamously known as the "Muslim ban," based on Trump's campaign exhortation for "a total and complete shutdown of Muslims entering the United States," this policy was effectuated through a series of unilateral directives iteratively issued in response to recurring legal challenges to the president's authority in this area. The ban relied on broad grants of discretion from the 1965 Immigration and Nationality Act (INA), including 8 USC § 1182(f):

> Whenever the President finds that the entry of any aliens or of any class of aliens into the United States would be detrimental to the interests of the United States, he may by proclamation, and for such period as he shall deem necessary, suspend the entry of all aliens or any class of aliens as immigrants or nonimmigrants, or impose on the entry of aliens any restrictions he may deem to be appropriate.

Opponents called for the policy's invalidation, arguing that Trump's ban exceeded the authority delegated to him by the INA and decrying the religious animus inherent in its adoption.[1] The Supreme Court, however, sided with the administration and upheld the orders. Writing for the majority in *Trump v. Hawaii* (2018), Chief Justice John Roberts contended Trump had sufficient power under the INA to impose the travel ban:

By its terms, §1182(f) exudes deference to the President in every clause. It entrusts to the President the decisions whether and when to suspend entry, whose entry to suspend, for how long, and on what conditions. It thus vests the President with "ample power" to impose entry restrictions in addition to those enumerated in the INA.

This episode from the Trump administration illustrates the pivotal role of discretion—in other words, the leeway Congress grants to the executive branch in using delegated authority—in US policymaking. Congress regularly empowers presidents and agencies to impose policy decisions with few instructions. Other times, however, it provides specific instructions allowing less executive maneuvering when implementing policy, such as in the case of tax rates (Epstein and O'Halloran 1999). How do Congress and other legislatures decide how much policymaking discretion to cede to executive actors?

Decades of research has investigated this central question in American politics, predominantly elevating interbranch policy conflict as the primary impetus. The consensus from this mostly theoretical work is that legislatures grant less discretion to ideologically distant executives to prevent bureaucratic drift, a well-known prediction called the ally principle. However, restricting executive branch discretion is costly, requiring legislatures to write detailed policies based on complicated policy information. Accordingly, this chapter highlights legislative capacity as the key to overcoming these associated costs. It is thus an important, yet understudied, determinant of discretionary endowments.

In contrast to previous work, we do not assume Congress retains enough capacity to adjust executive branch discretion at will. Instead, as highlighted in chapter 3, it has often lacked the requisite resources for executive constraint. Such deficits in capacity, we argue, inhibit Congress's ability to regulate the discretion of executive branch actors, chiefly those with divergent preferences. When equipped with sufficient resources, however, legislators can limit discretion to advance their preferred policy outcomes. In this way, the ally principle crucially depends on congressional capacity.

To test these theoretical arguments, we use a new measure of discretion based on the appropriations process from fiscal years 1960 to 2012, along with four indicators of resource capacity—committee staff sizes, staffer experience, committee member experience, and chair experience. We employ panel regression models, which improve upon previous cross-sectional designs that do not account for policy area or time-related confounders. This approach, combined with our measurement strategy, overcomes selection problems inherent in previous analyses and allows for more credible inferences about discretion. When staff or experience is low, we find interbranch conflict is unrelated to congressional discretionary decisions. As committee resources increase, however, the ally principle obtains.

Overall, we provide critical evidence for the policy effects of capacity on executive discretion, a fundamental feature of separation of powers systems. While select studies show the relationship between capacity and discretion in other contexts like the US states (Huber and Shipan 2002), this chapter represents, to our knowledge, the first evidence that legislative capacity is a binding constraint on discretionary grants at the federal level. In this way, we demonstrate a pervasive scholarly assumption—that Congress consistently carries enough resource capacity to readily restrict discretion—is indeed mistaken.

What Is Discretion?

Discretion is a central concept in separation of powers politics. Here, we are referring to the degree of freedom an executive actor (e.g., the president or an agency) has in implementing policy, based on the magnitude of authority *delegated* by Congress and the *constraints* placed on the use of that authority. We therefore adopt the conceptual definition of discretion advanced by Epstein and O'Halloran (1999) as delegation net of constraints.

Congress has considerable incentives to delegate policymaking authority to the executive branch. As a generalist institution, it is required to create policies in every imaginable facet of governance, from renaming a post office to overhauling the nation's health insurance system. Consequently, legislators and their staffs lack sufficient information to craft detailed policies in every area, particularly about how their policy *choices* will translate into actual policy *outcomes*. For example, what will the effects of marginal tax rates on businesses be on employment and tax revenue?

To reduce this uncertainty, Congress delegates policymaking authority to better-informed policy actors, typically specialized executive branch agencies. Expert bureaucrats can better discern the mapping between choices and outcomes to mitigate the possibility of extreme policy outcomes. Delegating authority, however, might also be costly for Congress since executives can use that authority to implement policy in a manner that is inconsistent with legislative preferences (see, e.g., Bendor and Meirowitz 2002 for an overview of these dynamics).

Yet Congress has numerous tools at its disposal to prevent bureaucratic drift (Epstein and O'Halloran 1999). It can write specific instructions for how delegated authority is to be used, thereby limiting the range of policy options agencies can consider. It may also reduce the scope of agency actions through a multitude of restrictions. Importantly, procedural requirements—such as those delineated in the Administrative Procedure Act—dictate the processes agencies must follow when promulgating policies. Congress likewise guides agency decision-making processes through other provisions, like requiring the consideration of particular types of information, mandating consultations with other public and private entities, and imposing deadlines.

Discretion, as we and others conceive of it, is a combination of delegation and constraint. Delegations vary in magnitude based on the task Congress wants an agency to execute, while constraint may be scaled to those tasks. What, then, determines when Congress alters discretion in this way? We theoretically consider this question in the following section.

Theoretical Underpinnings of Congressional Capacity and Discretion

Following previous work, we assume Congress strategically alters discretion to produce policy outcomes most favorable to its preferred position, while balancing concerns of bureaucratic drift with the desire to reduce policy-making uncertainty. Confident in their ability to implement agreeable outcomes, Congress should relinquish greater discretionary authority to executive actors that share its policy preferences, rather than ideological opponents likely to shift policy in a different direction. This result, known as the ally principle, is common to many theories of delegation and discretion (e.g., Epstein and O'Halloran 1999).

Restricting discretion is no small feat, however, and depends on Congress's capacity to pay the costs of doing so. Previous studies largely ignore the role of congressional capacity and instead implicitly assume Congress maintains enough opportunities and resources to limit executive discretion at will. Following work in other contexts (e.g., Huber and Shipan 2002), we relax this assumption. Conditional on sufficient policymaking capacity, discretionary restrictions require ample resources to write laws curbing executive behavior. Legislators must understand the policymaking environment and processes, the range of policy alternatives and related information, and the scope of authority that would incentivize the use of agency expertise.

These are big asks of low-capacity legislatures, which lack the staff and legislator expertise, experience, and labor to translate this information into policy instruments that can meaningfully confine executive actors. Without these resources, broad delegations of authority are the only feasible ones. These considerations were prominent in the passage of congressional reforms. The 1946 Special Committee on the Organization of Congress's report on the LRA draft, for instance, outlined the relationship between legislative capacity and executive discretion: "Congress has long lacked adequate facilities for the continuous inspection and review of administrative performance. We often delegate the rule-making power to administrative departments and commissions, without making any provision for follow-up to see if administrative rules and regulations are in accord with the intent of the law."[2]

On average, we expect Congress to endow greater discretionary authority to the executive branch when it is lower in capacity and yield less discretion when resources are abundant. Even when facing ideologically aligned agencies, high-capacity legislatures have some incentives to constrain executive authority in this way. For instance, reelection-seeking legislators may curtail discretion in response to constituent demand for executive restraint or government resources, regardless of interbranch alignment. In these cases, electoral concerns could outweigh ideological preferences. Such electoral considerations, however, may be more acutely activated by higher-profile activities capturing the public's attention, such as oversight, rather than comparatively opaque processes like discretion. Thus, the direct effect of congressional capacity may be more pronounced when explaining oversight (examined in the next chapter), as compared to discretionary grants.

Prediction 4.1: Conditional on high policymaking capacity, as legislative resource capacity increases, congressional actors will decrease overall levels of discretion given to the executive branch.

Though high-capacity legislatures generally want to curb executive discretion, we argue this incentive is greatest when their preferences diverge. Consistent with the ally principle, discretionary levels decrease in the ideological distance between Congress and executive actors. Congress cannot act on this impulse, however, if it lacks the necessary resources to regulate discretion. In those cases, legislators cannot differentiate discretionary grants between executive allies or foes. Hence, whether the ally principle manifests hinges on congressional resources.

> **Prediction 4.2:** Conditional on high policymaking capacity, when legislative resource capacity is high, ideological divergence between congressional actors and the president will be associated with lower levels of discretion. When resource capacity is low, ideological divergence will have little relation to discretion levels.

To be clear, we are not the first to advance this conditional argument about discretion. Indeed, Huber and Shipan (2002) present similar theoretical claims and empirical evidence cross-nationally and in the US states. Here, we contend the same incentives and constraints for legislatures likewise apply to Congress, where this argument has not been applied. Most studies of federal-level discretion (e.g., Epstein and O'Halloran 1999) instead assume Congress consistently maintains the requisite capacity to restrict discretionary authority.

Measuring Discretion

The first nontrivial task for testing these predictions is to measure the concept of discretion. A valid measure of discretion will have three desiderata. First, it should cleanly capture the constituent components of the concept—delegation and constraint. Second, it must be based on the observed behaviors of Congress, but the timing and form of those observations cannot be easily manipulable in ways that would lead to selection concerns in using the measure. Finally, it should be comparable over time within units of interest, to make credible inferences.

Congress can bestow discretion on the executive branch in many ways, most notably through the authorizing and appropriations processes. Previous measures have primarily examined the former. Epstein and O'Halloran (1999) use *Congressional Quarterly Almanac* summaries to combine indications of delegations and constraints within laws into an index of discretion. Huber and Shipan (2002) operationalize it as the length of statutes, with longer ones corresponding to more specificity and thus less discretion. While these measures have much to recommend, they also present drawbacks due to their reliance on the authorizations process. Authorizing statutes are by nature irregular occurrences, thus creating selection issues based on when they are enacted. The programs Congress authorizes or reauthorizes in a given year are nonrandom, making credible inferences challenging (Canes-Wrone 2010; Howell and Jackman 2013). Furthermore, authorizing legislation may address different programs or agencies from year to year, even within a single issue area, further complicating over-time comparisons. These laws also delegate authority to many different executive actors at a time, which is problematic given theories of delegation typically center around one principal and one agent.

To overcome these various challenges, we rely on a measure of discretion based on congressional outputs during the annual appropriations process (Bolton and Thrower 2019). The appropriations process happens on an annual basis for (almost) all agencies, eliminating selection bias concerns. Decisions are clearly targeted to specific agencies, which allows researchers to isolate the single and appropriate principal-agent relationship underlying existing theoretical arguments, while controlling for policy area and organizational unit. While neither an appropriations-based or authorization-based measure characterizes the sum of all agency discretion, we spotlight the former as an important policymaking venue in which discretionary decisions are made with appealing features for study. However, we recognize the importance of authorizations and show in the online appendix that accounting for such activity does not affect the performance of our appropriations-based measure in the empirical analyses.

An Appropriations-Based Measure

We measure discretion as the amount of budget authority congressional subcommittees appropriate to agencies divided by the number of pages of instructions given to agencies on how they are to use those appropriated funds.[3]

In particular, our measure of discretion granted to agency i in year t takes the following form:

$$\text{Discretion}_{it} = \ln \left(\frac{\text{New Budget Authority}_{it}}{\text{Pages}_{it}} \right)$$

The ratio of spending to pages has an intuitive and substantive meaning that accords nicely with the idea of discretion. In appropriating funds, Congress is delegating authority to the executive branch. This authority, however, is circumscribed by the level of detail in the accompanying instructions. When Congress delegates more money per page of report, it affords agencies wider leeway to expend funds. When this ratio decreases, so does the discretion of the agency receiving the funds.

In general, Congress delegates its appropriations decision-making (subject to floor approval) to subcommittees of the House and Senate Appropriations Committees. These subcommittees determine discretionary funding levels for federal agencies across the government for the coming fiscal year. They likewise write accompanying reports with their recommendations providing agencies detailed instructions on how the subcommittee believes the funds ought to be spent according to its policy preferences. In more recent years, scholars have noted an increasing centralization of appropriations policymaking power in committee and chamber leadership (Hanson 2014). We account for this trend in several ways described later in our analyses.

We construct this measure for fiscal years 1960–2012 using the reports on bills written by appropriations subcommittees. The level of new budget authority recommended by the subcommittee was coded for each agency in every report and adjusted for inflation to 2009 dollars, representing the delegation portion of our discretion measure. With respect to constraint, we coded those reports for the number of pages of instructions given to agencies on how to use these funds, to the nearest quarter of a page. Essentially, then, our measure of discretion is the amount of money appropriated per report page.[4] A larger ratio corresponds to Congress giving an agency more money with fewer strings attached. On the other hand, the ratio decreases because of either less funding or more constraints.

Overall, the average level of discretion in our dataset corresponds to $83.6 million per report page, with a standard deviation of $8.94 million per page. Of course, there is also substantial variation in these amounts by agency. Figure 4.1 displays the average discretion levels for the fifteen Cabinet departments in our dataset, along with 95 percent confidence intervals. As we discuss later in the chapter, however, we are cautious about making cross-agency comparisons in discretionary levels since the different missions and tasks of organizations in part drive these differences. One advantage of our measure relative to others is the ability to make inferences based on within-agency differences, given appropriations decisions are annual and not subject to the same selection biases associated with examining potentially one-off authorizations.

Average Cabinet Agency Discretion, FY 1960-2012

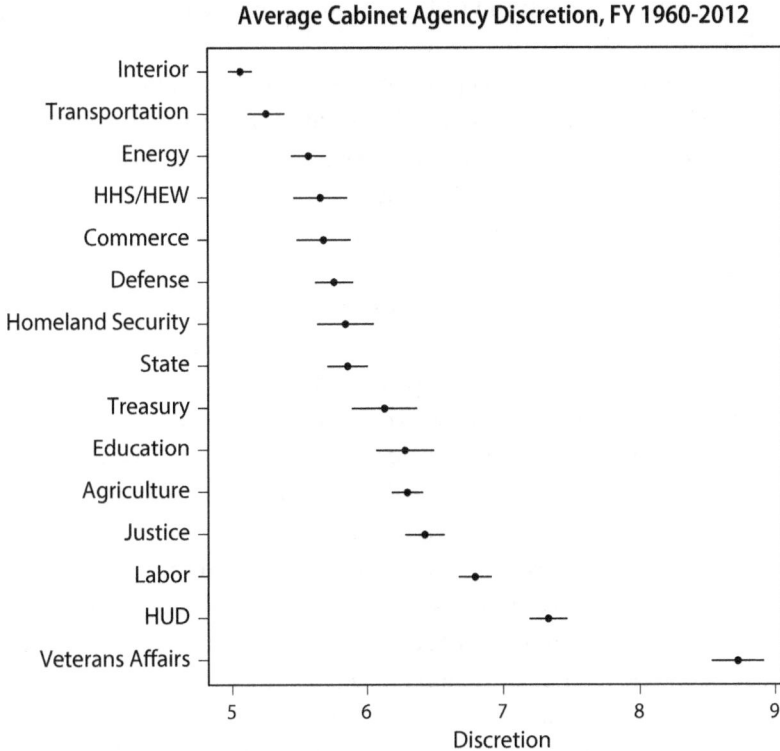

FIGURE 4.1. Average discretion by Cabinet agency, with 95 percent confidence intervals.

Assessing Validity

We argue our measure has high content validity—that is, the amount of money appropriated per page of report meaningfully captures the concept of discretion. Appropriations represent clear statements of delegation to the executive branch. Agencies rely on appropriated funds to carry out all non-mandatory functions. Without funds, an agency cannot design new programs, implement existing ones, pay its employees, enter into and pay out contracts, or carry out its functions more generally (see, e.g., Fenno 1966; Kiewiet and McCubbins 1991; Schick 2008). As Kiewiet and McCubbins (1991, 3) write, appropriations decisions are "the clearest statements of policy that exist." Other studies, in both the context of American politics and elsewhere, have used the assignment of budgetary resources as an indicator of delegation, either from a conceptual, theoretical, or empirical standpoint (e.g., Brown

2010; Calvert, McCubbins and Weingast 1989; Kiewiet and McCubbins 1991; McCarty 2004; Ting 2001).

Of course, the size of the appropriation will limit that authority to some degree. However, it alone is not sufficient to characterize the constraints placed on agencies, but instead reflects the magnitude of delegated authority. The degree of agency flexibility in determining how to use the delegated authority depends instead on the instructions accompanying the budget authority.[5]

Perhaps more controversial is how we capture these additional restrictions in our measure. We rely on the instructions within Appropriations sub-committee reports that coincide with spending recommendations. The length of these reports is positively correlated with the level of constraint contained therein. Longer reports yield more instructions and therefore limit agency actions to a greater degree, holding funding levels constant.

It may seem more straightforward to use the texts of the appropriations laws to ascertain the levels of constraint. By tradition, however, the vast majority of instructions given to agencies are enclosed in the appropriations reports (Fenno 1966; Schick 2008). As Kiewiet and McCubbins (1991, 17) argue, "In actuality, the level of aggregation in appropriations line items is a poor indicator of the amount of discretion allowed in making expenditures. Far more detailed directives are communicated in the hearings and reports of Appropriations subcommittees than in the text of bills."

The instructions of committee reports are not law. Agencies cannot face legal repercussions for flouting these congressional directives. Instead, "enforcement" emanates directly from Congress. Observers of the appropriations process have long noted vigorous compliance with subcommittee instructions (e.g., Schick 2008). As Fenno (1966, 292) commented in his landmark appropriations study, "Agency obedience to the law is hardly worthy of comment. But an agency's religious adherence to the direction, admonitions, suggestions, and intentions written in the Committee report is noteworthy as a measure of its desire for harmonious relations with the Committee." More recent investigations of report language reiterate agency adherence to appropriations instructions (Ginieczki 2010). The reason behind such deference to nonstatutory pronouncements is the repeated nature of agency-committee interactions. Agencies come to Congress on an annual basis, hat in hand, asking for more funds. If they disregard congressional instructions, they may face costs, such as the wrath of their overseeing committee, more restrictive spending limitations, or even less overall funding.

Additional information on the content and construct validity (i.e., its ability to reproduce well-known findings) of this measure is available in Bolton and Thrower (2019) and the online appendix to this chapter. In particular, we (1) provide further examples of common constraints present in committee reports; (2) show that report page length is strongly and positively correlated with a hand count of actual constraints taken from a random sample of reports; (3) demonstrate that our page length measure is correlated with bureaucrats' own perceptions about how constrained they are in the appropriations process, based on recent surveys; (4) show that the budget authority portion of the measure *does not* map onto these constraints in the same way, suggesting the two components of the ratio are tapping into fundamentally different concepts of delegation and constraint; (5) show the unconditional ally principle is reproduced by the measure; and (6) demonstrate inferences based on the measure are not affected by activity in the authorizations process, agency funding structures, strategic interactions between chambers or the president and Congress, or changes within agencies over time. With this validated measure of discretion in hand, we can now empirically evaluate our theoretical arguments concerning its relationship to legislative capacity.

Data and Measurement

Dependent Variable

The unit of analysis for our study is the subcommittee-year. We examine subcommittees instead of the full appropriations committees given our discretion measure is produced by the reports of the former. Because subcommittees oversee many agencies under their jurisdictions, we aggregate our measure of discretion (which is calculated at the agency level) to the subcommittee level to serve as our dependent variable. To do this, we sum all the budget authority for the agencies contained in each subcommittee report in every fiscal year as well as the length of the reports for each agency in that subcommittee's jurisdiction in a fiscal year. We then divide the former by the latter and take the natural logarithm of that value.

Subcommittee Resource Capacity

We create four new measures of resource capacity at the subcommittee level: majority party staff quantity as well as the average experience of these staffers, the subcommittee chair, and all subcommittee members.[6] While most studies examine a single indicator of resources, we expand the scope of our analysis to gain greater confidence that its results are not idiosyncratic to one measure. Each indicator directly channels the conceptual definition of resource capacity developed in chapter 2. Larger numbers of staff with greater levels of experience provide subcommittees with the time and human capital necessary to translate member preferences into both funding amounts and reports that meaningfully constrain executive branch actors. Similarly, chairs and members alike may gain expertise and substantive knowledge with increasing years of service on a subcommittee. All of these factors lower the subcommittee's marginal costs of limiting executive branch discretion.

Our first measure is the number of majority party staffers employed by the subcommittee in a given year. We focus on majority staff because, per our discussion in chapter 2, they are likely the most involved in the production of new policies given the subcommittee chairs' power and growing centralized leadership control in the appropriations process (Hanson 2014).[7] Formal authority for staffing decisions rests with the chairs of the full Appropriations Committees, but is often executed by the committee's staff director or chief clerk (Aldrich and Rohde 2000; Fenno 1966). In recent years, committees provide for subcommittee chairs and ranking members to make independent decisions about staffing.[8]

We compile an original dataset of staff allocations to the subcommittees of the House and Senate Appropriation Committees using information from the *Congressional Staff Directory*. This directory contains the names of staff members on each subcommittee, published at least once per year since 1959.[9] For consistency, we examine the summer issues of these directories, released annually in June or July.[10] We opt for this data source primarily for the longevity of the records available.[11]

For each year between 1959 and 2011, we count the number of staff members on each Appropriations subcommittee in both chambers. From these counts, we remove staffers assigned to assist the minority.[12] The average number of professional majority staff members on any given committee during this time period is four, with a minimum of one staffer and a maximum of sixteen (the House Defense subcommittee in 2007). Most subcommittees have fewer than ten dedicated majority staffers throughout the period of study.[13]

One could imagine other measures of resource capacity for subcommittees, such as the overall budget for the committee itself. Budgets might be especially important if subcommittees are using funds to, for instance, hire outside contractors to assist them with their policy work. Unfortunately, this data is not available in earlier years of our analysis in a consistent way. However, the data that does overlap with our dataset suggests a substantial portion of committee expenditures is devoted to payroll. For instance, according to its quarterly disbursement reports, the House Committee on Appropriations spent $2,775,713.80 in 2017, more than 90 percent of which was devoted to personnel compensation.

We develop three additional measures characterizing the subcommittee's human capital, based on the average number of years of experience for affiliated staffers, legislators, and chairs.[14] Here, we take subcommittee expertise to be nonsubstitutable across subcommittees. In other words, service on the Defense Subcommittee does not have spillover effects into work on, for instance, the Labor, HHS, and Education Subcommittee. In practice, members and staffers tend to inhabit the same subcommittee(s) over time, so possible overlap should have little impact on the analysis. However, it does mean that when new subcommittees are (infrequently) created, our measure conservatively records those members as having no experience on that subcommittee. To the extent this coding does not reflect the value of experience, our measure will only understate the subcommittee's capacity and bias against our expected results.

To create the member and chair measures of experience, we use the congressional directories to determine the membership of each subcommittee beginning in 1959.[15] To capture overall member experience, we simply take the average years of service for all members of the subcommittee. For chairs, we use their total years of experience leading the subcommittee. The measure of staff experience is constructed similarly, linking individuals in successive directories.[16]

Figure 4.2 plots the annual averages of each of these capacity measures across subcommittees. The graphs are instructive for observing broad trends and identifying the sources of variation in the measures. In general, subcommittee staff increases over time, similar to the overall staffing patterns described in chapter 3. The inflection point appears to be in 1970, corresponding to the passage of the Legislative Reorganization Act authorizing greater subcommittee staffing resources. There is a dip and stagnation in the 1990s, when Republicans assumed control of Congress and imposed massive staffing cuts. We do not observe the same dramatic decrease here as in Congress as a whole, however.

Chair experience declined somewhat over time as well. Overall, subcommittee chairs held an average of 4.84 years of experience, ranging from

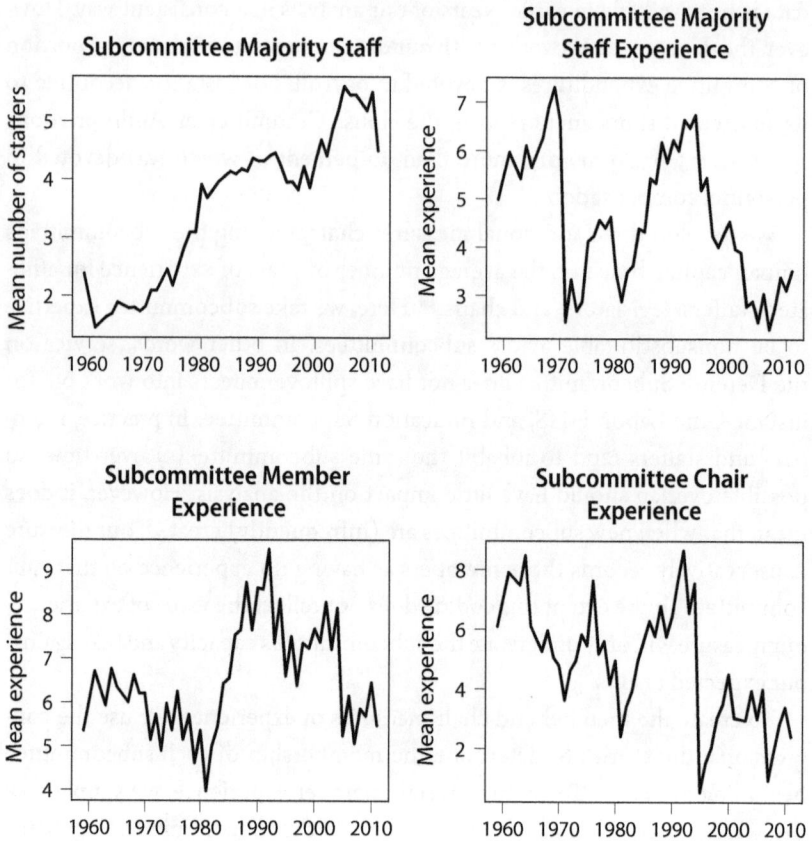

FIGURE 4.2. Annual averages for the four capacity measures, between FY 1960 and 2013.

zero (when they first become the chair) to thirty-seven years (the tenure of Representative Jamie Whitten [D-MS] at the helm of the House Agriculture subcommittee). One notable impetus for over-time variation is shifts in chamber majority control that simultaneously alter all subcommittee chair assignments. Consequently, experience substantially decreases, as new and inexperienced chairs ascend to power. We observe relative reductions in chair experience in 1981 (when Republicans assumed power in the Senate for the first time in decades), 1995 (when Republicans freshly commanded the House and the Senate), and 2007 (when Democrats regained House and Senate majorities).

The average tenure of subcommittee members is 6.5 years, with a minimum of zero in their first year and a maximum of 16.2 years. The latter occurred on the Senate's Interior subcommittee in 2003, led by Senator Robert Byrd (D-WV) with members including a number of other long-serving senators, such as Daniel Inouye (D-HI), Patrick Leahy (D-VT), and Ted Stevens (R-AK). While the 1980s were a period of overall membership stability and thus rising experience, such trends reversed in the decades to follow.

Finally, average majority staff experience in our sample is 4.6 years. Overall, staff experience declined over time. The sharp recession in 1971 can be attributed to an influx of new staffers following the 1970 LRA passage, and numerous longtime staffers discontinuing their service for idiosyncratic reasons, as far as we can tell. Average staff experience likewise decreased in 1981 and the mid-1990s.

Overall, then, these measures of congressional capacity provide insights into fluctuations in the staff resources and human capital available to subcommittees in any given year. Such capacity has not consistently increased over time, but each measure exhibits ebbs and flows. While figure 4.2 displays averages over time, there is also considerable spread around those averages in any given year, with outliers on each dimension. To account for this dispersion, we take the natural logarithm of these measures in all of the analyses (Ln[Subcomm. Staff.], Ln[Subcomm. Chair Exp.], Ln[Subcomm. Member Exp.], Ln[Subcomm. Staff Exp.]).

Policy Disagreement

We operationalize executive-legislative policy disagreement using a partisan-based indicator of whether the Appropriations subcommittee chair and the president are from opposing parties (Divided).[17] We interact this variable with our measures of capacity as the key test of prediction 4.2.

One could imagine other ways of measuring ideological divergence, such as the distance between the subcommittee chair and agency career employees or appointees. In general, agency-based ideal points are not available for much of the time period we analyze and most subcommittees are delegating to multiple agencies. Hearteningly, in other work we show Congress is more responsive to presidential preferences than agency preferences when making discretionary decisions (Bolton and Thrower 2019).

Control Variables

We also control for several factors that could confound our inferences. First, we account for time-invariant subcommittee features that may affect all three variables of interest by including subcommittee fixed effects. For instance, some subcommittees may consider more complex policy areas that necessitate higher levels of staff and discretion granted by those subcommittees. We similarly include year fixed effects, to account for annual-level factors that impact all subcommittees. For example, economic shocks or the distribution of power between legislative leadership and committees may influence both the degree of policy autonomy subcommittees will give to the executive as well as their available resources.[18]

Notably, previous work has largely centered on cross-sectional regression analyses that do not control for time or policy areas. Because our measure allows us to observe the same subcommittees making comparable decisions every year, we can account for these previously neglected factors and generate more credible estimates of our relationships of interest.

We also include subcommittee-year covariates that may confound the relationship between capacity, policy disagreement, and discretion. To begin, we control for the percentage of overall discretionary appropriations under the subcommittee's jurisdiction (*Discretionary Percent*). We also measure the conservatism of the subcommittee chair, which could reflect their demand for lower staffing levels (*Chair Conservatism*). Given more members could intensify demands for staff and decrease the costs of writing constraining reports, we include the logged size of the subcommittee (*Ln[Subcomm. Size]*). We also use an indicator variable for the first congress in which a subcommittee exists, which directly implicates staff and member experience. It can likewise potentially impact discretion, as staff and members embark on discretionary decisions in new policy areas (*First Congress*).

Finally, we control for the salience of a committee's policy area in a given year, which might increase staff allocations and congressional urges to micromanage the administration. We use data from the Comparative Agendas Project (CAP) on annual responses to Gallup Poll's long-running question asking respondents, "What is the most important problem facing the nation?" The CAP aggregates responses in each year into one of twenty-five different issue categories, yielding a dataset of the percentage of individuals mentioning an issue in a given category as the most important for each year. We then take each Appropriations subcommittee and match it with the appropriate major topic categories from the CAP. Some subcommittees match to multiple codes, given that the agencies they oversee often operate in disparate policy areas. For instance, the Agriculture subcommittee is matched with the "Agriculture" policy area as well as the "Health" and "Banking, Finance, and

Domestic Commerce" policy areas, since it covers the Department of Agriculture, the Food and Drug Administration, and the Commodity Futures Trading Commission. Lastly, we sum and then log the percentage of respondents in each subcommittee-year who thought those associated issues were the most important problem (*Salience*).

Subcommittee-Level Analysis

The results of OLS regression analyses are reported in table 4.1, all of which include subcommittee and year fixed effects. Each uses different capacity measures: number of majority party staffers (models 1–2); chair experience (models 3–4), member experience (models 5–6), and staff experience (models 7–8).[19] In each pair of models, the first examines prediction 4.1 (i.e., the average effect of capacity) and the second evaluates prediction 4.2 (i.e., the conditional ally principle).

Overall, in models 1, 3, 5, and 7, we find little support for prediction 4.1; there is no consistent direct relationship between resources and discretion. In some cases, the coefficient is positive (staff size and member experience) and in others negative (chair and staff experience). The estimated coefficients, however, are never statistically significant. As previously discussed, these null results may reflect the possibility that discretionary grants do not activate legislators' reelection incentives due to their less visible nature.

On the other hand, we find strong support for prediction 4.2. Across these models, the coefficient on the interaction term is negative and sizable, indicating discretion is decreasing under conditions of policy disagreement. Figure 4.3 displays the estimated effect of shifting from chair-president alignment to disagreement on discretion, at varying levels of resource capacity. For each measure, interbranch discord significantly reduces discretionary grants, but only when capacity is high.

For instance, when a chair has no prior experience leading the subcommittee, policy disagreement is statistically indistinguishable from zero. This estimated effect, however, becomes negative after an individual has served in that position for about 1.7 years. At the 90th percentile of the distribution (twelve years of chair experience), partisan opposition to the president corresponds to a 28 percent decrease in discretionary levels. These effects are statistically significant, and the general patterns are replicated for all four measures of subcommittee resource capacity. Altogether, the inescapable conclusion is that congressional resource capacity has a substantial impact on

TABLE 4.1. The Effect of Subcommittee Capacity on Discretion

	Model 1	Model 2	Model 3	Model 4	Model 5	Model 6	Model 7	Model 8
Divided	−0.054	0.577	−0.068	0.179*	−0.079	0.728**	−0.073	0.318
	(0.119)	(0.359)	(0.102)	(0.106)	(0.095)	(0.340)	(0.113)	(0.195)
Ln(Subcomm. Staff)	0.155	0.433						
	(0.174)	(0.290)						
Ln(Subcomm. Chair Exp.)			−0.013	0.100**				
			(0.033)	(0.040)				
Ln(Subcomm. Member Exp.)					0.017	0.262***		
					(0.109)	(0.097)		
Ln(Subcomm. Staff Exp.)							−0.010	0.135
							(0.071)	(0.085)
Divided x Ln(Subcomm. Staff)		−0.396*						
		(0.217)						
Divided x Ln(Subcomm. Chair Exp.)				−0.201**				
				(0.079)				
Divided x Ln(Subcomm. Member Exp.)						−0.408**		
						(0.184)		
Divided x Ln(Subcomm. Staff Exp.)								−0.281**
								(0.126)

Discretionary Percent	0.050***	0.052***	0.061***	0.060***	0.060***	0.059***	0.047***	0.047***
	(0.016)	(0.016)	(0.016)	(0.016)	(0.016)	(0.016)	(0.016)	(0.016)
Chair Conservatism	−0.260	−0.231	−0.306	−0.291	−0.306*	−0.284*	−0.254	−0.275
	(0.183)	(0.179)	(0.186)	(0.179)	(0.175)	(0.163)	(0.179)	(0.178)
Ln(Subcomm. Size)	0.298**	0.233	0.484***	0.534***	0.490***	0.534***	0.357***	0.405***
	(0.132)	(0.144)	(0.110)	(0.116)	(0.111)	(0.114)	(0.133)	(0.133)
Salience	−0.750**	−0.781**	−0.949**	−0.932**	−0.948**	−0.881**	−0.726*	−0.784**
	(0.373)	(0.371)	(0.364)	(0.361)	(0.362)	(0.363)	(0.375)	(0.358)
First Congress	0.430**	0.438**	0.607**	0.679***	0.638***	0.828***	0.424**	0.508**
	(0.194)	(0.192)	(0.237)	(0.242)	(0.213)	(0.253)	(0.213)	(0.213)
N	846	846	971	971	972	972	825	825
Subcomm. FEs	✓	✓	✓	✓	✓	✓	✓	✓
Year FEs	✓	✓	✓	✓	✓	✓	✓	✓

OLS regression coefficients reported, with standard errors clustered by chamber-year in parentheses. Subcommittee and year fixed effects and constant are not shown. Significance codes: $*p < 0.10$, $**p < 0.05$, $***p < 0.01$, two-tailed tests.

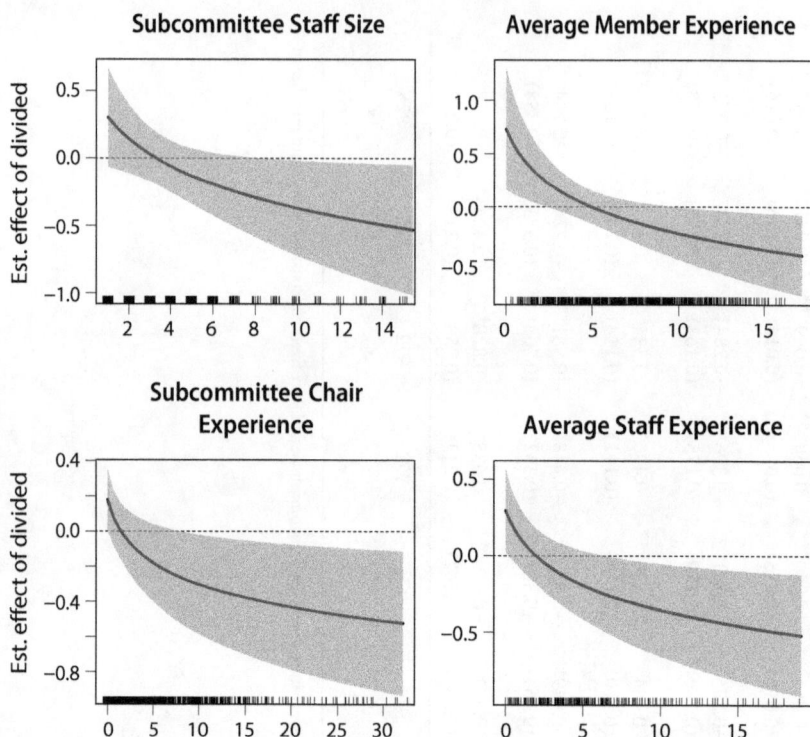

FIGURE 4.3. The marginal effects of president-chair partisan disagreement on discretion, while varying subcommittee resource capacity. Rug plots have been jittered for the staff size and chair experience measures to better represent the distribution of values observed in the dataset.

executive discretion, particularly in moderating the impact of interbranch conflict.

One concern with these results might be that Congress "staffs up" to constrain ideologically distant administrations, which might yield estimates affected by post-treatment bias. Though we showed interbranch division does not drive capacity in chapter 3, we only considered macrolevel reforms and analyses. Such endogeniety concerns could still manifest on a smaller scale at the subcommittee level. Though member and chair experience is likely not manipulable given members have strong property rights over committee assignments, staffing might be easier to ramp up in the face of ideological division.

To examine this possibility, we regress logged total staff and logged mean staff experience onto indicators of president-chair partisan alignment. For the former, we estimate a coefficient of 0.0004 (standard error = 0.065, $p = 0.995$) on *Divided*. In other words, the relationship between interbranch partisan division and staff sizes is essentially zero. For staff experience, we actually estimate a small and negative coefficient, which is the opposite of what would be expected if Congress were manipulating capacity to counter unfriendly presidents (beta = -0.077, standard error = 0.082, $p = 0.35$). These findings provide greater confidence that legislators do not wield capacity primarily as a partisan weapon, thus further validating our empirical analyses.

Summary and Conclusion

This chapter presents our first empirical evidence demonstrating the policy effects of legislative capacity at the congressional level. The qualitative account in chapter 3 presented capacity as critically important for carrying out core legislative tasks. Here, we provided systematic, quantitative analysis corroborating that story. We reveal a ubiquitous prediction in the theoretical literature on discretion—the ally principle—is contingent on congressional capacity. Our findings are reproduced using several measures of resource capacity, with improvements to research design and measurement that give us confidence in the results. These patterns cast doubt on the prevailing wisdom in the separation of powers literature that Congress can be assumed to have sufficient resources to restrict the discretion of ideologically opposed executive actors.

The centrality of discretion to separation of powers politics and policymaking suggests the importance of these results. As our discussion of the Trump travel ban illustrates, the substantive stakes of discretion could not be higher. It fundamentally delineates the authority of the president and executive branch in the policymaking process. When Congress gives specific instructions, the executive branch can be held to them. However, when it uses broad language that, in the words of Chief Justice Roberts, "exudes deference to the President in every clause," it can hardly expect anything other than to be subject to the whims of presidential preferences. Sometimes, Congress and the president will agree about policy outcomes, which causes little damage to legislative interests. When disagreements prevail, however, presidents will be well positioned to use broad, imprecise mandates to move policies in ways legislative majorities find objectionable. Whether discretion is narrow or expansive depends on interbranch divisions and, importantly, congressional resources to forge policy instruments that constrain executive actors.

Of course, ex ante mechanisms are just one way Congress affects executive branch behavior. Not only does constraint hinge on the degree of executives' discretion, but also on *how they use it*. If presidents ignore discretionary bounds or use their authority to unilaterally shift policies in ways disfavored by legislative majorities, then Congress's discretionary decisions provide little constraint at all. These ex ante constraints must be coupled with credible threats of ex post punishment. While the courts or other institutions might provide such checks, we argue Congress is the institution most motivated to protect its own interests after delegating. The next chapter examines perhaps the most important ex post instrument of congressional control: oversight.

5

Continuous Watchfulness? Legislative Capacity and Oversight

The 2016 election was marred by controversies surrounding the Russian government's interference and allegations that Trump campaign officials cooperated in these efforts. Intelligence reports before and after the election detailed Russian operations to hack and leak Democratic National Committee emails and spread anti–Hilary Clinton propaganda through social media. President Trump, however, denied or downplayed these findings, publicly stating on November 11, 2017, "Every time [Putin] sees me, he says, 'I didn't do that.'" . . . I really believe that when he tells me that, he means it."[1]

Despite Trump's initial denials, scrutiny over his campaign's possible collusion with Russia during the election mounted, leading to House and Senate Intelligence Committees investigations into the matter. On March 12, 2018, House Republicans announced an end to their probe, concluding they found no evidence of collusion. Rep. Adam Schiff (D-CA) criticized the Republican majority's decision as a political maneuver to safeguard the president, saying, "[The decision] is nonetheless another tragic milestone for this Congress, and represents yet another capitulation to the executive branch. By ending its oversight role in the only authorized investigation in the House, the Majority has placed the interests of protecting the President over protecting the country, and history will judge its actions harshly."[2]

The Senate Intelligence Committee likewise investigated Russian activities in the 2016 election. Though viewed as less partisan than the House's investigation, the Senate committee was nonetheless initially criticized for its slow pace, evidenced by its failure to conduct any major hearings or issue subpoenas in the first months of its inquiry. Some attributed these shortcomings to the committee's paucity of expertly trained and adequately experienced staffers. As *The Daily Beast* reported on April 23, 2017:

> Of the seven staffers so far assigned to review classified documents related to the Russia investigations, none of them has prosecutorial or investigative experience.... Most of them lack a background in Russia expertise.... The investigation already faces a series of obstacles that have heavy requirements on time: the classification of documents, the location of documents at various agencies, and an incredible volume of material. But of the seven staffers, none has been assigned full-time to the work of the Russia probe.... "To do a serious investigation would require not less than a dozen full-time staffers [with] counterintelligence, prosecutorial skills to do it, and people who have a very good sense of the forensic accounting world of Russia and Europe. Without that sort of expertise, you're not going to get anywhere," [attorney Scott] Horton said.[3]

The committee soon after devoted to the investigation more staffers with expertise in intelligence law, while allocating an additional $1.2 million toward this effort.[4] In the end, the Senate's probe proved far more extensive and damaging to the Trump administration's reputation than the one conducted by the House. After a three-year investigation, members of both parties on the Senate committee concluded Russian officials interfered in the 2016 presidential election. Yet there was dissent along partisan lines as to whether there was actual "collusion" between Russia and the Trump campaign. Six out of the eight Republican committee members agreed that "we can now say with no doubt, there was no collusion," while five of the seven Democratic senators concluded the report "unambiguously shows that members of the Trump Campaign cooperated with Russian efforts to get Trump elected."[5]

As these investigations demonstrate, legislators can strategically engage in oversight to politically damage executive branch actors and take public positions on important issues in front of their constituents. Divergent political preferences between the branches can certainly lead to more vigorous oversight (see, e.g., Kriner and Schickler 2016; Kriner and Schwartz 2008; Parker and Dull 2009). Investigations can depress presidents' popularity (Kriner and Schickler 2014), which has negative consequences for their legislative agendas (Rivers and Rose 1985; Beckmann 2010) and electoral fortunes. And preliminary evidence reveals the Russia investigations did just that for the Trump administration (Kriner and Schickler 2018). However, the relatively fulsome probe by the Republican-led Senate panel likewise illustrates how institutional imperatives may guide Congress's investigative activity.

While Congress may prefer to wield oversight as a political weapon against administrations, this example also shows its ability to do so may be inhibited by insufficient resources. Yet existing work linking capacity and oversight has yielded mixed results. Some scholars uncover little empirical evidence that staff capacity influences oversight activity (Aberbach 1990; Fowler 2015), while others find committee member experience can enhance oversight, but only during divided government (McGrath 2013). Thus, there is uncertainty in the literature as to whether, when, and what types of capacity matter for oversight.

In this chapter, we consider how resource capacity influences Congress's ability to use oversight to achieve its political and policy goals. Using data on investigations and hearings at the chamber level, we find legislative actors engage in less oversight activity when staff size is low. As these resources increase, Congress becomes able to command oversight as a political weapon more forcefully, particularly against administrations with conflicting preferences. We likewise track these enterprises at the committee level and find similar results, though with some nuance depending on the oversight activity and resources examined. Finally, we conduct a placebo test revealing the expected dynamics do not manifest in cases where committee agendas are dictated by outside forces, lending further credence to the importance of capacity in allowing legislators to pursue their goals.

Overall, then, this chapter further substantiates our theoretical argument, while offering important contributions to the existing literature on capacity and oversight. Whereas previous studies chiefly examine interbranch ideological or partisan differences as the primary impetus for oversight activity, we investigate the direct and interactive effects of legislative capacity on this ex post constraint. To this debate, we add rich data on oversight hearings and investigations, new measures of committee staff and their human capital, research designs that account for possibly confounding committee- and year-level factors, and placebo tests that bolster confidence in our conclusions. In doing so, we offer the most comprehensive examination of congressional oversight and capacity to date and offer clarifications of conflicting results in previous studies about the role of capacity.

What Is Oversight?

Aberbach (1990, 2) defines oversight as the "congressional review of the actions of federal departments, agencies, and commissions, and of the programs and policies they administer, including review that takes place during program and policy implementation as well as afterward." It is one of the most powerful congressional tools of executive branch control. Oversight occurs before, during, and after agency activities of interest, affording Congress opportunities for influence throughout the policy development and implementation processes. From the perspective of our theoretical argument, oversight is important for legislators to be able to ensure that discretion is used in ways that advance their interests and as a means to publicly sanction the executive branch when it is not.

Of course, oversight is not the only mechanism by which Congress punishes agency actions with which it disagrees. It could pass legislation penalizing executive actors for implementing unfavorable policies, withhold or reduce agency authority, or defund programs. However, such statutory mechanisms often require a supermajority to implement, a difficult task in highly polarized eras (Barber and McCarty 2015). Oversight, however, is an appealing and expeditious way for legislators to control the executive branch through retaliatory actions, requiring only the consent of the responsible committee or chair. In this way, it can influence the executive without the collective action problems attendant to lawmaking.

Congress oversees executive actors through formal and informal means. With respect to the former, legislators can hold formal oversight hearings to scrutinize agency actions, conduct program evaluations, direct agency audits, and consider reauthorizations. Committees can subpoena public and private actors, requiring their testimony. They also investigate specific accusations of executive branch misconduct, which often encompasses multiple hearings spanning months or years. Many investigations, such as those led by then-senator Harry Truman on wasteful and fraudulent government spending during World War II or the Church Committee's investigations into intelligence abuses during the 1970s, expose serious problems in governance and have lasting consequences for policy and agency behavior. Investigations can also serve legislators' political goals, who relish opportunities to appear to be "doing something" before their constituents. Indeed, the Truman-led hearings were arguably imperative in launching him from the Senate to the White House.

Members and their staffers likewise employ informal tactics, including phone calls, letters, emails, or in-person meetings to influence the executive branch. Informal communications occur much more frequently than hearings, while being far less visible. As such, the effectiveness, content, and frequency of informal contact between committees and agencies is difficult to observe, though some recent scholarship has made substantial headway in this regard (e.g., Lowande 2018; Ritchie 2018).

Despite its ubiquity, the Constitution does not explicitly authorize Congress to conduct oversight. Instead, the practice developed as an implicit congressional power and has been affirmed repeatedly by the courts.[6] Oversight hearings originated in the British Parliament and were subsequently imported by colonial legislatures (Feinstein 2017). The practice continued after the ratification of the Constitution. The first recorded congressional investigation, relating to a conflict between the US Army and Native American tribes, occurred in 1791 (Kriner and Schickler 2016).

Oversight activity was relatively stagnant until the 1910s, when it became more regularized. At the same time, the committee system institutionalized and oversight came to be dominated by new standing committees, instead of ad hoc ones. Congressional oversight continued to ebb and flow over the course of the twentieth century, with notable increases corresponding to the Teapot Dome scandal (1921–23), Watergate (1973–74), the Iran-Contra affair (1987), multiple wars (particularly Vietnam), and the creation of new governmental programs in the New Deal era (e.g., Aberbach 1990; Kriner and Schickler 2016).

Given the importance of oversight for separation of powers politics, substantial scholarly attention has been devoted to explaining the growth of oversight over time and why it has varied along the way. For example, Feinstein (2017) attributes the initial surge in the early 1900s to pressures from the Progressive movement and the rise of investigative journalism. Others associate oversight's ascension to reforms in legislative capacity, such as the Legislative Reorganization Acts of 1946 and 1970 that provided rules and resources for congressional oversight (see chapter 3).

In interviews with high-ranking congressional committee staffers conducted between 1978 and 1981, Aberbach (1990) asked respondents why they thought oversight had increased since the early 1970s. The most popular answer credited expansions in the size and scope of government over time. Interestingly, the next most cited explanation attributed this growth in oversight to increases in legislative capacity, specifically staff (27 percent) and other internal congressional reforms occurring during that time (22 percent). Parker and Dull (2009) also associate heightened oversight activity in the 1970s to an upturn in institutional capacity, but they do not directly test this claim. Aberbach (1990) examines the connection between committee staff sizes and oversight days between 1961 and 1977, but finds no statistical correlation. Fowler (2015) similarly finds little notable relationship between capacity and oversight in the realm of foreign affairs. Overall, though, surprisingly little scholarship has empirically scrutinized this relationship.

Instead, most studies debate whether partisan or ideological conflict impacts the volume of oversight. Although Mayhew (1991) finds no difference in the number of high-profile investigations covered in the *New York Times* under divided versus unified government, others uncover a positive correlation with alternative measures of investigative activities (Kriner and Schwartz 2008; Kriner and Schickler 2016; Parker and Dull 2009). Some scholars argue that the effects of divided government are moderated by other features of the political environment, such as majority party heterogeneity (Kriner and Schwartz 2008), polarization (Kriner and Schickler 2016), or retrospective behavior (MacDonald and McGrath 2016). Importantly, McGrath (2013) finds that while ideological divergence between the committee and president is positively correlated with oversight hearings, this effect decreases in committee member experience.

Altogether, then, the literature on oversight has provided inconsistent results about the relationship between capacity and oversight. Most studies do not consider it; those that do tend to study a single measure at a time, which often differs across studies. Disparate studies also measure various oversight outcomes, frustrating direct comparisons of their results. Some of these research designs, further, do not account for confounding factors at the committee level or ones that affect all committees in a given year. In the following sections, we advance a theoretical and empirical framework to overcome many of these challenges.

Theoretical Underpinnings of Congressional Capacity and Oversight

Several mutually reinforcing incentives impel members of Congress to pursue oversight. First, legislators possess strong reelection incentives. Oversight allows them to publicize executive branch activities and claim credit for correcting administrative actions that have harmed constituents (Fiorina 1977). Second, hearings or large-scale investigations often generate negative public attention and can mobilize political opposition against presidents. These forces have an adverse effect on the public standing of presidential administrations (Kriner and Schickler 2014) and jeopardize the success of their legislative agendas (Rivers and Rose 1985; Beckmann 2010). The public nature of oversight reinforces these electoral incentives to a substantially greater degree relative to other, less visible forms of constraint like discretion. Third, oversight is a means through which Congress asserts its power as an institution, irrespective of other policy and political goals (Schickler 2001). Notably, electoral and institutional incentives are more or less constant over time and do not necessarily change with partisanship.

Finally, substantial policy benefits may accrue to members of Congress, directly and indirectly. With respect to the former, oversight affords legislators the ability to learn about and correct executive policy implementation. Indirectly, oversight—or its threat—can induce greater responsiveness to legislative preferences because it imposes considerable costs on executive branch actors. Agencies must take time to prepare testimony and face public (often negative) scrutiny for their actions, which can damage their credibility and reputation. Consequently, oversight can deter executives from policy choices that would make legislative majorities worse off relative to the status quo. Because oversight can occur without supermajority support, its agenda is solely the prerogative of majority parties.

The foregoing discussion indicates legislators have incentives to employ oversight, regardless of executives' ideological orientation, to protect Congress's institutional power or augment their own individual prospects for reelection. Yet they have the *greatest* incentive to constrain executive power when they disagree ideologically with the executive branch. In these cases, there is a greater risk executive actors will implement policies that are unfavorable to congressional majorities.

Oversight, however, requires resources and policy expertise. Committees must identify fruitful areas for investigation as well as witnesses and documents useful for informing particular questions. They must take the time to question individuals with policy-relevant information and pore through the voluminous records requested from governmental and nongovernmental actors. Committee members must also analyze this data to determine what is credible and informative for addressing the questions at hand. These costs are easier to manage when Congress is high in resource capacity. Well-resourced committees can hire staff that can devote time to oversight activities. Experienced staffers and those with policy expertise are particularly valuable for these tasks. Similarly, members and chairs who have served on committees for many years have repeated interactions with agencies and acquire expertise in relevant policy areas.

In sum, capacity should have two primary effects. First, we expect a positive correlation between resources and oversight. This relationship reflects legislators' electoral and institutional incentives for oversight, irrespective of their ideological orientation toward the executive. This prediction differs from theoretical accounts contending legislative capacity is only useful during ideological and partisan division (e.g., McGrath 2013). Second, the impact of interbranch division on oversight should depend on resource capacity. When capacity is low, we expect no effect of interbranch preference divergence. As capacity increases, however, there should be a positive correlation between executive-legislative conflict and oversight activity. Based on these arguments, we empirically evaluate two distinct predictions:

Prediction 5.1: Conditional on high policymaking capacity, as legislative resource capacity increases, congressional actors will engage in more oversight of the executive branch.

Prediction 5.2: Conditional on high policymaking capacity, when legislative resource capacity is high, ideological divergence between congressional actors and the president will be associated with higher levels of oversight. When resource capacity is low, ideological divergence will have little relation to oversight levels.

Data and Measurement

Measuring Oversight

With some exceptions (e.g., Kriner and Schwartz 2008), most oversight studies examine particular activities in isolation. We recognize, however, that the frequency and intensity of oversight can be captured in many ways. Accordingly, we gather data on four different indicators of oversight activity: total hearings, hearings related to investigations of executive branch misconduct, days of hearings related to investigations, and pages in the CIS related to investigations. Our approach can help discern whether conflicting results in the literature represent differences in research design or real distinctions in the political dynamics underlying different indicators of capacity and oversight.

To begin, we use the Congressional Information Service (CIS) abstracts database, maintained online by ProQuest Congressional, to identify and collect a new dataset on *all published hearings* by standing, select, and special congressional committees between 1898 and 2014. We identify 111,087 oversight hearings published during this time period, 60 percent of which were conducted by the House, 38 percent by the Senate, and 2 percent jointly. On average, congressional committees held about 949 hearings per year, with a peak of 4,241 in 1992 and a low of 37 in 1899.

While this measure serves as a useful indicator of legislators' overall exercise of their oversight powers, hearings take many forms and may not always be about confronting executive branch actors. As such, we also employ data on congressional investigations into executive branch misconduct. Investigations are a narrower type of oversight centered on high-profile actions, often involving a long-lasting series of hearings. To measure investigations, we use the Kriner and Schickler (2014) dataset, who conducted CIS searches to identify all hearings related to investigative misconduct between 1898 and 2014.[7]

To construct a measure of *the number of investigative hearings*, we sum the number of hearings by CIS identification number, each of which is associated with a unique investigation. These counts produced a total of 5,627 hearings related to executive branch misconduct investigations (55 percent House, 45 percent Senate), averaging 48 per year (26 in the House, 22 in the Senate) and ranging from 2 to 242 per year. Second, following Kriner and Schwartz (2008), we count the *number of hearing days* related to high profile investigations, which was also provided in the Kriner and Schickler (2014) dataset. Finally, we aggregate the *number of pages devoted to each investigative hearings* identified in the CIS, collected by Kriner and Schickler. We take the natural logarithm of each of these measures.[8]

Given these three measures of investigative activity are related to the same concept, we combine them into a single index (*Investigative Activity*). To do so, we conduct factor analysis on the measures. Unsurprisingly, all three load highly onto a single factor. We use the predicted factor score as our measure of investigative activity.[9] This score ranges from -2.9 to 1.9 at the chamber level, with a mean of zero and a standard deviation of one.

To conduct our empirical tests, we construct two datasets on oversight: (1) by chamber-year; and (2) by chamber-committee-year. Our chamber-year level dataset contains an observation for both the House and the Senate in every year between 1898 and 2014. To construct the committee-level dataset, we use the CIS identification number associated with each hearing and investigation in the Kriner and Schickler (2014) dataset to identify the committee conducting the hearing or investigation in Congressional Proquest. With these committee matches, we assemble the oversight data by committee-chamber-year. Because most of our committee-level capacity measures are limited to 1967 through 2012, we confine ourselves to that time period in the second set of analyses. By leveraging these datasets, we can observe how macrolevel and within-committee changes in congressional capacity impact the relationships of interest.

Congressional Resource Capacity

In our chamber-year analyses, we use congressional staffing levels for all standing committees to measure legislative resource capacity ($Ln[Leg. Staff]$). We collect this data from *Vital Statistics on Congress*, gathering information on overall committee staffing levels between 1898 and 2014. Although this dataset extends back to 1891, staff data was not reported annually until 1970. Thus, we use linear interpolation to supplement missing data in the earlier years.

At the committee level, we rely upon four measures of resource capacity similar to those introduced in the last chapter for the appropriations committees: majority staff size ($Ln[Comm. Staff]$), majority staff experience ($Ln[Comm. Staff Exp.]$), member experience ($Ln.[Comm. Member Exp.]$), and chair experience ($Ln[Comm. Chair Exp.]$). To obtain staff majority size, we count the number of staffers by committee listed in the congressional staff directories, which are consistently available between 1967 and 2012 for all committees in each year. We identified 25,227 unique congressional staffers and traced their careers to create the experience measure by averaging the number of years each staffer has served on a particular committee for each committee-year.[10] As in chapter 4, we omit staffers designated as working for the minority party.[11]

We likewise create a measure of average committee member experience between 1967 and 2012. Here, we identify the members for each committee using two different datasets collected by Nelson, Stewart, and Woon to determine how many years each member served on a given committee.[12] We then average the experience of all members on the committee for each committee-year observation in our dataset. We use an analogous procedure to determine the number of years a committee chair has served in that position as another measure of experience.[13] Taken together, we can characterize the number of majority party staff as well as the experience of staff, committee members, and chairs at the committee level in each year.

Many of the trends in committee staffing mirror those described in chapter 4 for the appropriations committees. Average majority committee staff increased markedly from around twenty individuals in 1967 to fifty-three in 1980. Staff sizes peaked in 1992, averaging fifty-four majority staffers per committee. As would be expected from chapter 3, staffing dramatically declined beginning in 1995, when Republicans gained control of the House, reaching thirty-one in 2001.

The mean experience of majority committee staffers initially peaked at 7.8 years in 1967, but steadily decreased to a low of 2.1 years in 1981. As noted in chapter 4, the 1970 Reorganization Act is the likely culprit for this decline given the influx of new committee staffers following its passage. Staff experience swelled again in the 1980s. Overall, majority committee staff experience averages about 3.7 years over time, with a standard deviation of 1.3 years.

Average committee member experience has remained remarkably steady, at least in the aggregate, ranging from 3 years in 1981–82 to 4.7 years in 1991–92. Finally, the average experience of committee chairs steadily deteriorated since its peak of 4.2 years in 1967. Chair experience did rise between 1983 and 1992, but subsequently descended again to a nadir of 1.2 years in 1996. This measure has fluctuated ever since. Overall, the mean years of chair experience is 2.5 years, with a standard deviation of 0.86 and a maximum of 12 years.

Partisan Disagreement

On the chamber level, we use an indicator variable for whether the president and the chamber majority are from opposing political parties. At the committee level, we measure when the president and committee chair are from opposing parties (both are denoted *Divided* in the tables below).[14] To test prediction 2, we include an interaction term between our measures of resource capacity and *Divided*.

Control Variables

We control for numerous variables that could influence both congressional oversight and capacity. We describe these variables first at the chamber level and then at the committee level. To begin, the electoral incentives of legislators may strongly motivate their decisions to increase executive branch oversight (Kriner and Schwartz 2008; Kriner and Schickler 2016; Lowande and Peck 2016). Previous research demonstrates Congress often engages in oversight activity to discredit presidents in the eyes of the public. When presidents have strong public standing, however, Congress may shy away from oversight given presidential resilience to congressional attacks (Kriner and Schwartz 2008). Furthermore, legislators maintain electoral incentives to align themselves with a popular president, to garner public favor (Parker and Dull 2009). Presidential popularity may also shape congressional decisions about capacity, given the public opinion dynamics discussed in chapter 3. To measure the president's standing with the public, we include the yearly averaged presidential approval rating from the Gallup Poll (*Pres. Approval*).

Relatedly, presidents and members of Congress tread more carefully during election years when public scrutiny is particularly high. During these years, executive actors may avoid acting outside the scope of their powers, while legislators may do the same. Congress could also be reticent to increase its own resources in election years. As such, *Election Year* is coded as "1" in every presidential election year and "0" otherwise.

Economic conditions might leave executive actors more vulnerable to oversight (Kriner and Schickler 2016). Since the economy is frequently a high-salience issue, the public may hold public officials accountable for economic downturns and reward Congress for seeking accountability from the executive branch when they occur. Thus, we might expect an uptick in oversight during economic turbulence. These considerations could likewise motivate Congress's decisions about its own resources, perhaps disincentivizing investments in legislative capacity. We use the annual *Unemployment* and *Inflation* rate as measures of the economy's health. The former is only available since 1947 from the Bureau of Labor Statistics, which limits the scope of our regression analyses.

Instances of war have historically been the impetus for congressional investigations of the executive branch. Following Cohen (2012), we measure *War* as an indicator for when the United States was involved in the following military conflicts: World War I, World War II, the Korean War, the Vietnam War, the Gulf War, and the most intense combat of the wars in Iraq and Afghanistan (2001–3).[15]

Next, we control for the *Chamber Polarization* of each congressional chamber by using the absolute distance of the NOMINATE scores between party medians. Oversight may serve as a substitute for legislation when gridlock is high, enabling Congress's continued influence over policymaking (Bolton 2021). Polarization could also rouse Congress's desire for resources facilitating these tasks.

During their "honeymoons" in office, presidents generally hold higher public and congressional standing, which may lead to less oversight. *Honeymoon* is coded as "1" if the president is in their first two years in office and "0" otherwise. Additionally, we control for annual government activity, as that may increase the staff sizes of committees and the demand for oversight, with two variables. *Spending as % GDP* examines annual government spending normalized to the size of the economy, while *Ln(Exec. Expenditures)* is an absolute measure capturing the overall level of government spending by executive agencies in a given year.

Further, we include an indicator variable for whether an observation corresponds to the Senate. Previous scholars note oversight should be more active in the House given rules empowering leaders and committees, while Senate rules might advantage minority parties that make oversight activities more difficult (Kriner and Schwartz 2008; Kriner and Schickler 2016; Parker and Dull 2009). There are also potential differences across chambers in staffing levels based on committee size and numbers.[16] Finally, the chamber-level models include a linear time trend and presidential fixed effects. The latter capture any time-invariant features of an administration that could confound our results, while the former accounts for any secular trends in either capacity or oversight.

In the committee-level analyses, we include fixed effects for every year to account for the effect of time, identifying ideological effects from instances where the House and Senate are controlled by different parties. In this way, we control for those factors in a year affecting all committees equally that could confound the results. For instance, economic conditions in a particular year might dictate staffing levels and executive overreach in dealing with potential crises, both of which could influence the likelihood of congressional investigations. These fixed effects also control for features of Congress in a given year that may impact its operations, such as the relative power in committees versus leadership. Additionally, we include committee fixed effects to account for time invariant features of committees and their work that could shape our results. The technical nature of a committee's policy area, for example, might affect both its staffing levels and the productivity of human capital, which could in turn influence that committee's oversight output. Previous studies of oversight at the committee level typically do not employ both committee and year fixed effects, leaving relationships vulnerable to confounding forces like those mentioned above.

Since we are employing these fixed effects in the committee-level analysis, we only need to control for factors varying within years and over-time within committees. We utilize committee-year level control variables in our specifications that are similar to the subcommittee controls used in chapter 4. First, we include a measure of the committee chair's conservatism, using DW-NOMINATE scores, to account for her own ideological preferences that could influence oversight activity and staffing levels (*Chair Conservatism*). Second, we capture the salience of a committee's policy area in a given year, by assigning each a CAP committee policy code and matching it to the percentage of responses identifying an issue related to that policy area as the most important problem measured by Gallup Poll. Thus, *Salience* is the logged percentage of these matched responses. Next, we include the logged size of each committee in any given year (*Ln[Comm. Size]*) to account for the possibility that high membership increases staff sizes, thus influencing the efficiency and production of oversight. Finally, new committees possess fewer and less experienced staffers. Thus, the novelty of the policy area or task may implicate oversight activity. As such, we include a dummy variable for the first two years of a new committee's life (*First Congress*).

Chamber-Level Analysis

To begin, we conduct *t*-tests comparing oversight activity during low-capacity (pre-1945) and high-capacity periods (post-1945). Congress held 148 hearings per chamber year during the former, and 446 in the latter. This difference is statistically significant ($p < 0.001$). Similarly, the average investigative activity score grew from −0.32 to 0.22 when transitioning between these periods, an increase of about one half of a standard deviation on the scale ($p < 0.001$).

We more rigorously test prediction 5.1 by regressing oversight activity onto our more direct measure of capacity available at the chamber level, *Ln(Leg. Staff)*.[17] We adopt OLS regressions with standard errors clustered by chamber and congress number to model the relationships of interest. The coefficients for these baseline models are reported in columns 1 and 3 of table 5.1 for total hearings and the investigative scale, respectively.

We estimate a positive and statistically significant coefficient on *Ln(Leg. Staff)* for both outcomes. Specifically, a standard deviation expansion in staff corresponds to an increase of 31 percent in total hearings and a two-thirds

TABLE 5.1. Chamber-Level Analysis: The Effect of Resource Capacity on Total Hearings and Investigative Activity

	Model 1 (Total Hearings)	Model 2 (Total Hearings)	Model 3 (Investigations)	Model 4 (Investigations)
Divided	0.147***	−0.989*	0.233	−5.750**
	(0.046)	(0.584)	(0.165)	(2.336)
Ln(Leg. Staff)	0.269**	0.171	0.667**	0.152
	(0.118)	(0.119)	(0.306)	(0.362)
Divided x Ln(Leg. Staff)		0.168*		0.883***
		(0.085)		(0.333)
Chamber Polarization	1.726***	1.706***	2.388**	2.282**
	(0.328)	(0.313)	(1.194)	(1.083)
Unemployment	0.011	0.016	−0.118	−0.092
	(0.022)	(0.021)	(0.089)	(0.085)
Inflation	−0.007	−0.002	−0.044	−0.021
	(0.011)	(0.011)	(0.029)	(0.027)
War	−0.061	−0.087	0.097	−0.041
	(0.058)	(0.061)	(0.168)	(0.170)
Election Year	−0.186***	−0.173***	−0.129	−0.062
	(0.046)	(0.047)	(0.116)	(0.115)
Pres. Approval	−0.004*	−0.004*	−0.011*	−0.010*
	(0.003)	(0.003)	(0.006)	(0.006)
Honeymoon	−0.180***	−0.184***	−0.208	−0.227
	(0.060)	(0.058)	(0.180)	(0.178)
Ln(Exec. Expenditures)	0.139	0.181	0.449	0.670
	(0.132)	(0.125)	(0.431)	(0.440)
Spending as % GDP	0.029	0.018	0.088	0.030
	(0.019)	(0.018)	(0.065)	(0.058)
Senate	−0.183***	−0.177***	−0.005	0.028
	(0.039)	(0.038)	(0.201)	(0.198)
Trend	−0.074***	−0.082***	−0.128**	−0.168**
	(0.015)	(0.015)	(0.063)	(0.070)
N	134	134	134	134
President FEs	✓	✓	✓	✓

OLS regression coefficients reported, with standard errors clustered by chamber-congress in parentheses. Presidential fixed effects and constant are not shown. Significance codes: *$p < 0.10$, **$p < 0.05$, ***$p < 0.01$, two-tailed tests.

standard deviation increase on the investigative activity scale. Thus, consistent with prediction 5.1, resource capacity is associated with increases in oversight and investigative activity, even after controlling for partisan division. *Divided* is also significantly correlated with the number of hearings. When the chamber is not controlled by the president's party, it produces 15 percent more hearings per year.

Marginal Effect of Divided on Total Hearings at Different Levels of Staff

Marginal Effect of Divided on Investigative Activity Index at Different Levels of Staff

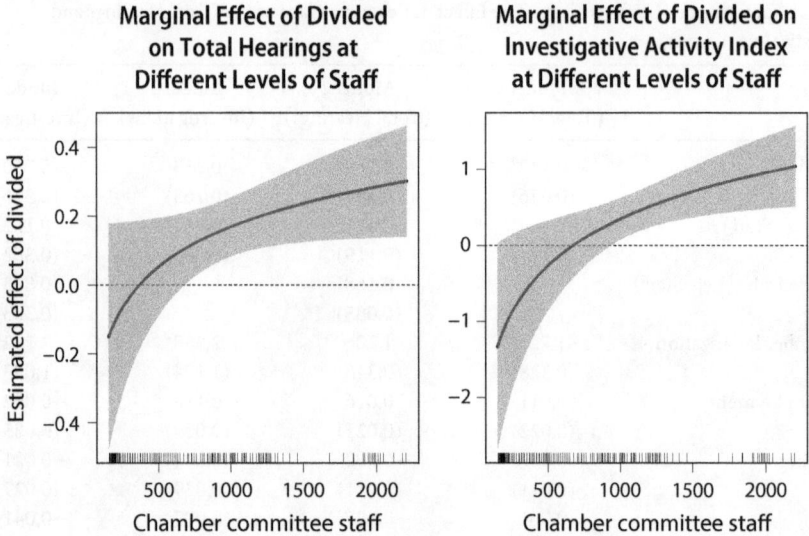

FIGURE 5.1. The marginal effects of *Divided* on each oversight measure, while varying chamber staffing. Reported with 95 percent confidence intervals.

Next, we evaluate the conditional relationship between executive-legislative disagreement and resource capacity posited in prediction 5.2. We interact *Ln(Chamber Staff)* with *Divided* for both measures of oversight in columns 2 and 4 of table 5.1. Both interaction terms are positive, as expected. The coefficients for the *Ln(Chamber Staff)* variable are still positive in these models, though statistically insignificant, suggesting the effect of staff is greatest during divided government.

The estimated marginal effects of *Divided* at different increments of staffing are depicted in figure 5.1. At low staffing levels, partisan division does not have a statistically significant impact on either hearings or investigative activity. As committee staff increases, however, this effect becomes positive and statistically significant for both oversight measures. More precisely, when staffing is at the 25th percentile of the observed distribution (329 staffers), a shift from unified to divided government has no statistically significant impact on either outcome, in line with our theoretical expectation that Congress is unable to act on its ideological impulses when its capacity is relatively low. At the 75th percentile of the staffing distribution (1,909 staffers), however, partisan division is positively and significantly correlated with oversight. In particular, *Divided* is associated with a 32 percent increase in total hearings and a nine-tenths standard deviation gain in investigative activity. One may wonder whether the meaning of divided government changes over time, based on evolving partisanship. We also analyzed models using ideological, rather than partisan, measures of conflict and find identical results. We likewise interacted divided government, resource capacity, and a linear trend, which yielded an insignificant relationship.

Committee-Level Analysis

Next, we conduct analyses with the chamber-committee-year dataset, using OLS regressions and committee-year level control variables across every model. The tables report the effects of resources on each measure of oversight activity: total hearings (table 5.2) and investigative activity (table 5.3). Each column uses a different independent variable for resource capacity: $Ln(Comm. Staff)$ in model 1; $Ln(Comm. Staff Exp.)$ in model 2; $Ln(Comm. Member Exp.)$ in model 3; and $Ln(Comm. Chair Exp.)$ in model 4. In general, we find evidence that resource capacity influences oversight at the committee level, though not uniformly across measures.

Table 5.2 examines the effects of resources and partisan division on total hearings. We find strong support for prediction 5.1 in model 1. That is, a standard deviation enlargement in staff size is significantly associated with a 16.2 percent increase in oversight hearings, irrespective of interbranch division. We uncover no evidence in favor of prediction 5.2 in this context, however. Total staff size does not moderate the effects of interbranch conflict. On the other hand, majority staff experience and member experience—important features of staff and member human capital—do appear to moderate the impact of partisan division, as displayed in the two rightmost panels of figure 5.2. At low levels of majority staff and member experience, we find generally insignificant effects of preference divergence. Yet these effects become positive and significant as staffing increases. Indeed, at the 75th percentiles of majority staff and member experience, committee-executive partisan division boosts total hearings by 56 and 59 percent, respectively. Chair experience, however, does not have a statistically significant effect. In sum, we find strong evidence for prediction 5.1 when considering total staff, and additional support for prediction 5.2 with the staff and member experience measures.

Table 5.3 conducts these analyses using investigative activity as the dependent variable, uncovering the importance of different types of resources. Consistent with prediction 5.2, model 1 reveals total staff is a critical moderator of partisan division. These effects are depicted in the left panel of figure 5.2.

TABLE 5.2. Committee-level Analysis: The Effect of Resource Capacity on Total Hearings

	Model 1	Model 2	Model 3	Model 4
Divided	0.281	−0.152	−0.656***	0.048
	(0.201)	(0.128)	(0.200)	(0.115)
Ln(Comm. Staff)	0.168**			
	(0.068)			
Divided x Ln(Comm. Staff)	−0.060			
	(0.054)			
Ln(Comm. Staff Exp.)		−0.332***		
		(0.065)		
Divided x Ln(Comm. Staff Exp.)		0.170**		
		(0.079)		
Ln(Comm. Member Exp.)			−0.819***	
			(0.115)	
Divided x Ln(Comm. Member Exp.)			0.459***	
			(0.122)	
Ln(Comm. Chair Exp.)				−0.100
				(0.086)
Divided x Ln(Comm. Chair Exp.)				−0.024
				(0.098)
Ln(Committee Size)	−0.166	−0.131	−0.056	−0.092
	(0.165)	(0.163)	(0.155)	(0.164)
First Congress	0.010	−0.153	−0.228	0.031
	(0.127)	(0.118)	(0.138)	(0.132)
Salience	0.055**	0.055**	0.037	0.036
	(0.026)	(0.026)	(0.025)	(0.026)
Chair Conservatism	0.198**	0.157*	0.038	0.102
	(0.087)	(0.081)	(0.083)	(0.081)
N	1,415	1,415	1,463	1,477
Committee FEs	✓	✓	✓	✓
Year FEs	✓	✓	✓	✓

OLS regression coefficient reported, with standard errors clustered by chamber-congress in parentheses. Committee and year fixed effects and constant are not shown. Significance codes: $^*p < 0.10$, $^{**}p < 0.05$, $^{***}p < 0.01$, two-tailed tests.

At the 25th percentile of majority staff size, partisan division corresponds to a 0.36 standard deviation spike in investigative activity. This effect yields an even greater increase of 0.55 standard deviations at the 75th percentile of total staff. Staff experience heightens investigative activity regardless of partisan division (in line with prediction 5.1), but does not moderate the effect of interbranch conflict. A standard deviation uptick in staff experience is associated with a tenth of a standard deviation increase on the investigative activity scale,

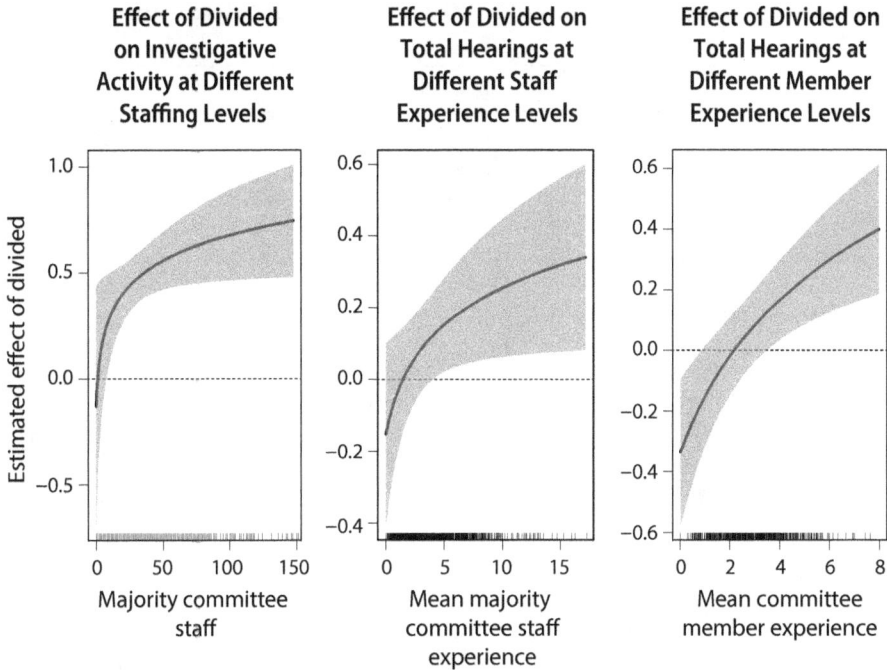

FIGURE 5.2. The marginal effects of *Divided* on oversight, while varying committee resource capacity for selected measures. Reported with 95 percent confidence intervals.

even during periods where the presidency and committee are controlled by the same party. Notably, we see no effects of member human capital on investigative activity, contrary to our previous findings for total hearings and those uncovered by McGrath (2013).

As in the last chapter, readers may be concerned that capacity is caused by interbranch conflict. To address these endogeneity concerns, we again regress logged staff onto divided government, finding the effect is small and statistically insignificant (coefficient = -0.003; standard error = 0.05). We find similarly insignificant effects for the other measures of capacity. Thus, there is no clear evidence that partisan division impacts capacity in problematic ways for our inferences.

What, then, to make of these analyses? The results reported here provide some general support for our theoretical framework. However, the precise operationalization of oversight and resource capacity clearly impacts one's exact conclusions. Our approach of examining varied indicators of the concepts, while keeping constant the research design accounting for

TABLE 5.3. Committee Level Analysis: The Effect of Resource Capacity on Investigative Activity

	Model 1	Model 2	Model 3	Model 4
Divided	−0.129	0.655***	0.353	0.584***
	(0.284)	(0.136)	(0.249)	(0.119)
Ln(Comm. Staff)	−0.044			
	(0.070)			
Divided x Ln(Comm. Staff)	0.175**			
	(0.080)			
Ln(Comm. Staff Exp.)		0.202***		
		(0.070)		
Divided x Ln(Comm. Staff Exp.)		−0.121		
		(0.088)		
Ln(Comm. Member Exp.)			−0.132	
			(0.139)	
Divided x Ln(Comm. Member Exp.)			0.064	
			(0.150)	
Ln(Comm. Chair Exp.)				0.101
				(0.092)
Divided x Ln(Comm. Chair Exp.)				−0.141
				(0.111)
Ln(Committee Size)	−0.060	−0.103	−0.062	−0.080
	(0.145)	(0.149)	(0.136)	(0.139)
First Congress	−0.034	0.080	−0.017	0.043
	(0.162)	(0.170)	(0.175)	(0.156)
Salience	0.031	0.036	0.030	0.030
	(0.040)	(0.040)	(0.039)	(0.039)
Chair Conservatism	0.167*	0.169*	0.095	0.109
	(0.084)	(0.086)	(0.086)	(0.083)
N	1,415	1,415	1,463	1,477

OLS regression coefficient reported, with standard errors clustered by chamber-congress in parentheses. Committee and year fixed effects and constant are not shown. Significance codes: $*p < 0.10$, $**p < 0.05$, $***p < 0.01$, two-tailed tests.

committee- and year-level confounding variables, allows these nuances to come into plain sight. These findings also help clarify divergent results in previous work and open up space for future theoretical development, as detailed in the conclusion.

Placebo Test

One possible concern with the conclusions we draw from our results is that they may also imply a mechanical relationship between staff and legislative outputs unrelated to calculations regarding interbranch constraint. Such a scenario would arise, for instance, if congressional staff were simply expected to engage in oversight activity irrespective of the broader political environment. This concern might be especially pressing in light of our empirical analyses revealing a positive correlation between staff and oversight, even during unified government (prediction 5.1).

We investigate this possibility with a *placebo test*. The logic behind a placebo test is that researchers identify a context in which the theorized mechanism should *not* apply and examine if an effect still manifests. In our case, we only expect to observe strategic behavior in areas where congressional majorities can fully control the agenda. When their agenda is externally driven, capacity and interbranch preference divergence should not influence oversight activity. We identify two areas of committee activity where congressional actors have relatively less control over their agendas: nominations and treaties. Here, presidents determine the agenda through their submissions of nominations and treaties for Senate consideration. Of course, presidents could strategically time these submissions for when Congress has lower capacity. But this possible strategy has drawbacks in terms of time loss or diminished influence without confirmed appointees or negotiated treaties. Congress might also use their resources to devote more or less hearings to nominees or treaties. This scenario might be less of a concern for appointments, most of which receive only one hearing. It may, however, be potentially problematic for treaties, and readers should thus be mindful of this limitation when evaluating our empirical results.

To examine these areas, we use the Fowler (2015) dataset, which codes public and executive session hearings of the Senate Armed Services and Senate Foreign Relations Committees from 1947 to 2008. Importantly, it also distinguishes the contents of different hearings. From this committee-year level dataset, we employ three dependent variables: the logged number of all hearings (not including nominations and treaties), the logged number of treaty hearings, and the logged number of nomination hearings. The key independent variables are an indicator for when the president and Senate majority are of different parties (*Divided*), the logged number of congressional staff (*Ln[Comm. Staff]*), and their interaction (*Divided* × *Ln[Comm. Staff]*).[18]

We include several control variables, based on our previous analyses and those in Fowler (2015). First, we control for the salience of policy topics in the jurisdiction of the relevant committee, based on the most important problem data discussed above (*Salience*). Second, we include the logged budget size for executive agencies under the committees' jurisdictions using data collected by

Fowler (*Ln(Budget)*). We also control for whether or not the United States is involved in a major armed conflict (*War*) and presidential approval (*Pres. Approval*), both measured in the same ways as described previously. Following Fowler, we control for polarization within the Senate, operationalized as the absolute value of the difference between the DW-NOMINATE scores of the party medians (*Chamber Polarization*). Finally, we include an indicator variable for whether the hearing was conducted by the Foreign Affairs Committee, which captures time-invariant features of the committees that may confound the results.

Table 5.4 reports the results from six OLS regression models, with standard errors clustered by Congress. Each model includes fixed effects for committee and president, to account for their particular idiosyncrasies. We employ models with and without control variables, for each dependent variable.

In models 1 and 2, we examine the effects of our key independent variables on all oversight activity, except those related to nominations or treaties. Across both specifications, staffing is positively correlated with hearings under unified and divided government, providing further evidence that legislators are not simply driven by ideological disagreement—in support of prediction 5.1. Consistent with prediction 5.2, we find the negative effect of divided government is significantly moderated by greater staffing resources.

We explore treaty hearings in models 3 and 4. As expected, we find a null effect in our key variables (i.e., staffing, divided government, and their interaction). We uncover similar patterns when analyzing nomination hearings (models 5 and 6). We do find a large negative effect of divided government in model 5, though the estimate shrinks nearly in half and becomes statistically insignificant when relevant controls are added.

In summary, these placebo tests offer additional support for our larger theoretical argument. Congressional majorities only strategically engage in executive branch oversight based on partisan division and capacity in areas where they can control the agenda. For externally set agenda items, such strategic dynamics do not manifest. These results provide evidence that capacity does not merely raise all legislative activity, but serves the broader purpose of advancing congressional priorities in the ways we hypothesized.

Summary and Conclusion

In this chapter, we spotlight one of Congress's most powerful tools for preventing bureaucratic drift and disciplining the executive branch: oversight.

TABLE 5.4. The Effect of Committee Staffing on Armed Services and Foreign Affairs Hearings

	Model 1	Model 2	Model 3	Model 4	Model 5	Model 6
Divided	−0.639**	−0.724**	0.532	0.496	−1.360**	−0.709
	(0.172)	(0.260)	(0.486)	(0.572)	(0.566)	(0.971)
Ln(Comm. Staff)	0.239**	0.217*	−0.00150	0.0966	0.226	0.446
	(0.115)	(0.116)	(0.265)	(0.319)	(0.263)	(0.340)
Divided x Ln(Comm. Staff)	0.141**	0.173**	−0.131	−0.0596	0.317	0.146
	(0.0564)	(0.0806)	(0.178)	(0.186)	(0.194)	(0.300)
Salience		−0.0171		−0.0201		−0.201**
		(0.0408)		(0.0893)		(0.0980)
Ln(Budget)		0.0346		0.309		0.124
		(0.0733)		(0.196)		(0.320)
War		−0.0330		−0.131		0.202
		(0.0787)		(0.165)		(0.314)
Chamber Polarization		−0.686		−4.284		−0.0636
		(1.215)		(2.673)		(4.044)
Pres. Approval		0.000160		−0.00383		0.00429
		(0.00290)		(0.00798)		(0.00749)
N	124	120	124	120	124	120
Committee FEs	✓	✓	✓	✓	✓	✓
President FEs	✓	✓	✓	✓	✓	✓
Type of Hearings	All Other	All Other	Treaty	Treaty	Nominations	Nominations

OLS regression coefficients reported, with robust standard errors clustered by Congress in parentheses. Committee and presidential fixed effects and constant are not shown. Note there is missing? most important problem? data from the Comparative Agendas Project for 1953 and 1955 that leads to four observations being omitted in models 2, 4, and 6. Significance codes: $*p < 0.10$, $**p < 0.05$, $***p < 0.01$, two-tailed tests.

We offer one of the most comprehensive quantitative examinations of oversight to date, with multiple measures capturing the frequency and intensity of these activities at the chamber and committee levels. Unlike in the case of discretion, we find stronger evidence here in favor of the direct effects of capacity, perhaps reflecting the reelection incentives surrounding the public nature of oversight.

Also consistent with our theory, we reveal legislative resource capacity moderates the effects of congressional-presidential conflict on oversight activity. Chambers and committees are only able to actively oversee their ideological opponents in the executive branch when they have sufficient capacity to do so. In this way, familiar findings in the literature about divided government and oversight disappear when congressional resources are relatively low. These results, however, depend on the particular oversight activity and indicator of capacity under examination. We think of this revelation not as evidence our theoretical framework is wholly inapt, but rather as an invitation for future work to clarify why different types of capacity are more salient for some oversight activities than others.

Overall, this chapter and the last demonstrate how resource incapacity affects discretionary grants to executive actors and the oversight of whether that discretion is used to implement policies consistent with congressional preferences. These ex ante and ex post activities work together, allowing Congress to check executive unilateralism and maintain its relative standing in the separation of powers system.

As argued in chapter 2, the effects of capacity are unlikely to be confined to the legislative branch. Instead, the structure of American governance ensures they will diffuse throughout the separation of powers system. With Congress less able to impose constraints, presidents inherit greater opportunities to unilaterally advance policies they might not otherwise obtain when up against better-resourced legislators. Here, executives can be assured their policies will not be undermined and that they will not incur costs if they use their discretion in ways unpalatable to legislative majorities. These incentive effects of legislative (in)capacity for chief executives are the subject of the next two chapters.

6

The Pendulum of Power

PRESIDENTIAL UNILATERAL POLICYMAKING

We're not just going to be waiting for legislation in order to make sure that we're providing Americans the kind of help they need. I've got a pen and I've got a phone. . . . And I can use that pen to sign executive orders and take executive actions and administrative actions that move the ball forward. . . . One of the things that I'm going to be talking to my Cabinet about is how do we use all the tools available to us, not just legislation, in order to advance a mission that I think unifies all Americans.

—PRESIDENT BARACK OBAMA

Ahead of his first Cabinet meeting of 2014, President Obama broadcasted his intention to unilaterally propel his policy agenda in the face of what he viewed as an obstructionist Congress.[1] Such rhetorical threats were a routine occurrence after Republicans seized the House in 2011. Not long after, the White House debuted the "We Can't Wait" campaign, publicly tracking its efforts to act administratively in areas where legislation stalled. In announcing this initiative, Obama proclaimed, "We can't wait for an increasingly dysfunctional Congress to do its job. Where they won't act, I will."[2]

His approach to unilateralism was considered emblematic of presidents facing recalcitrant congresses by the media and some academics. The *New York Times*, for example, reported, "The Obama administration's pattern reflects how presidents usually behave, especially during divided government, and appears aggressive only in comparison to Mr. Obama's having been 'really skittish for the first two years' about executive power" (Savage 2012). This account of unilateralism, wherein presidents use directives to bypass legislative opponents and impose their own will, is often referred to as the "evasion" view (e.g., Martin 2000; Mayer 2010).

Despite the intuitive allure of the evasion account, the data suggests presidents are, on average, not pursuing this strategy. Obama actually signed fewer executive orders under Republican congressional control, as compared to earlier in his term under Democratic leadership. Despite his confrontational rhetoric, many of his seemingly controversial unilateral actions were well within his legal authority and hardly unprecedented. For instance, he unilaterally raised the minimum wage instituted by federal contractors, an action long settled as being authorized under the Federal Property and Administrative Services Act of 1949.[3]

Obama was not unique in his apparent deference to congressional preferences or discretion in the law. Empirical studies have repeatedly confirmed presidents issue fewer unilateral directives under divided government (Bailey and Rottinghaus 2014; Chiou and Rothenberg 2017; Fine and Warber 2012; Howell 2003; Young 2013). They seemingly exercise restraint, not force, in the face of congressional opposition, when the incentives for evasion are ostensibly the highest. Why presidents are apparently so deferential, even when these actions do not require direct legislative approval, is an enduring puzzle in American politics. As one prominent scholar opined, "We do not have a complete understanding of the interbranch dynamics of unilateral actions" (Mayer 2010, 441).

Indeed, the precise underpinnings of presidential constraint have remained somewhat opaque within scholarly discourse. Some recent work doubts whether Congress, mired in gridlock and partisan conflict, plays any role in producing these patterns through exercising their institutional powers. Instead, scholars argue that constraint might emerge from other sources, such as from public distaste for unilateralism or negative opinions about presidential actions (e.g., Christenson and Kriner 2020; Posner and Vermeule 2010; Reeves and Rogowski 2018). However, if these checks really are at the core of constraint, why do presidents appear so deferential to *congressional* preferences? We think it is because Congress actually can provide meaningful restraints. And, if true, presidential strategies should depend on congressional capacity.

As we demonstrate in chapters 4 and 5, Congress's command over the executive branch critically depends on its resource capacity. In this chapter and the next, we consider how capacity impacts the incentives of executives contemplating whether to go it alone. Limited discretion diminishes their potential policy gains from unilateralism. Impending retaliatory mechanisms like oversight deter chief executives from wielding what discretion they do have in ways congressional majorities find objectionable. As such, under conditions of high capacity, self-restraint is an attractive strategy for presidents. However, when ex ante or ex post constraints are diminished due to low congressional capacity, presidents can press their advantage and evade unfriendly majorities.

We empirically evaluate our predictions using presidential executive orders issued between 1905 and 2019, a longer time frame than the post–World War II era typically studied in the literature. This data allows us to leverage the ups and downs of congressional resources during this time, as described in chapter 3. Because congressional policymaking capacity is sufficiently high throughout this period, we analyze the links between resources and presidential behavior. Consistent with our theoretical expectations, we find robust evidence that resource capacity moderates the relationship between divided government and executive order activity.[4] Moreover, we report analyses directly connecting the discretion Congress provides presidents to their unilateral behavior in specific policy areas. In doing so, we affirm the centrality of discretion and congressional activity for executive unilateralism.

Presidential constraint is neither universal nor inevitable. Indeed, evasion was the rule in some time periods. The analyses in this chapter identify mechanisms underlying the patterns of constraint observed in the modern area, thus shedding light on a long-standing puzzle in the study of the presidency and American politics about why presidents appear constrained by congressional preferences. Taken together, this chapter provides powerful confirmation that Congress and its capacity are the keys to containing executive power.

The Foundations of Unilateral Power

While many readily associate presidential powers with those explicitly listed in the Constitution, inherent authority and powers presidents read into the Constitution have evolved into mainstays of executive governance. Vague language in Article II, including the Vesting Clause,[5] the Oath Clause,[6] and the Take Care Clause provide ample opportunities for presidents eager to justify expanding the scope of their powers.[7] It is from these constitutional interstices that unilateral actions, such as executive orders, arise (Calabresi and Yoo 2008).

Two features of unilateral actions make them particularly attractive for presidents wanting to push their programs (Howell 2003). First, they give presidents a first-mover advantage. Presidents can alter status quo policies in beneficial ways relative to what they might have obtained through legislation. Since these actions occur outside of the statutory process, the burden of response falls squarely on Congress. Reversing unilateral actions, however, is difficult for legislators facing internal gridlock. Second, when presidents act unilaterally, they act alone. Congress is encumbered by massive collective action problems associated with coordinating the activities of 535 members across two chambers. Presidents, conversely, are the unequivocal heads of the executive branch and can directly issue orders themselves. To be sure, they likewise face challenges harmonizing across the bureaucracy, given many unilateral directives are subject to inter-agency review processes (Rudalevige 2012). Yet chief executives exclusively maintain authority over the issuance and content of these directives. Unilateral tools are therefore powerful devices in which presidents can sidestep the legislative process.

There are many varieties of unilateral action (e.g., proclamations, memoranda, national security directives), but we focus on executive orders for several reasons. First, these directives instruct agencies to take actions and are thus important for influencing executive branch policies. Proclamations target individuals outside of the government, while executive agreements tend toward an international audience. Second, executive orders are viewed as having the force of law, further cementing their importance for public policy. Similar policy instruments, such as memoranda, have ambiguity surrounding their legal status, given courts' silence on the issue. Finally, these orders are required by law to be published in the *Federal Register*, facilitating consistent and transparent analysis. Presidents can decide whether to publish memoranda, while national security directives are mostly kept classified.

Exclusively analyzing executive orders may limit the scope of our conclusions about unilateralism if they are used differently from other policy devices. For instance, if presidents substituted memoranda for executive orders during divided government, this would produce a misleading portrait of how their unilateral activity responds to congressional preferences. Fortunately, previous studies find similar patterns of constraint for other unilateral tools (e.g., Lowande 2014). Our robustness checks, presented later in this chapter, further substantiate these claims.

Defining Executive Orders

Executive orders are written presidential directives instructing executive branch agencies or officials about how to implement, interpret, or execute the law. They serve a variety of functions, ranging from the truly mundane to some of the most consequential policy actions in US history. On the ceremonial end, they can create awards or medals, design flags or seals, commemorate a holiday, or mourn a death. Most orders, however, affect policy.

Presidents often use them to establish new policy initiatives. For instance, Franklin Roosevelt created the Federal Civil Works Administration (EO 6420-B, November 9, 1933) to promote job creation through public work projects. In 2001, George W. Bush formed the White House Office of Faith-Based and Community Initiatives, an agency used to support faith-based and community organizations in accordance with one of his key agenda items (EO 13199). Indeed, unilaterally creating White House agencies to shepherd presidential priorities is a common administrative strategy. During the Obama administration alone, forty-one offices or agencies originated from executive orders, such as the White House Office of Urban Affairs (EO 13503) and the White House Office of Health Reform (EO 13507) in 2009.

Presidents likewise employ these orders to regulate government contractors, which can have broad economic and social effects. Perhaps most famously, Johnson signed EO 11246 on September 24, 1965, prohibiting government contractors from discriminating on the basis of "race, creed, color, or national origin" when hiring employees. Nixon, Clinton, and Obama extended this definition to include sex, religion, age, disability, sexual orientation, and gender identity (EO 11478, EO 13087, EO 13672). As discussed earlier, presidents have also used executive orders to adjust the minimum wage for government contractors. For instance, Obama's minimum wage order followed exhortations in his 2014 State of the Union Address for Congress to implement these changes nationwide. In remarks announcing this executive order, he criticized Congress's failure to overcome gridlock and pass a federal minimum wage bill: "While Congress decides what it's going to do . . . today I'm going to do what I can to help raise working Americans' wages." Although this order did not achieve Obama's most preferred policy of increasing wages for all workers, it did allow him to better advance his goals than what a gridlocked Congress would have produced if left to its own devices.

Many early executive orders transferred land and other property between varied agencies managing its care, or leased it to other nongovernmental actors. While this exercise commonly occurred under Theodore Roosevelt, Taft, and Wilson, it dates back to presidents as early as James Monroe. These transfers are particularly useful for controlling military and natural resources. Indeed, one of the most sensational scandals in US political history, Teapot Dome, was triggered by Warren Harding's executive order shifting the management of oil reserves from the US Navy to the Department of the Interior (EO 3474, May 31, 1921).

Presidents have long turned to executive orders in response to international and domestic crises. During World War I, Wilson issued several orders related to the war effort, including ones facilitating hiring into the military departments, the sale of property for war funds, and the seizure and transfer of lands for military purposes. Carter deployed a series of executive orders negotiating the release of Americans during the final days of the Iran hostage crises in January 1981. A year prior to these negotiations, Carter unilaterally placed sanctions on Iran via executive order (EO 12205, April 7, 1980, and EO 12211, April 17, 1980). Subsequent presidents have continued the practice of unilaterally sanctioning countries like Libya, Iraq, Yugoslavia, Liberia, Sudan, North Korea, Syria, and Russia. With respect to economic management, on August 15, 1971, Nixon famously signed EO 11615 aimed at managing rising inflation by stabilizing prices, rents, wages, and salaries. Franklin Roosevelt likewise signed countless executive orders regulating the economy amid the Great Depression and World War II. Indeed, the National Industrial Recovery Act of 1933 mandated that Codes of Fair Competition structuring industry production targets and worker wages be approved and promulgated through presidential order. Facing the deadly coronavirus pandemic, Trump deployed executive orders facilitating the production of medical and other critical resources.

Executive orders also serve to directly supervise agencies and their employees. They can create, alter, or eliminate agencies; establish lines of succession; adjust salaries; appoint individuals to executive positions; provide exemptions from retirement; place or remove certain positions from civil service schedules; impose agency-wide efficiency requirements; or make other changes to civil service regulations. Executive orders were an important way in which the federal civil service system was extended for the first decades of its existence. Between 1884 and 1913, presidents added 131,834 positions to the classified service, often in ways that advanced their own partisan or governance objectives at the expense of congressional interests. Indeed, patronage and civil service were a primary axis of political conflict in this era, with unilateral power at its center (Johnson and Libecap 1994).

Another consequential use of these orders is structuring regulatory processes across the executive branch. Presidents since Nixon have issued executive orders establishing procedures for White House oversight of agency regulations (Rudalevige 2018). Perhaps most notably, Reagan signed EO 12291 shortly after his inauguration mandating agencies to submit regulations to the Office of Information and Regulatory Affairs, a subunit of the OMB within the White House, for approval before being finalized and published. Subsequent presidents have altered this process though the basic structure of central clearance remains, affording them substantial control over regulatory outcomes.

Executive orders, furthermore, initiate specific regulatory efforts. For instance, the Department of Labor promulgated regulations increasing the minimum wage used by federal contractors shortly after Obama issued his aforementioned 2014 executive order. To fulfill a campaign promise of deregulation, Trump signed his "two-for-one" executive order (EO 13771) in 2017, mandating agencies eliminate two existing regulations for every new one proposed. During a 2011 drug shortage crisis resulting from manufacturers' discontinuing the production of critical drugs without prior notification, Obama penned an executive order interpreting a section of the Food, Drug, and Cosmetic Act to allow the Food and Drug Administration greater authority to enforce prior notifications of production discontinuances (EO 13588). The FDA subsequently crafted a rule imposing greater enforcement of this legal provision, and drug shortages eventually decreased.

Executive Order Use over Time

Although the first recorded *numbered* executive order was issued by Abraham Lincoln in 1862, earlier presidents likewise deployed them to direct bureaucratic activities. Unfortunately, orders signed prior to the twentieth century were not systematically recorded or centrally cataloged. At the direction of Theodore Roosevelt in 1905, the Department of State created a repository of executive orders, requesting each agency submit its own records of orders it had maintained. In 1907, the Department of State retroactively assigned numbers to all previous orders submitted and to every new one issued in chronological order. This collection became known as the numbered series of executive orders (Mayer 2002).

Some agencies failed to submit executive orders to the Department of State by 1907. These directives were later discovered, but were not given a number. Instead, they became part of an unnumbered executive order series.

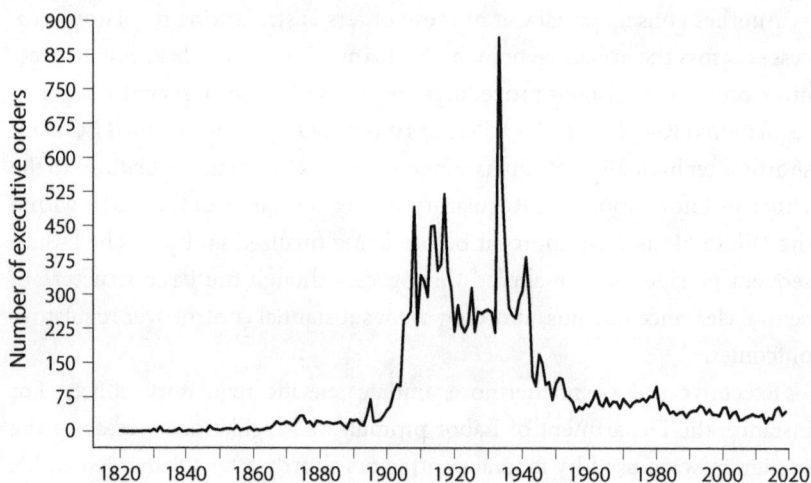

FIGURE 6.1. The total number of executive orders issued between 1820 and 2019.

As detailed in chapter 3, the Federal Register Act of 1935 provided a process by which all executive orders and proclamations had to be published in the *Federal Register* beginning in 1936. Since there appears to be no systematic substantive differences in content between numbered and unnumbered executive orders, we include both types in our study. We are reasonably confident that we are accounting for most executive orders with the inclusion of these two series.

Figure 6.1 shows the total numbered and unnumbered executive orders over time. By our count, the first one was issued on February 29, 1820 (forty-two years prior to the first numbered order) by James Monroe, who commanded the withdrawal of public lands in Louisiana for naval purposes. In fact, many of these early orders dealt with public lands and the establishment of military bases, particularly after the Civil War. Following Reconstruction, executive order use increased. In particular, the late nineteenth century ushered in surges in unilateral action after the implementation of the Pendleton Act and other civil service reforms.

Notably, the number of orders swelled at the beginning of Theodore Roosevelt's second term in 1905 for purposes related to the management of land, the civil service, the military, labor policy, and government commissions. Before 1905, presidents issued a mean of 12 orders per year and just 2 per year before 1866. Roosevelt averaged 312 orders annually during his second term. In contrast, 145 executive orders were deployed on average across all presidents between 1905 and 2019. Roosevelt's use of executive orders generally accords with historical accounts of him being an advocate for an energetic executive, often at the expense of Congress (Dodds 2013).

Even following Roosevelt's presidency, order frequency remained elevated, with peak activity in the 1930s and 1940s corresponding to economic crises and World War II. Following the war, however, executive order numbers decreased throughout the end of the century and into the next. This decline is in direct contrast to the prevailing public narrative of aggressive unilateralism in contemporary eras. In fact, the mean number of executive orders peaked during the Wilson administration at 378 and has steadily waned since the mid-twentieth century. Order issuance reached its nadir (since Grover Cleveland) during Obama's presidency, who averaged only 35 per year.

Explaining the Variation

Even with the persistent decline of executive orders, significant disparities remain over time and within presidencies. Given its importance as a unilateral tool of policy implementation, a robust literature is devoted to explaining its variation. Prominent accounts highlight administration changes, presidential approval ratings, executive branch size, electoral concerns, partisanship, international crises, foreign policy issues, and economic distress (Christenson and Kriner 2019; Dickinson and Gubb 2016; Krause and Cohen 1997; Marshall and Pacelle 2005; Mayer 1999; 2002; Shull 2006; Rottinghaus and Warber 2015; Young 2013).

One central and recurring question, however, remains. Do presidents use unilateral actions to bypass legislative opponents or are they constrained by congressional preferences? The answer to this question speaks fundamentally to the balance of power in a separated system and the issue of whether presidents can unilaterally undermine Congress's position in the policymaking process. Media reports and conventional wisdom widely indicate they do. They believe presidents benefit most from unilateral actions that bypass oppositional congresses and will thus use them more forcefully amid interbranch conflict.

Despite the intuitive logic of this so-called "evasion" view of unilateralism, scholars largely find the exact opposite. That is, presidents actually issue fewer executive orders under divided government, indicating they are considerably constrained by congressional preferences (Bailey and Rotting-haus 2014; Chiou and Rothenberg 2014; Fine and Warber 2012; Howell 2003; 2005; Young 2013). Increased legislative success and seat shares for the pres-ident's party likewise augment the volume of executive orders (Gleiber and Shull 1992; Krause and Cohen 1997; Shull 2006; Young 2013). That said, some studies do yield mixed or insignificant results when investigating this relation-ship (Deering and Maltzman 1999; Dickinson and Gubb 2016; Krause and Cohen 1997; 2000; Mayer 1999; 2002; Mayer and Price 2002; Rottinghaus and Warber 2015).

Overall, the literature implies presidents are deterred by legislative oppo-nents when contemplating unilateral action. Existing studies, however, do not offer a clear explanation for these findings. We argue legislative capacity is critical for containing presidential power. By ignoring capacity, previous work has elided the mechanisms underlying executive restraint, while also obscur-ing presidential opportunities for evasive unilateral behavior. In the following section, we revisit our theory regarding how congressional capacity motivates presidential incentives for unilateralism.

Theoretical Underpinnings of Legislative Capacity and Presidential Unilateralism

Executive orders provide a powerful means for presidents to enact their pol-icy preferences (see, e.g., Eskridge and Ferejohn 1992; Ferejohn and Shipan 1990; Ferejohn and Weingast 1992) and are particularly appealing when their legislative agendas are stalled, quashed, or watered down. In this way, presi-dents can use executive orders to achieve more favorable policies than what the statutory process might yield. These orders, however, are not perfectly substitutable for legislation and are costly to create. Drafting an order often involves a lengthy bargaining process between the White House and agen-cies, which requires time, resources, and administrative attention (Rudalevige 2012). Additionally, executive orders often generate negative media attention, public backlash, and mobilized opposition groups—all of which can dam-age presidents' legislative and administrative agendas (Cooper 2002; Warber 2006).

Presidents prefer to avoid these costs if an executive order will not yield substantial policy benefits or is likely to garner damaging congres-sional retribution, which might offset any potential policy gains. If they do expect Congress to impose ex post costs, they will only move policy within congressionally set discretionary windows and use that discretion consistent with the preferences of legislative majorities. Such presidential self-restraint, however, will only manifest when Congress has the capacity to actually narrow discretion and credibly retaliate. In its absence, executive evasion will reign.

When resource capacity is impaired, Congress lacks the time, staff, expertise, and policy information to write sufficiently constraining laws and oversee policy implementation.[8] Low-capacity congresses are thus less able to restrict executive branch activities, both before and after an order is issued. These congresses cede more discretion to presidents, who can then expect greater policy benefits from unilateral action. Deficits in resource capacity likewise reduce the threat of ex post constraints, lowering the likelihood of retaliation against orders congressional majorities disfavor relative to the status quo. As such, presidents' incentive for unilateralism is heightened during periods of low congressional capacity in the absence of these constraints.

As congressional resources increase, discretion wanes and retaliatory threats become credible. Indeed, as discussed in chapter 2, capacity can have a direct effect on discretion and oversight, irrespective of a president's party or ideology relative to Congress's. With less discretion (when the potential policy benefits from unilateralism are lower) and a greater likelihood of ex post costs, the attractiveness of unilateralism decreases as capacity increases. Following this logic, our first prediction states:

Prediction 6.1: Conditional on high policymaking capacity, presidential use of executive orders decreases as congressional resource capacity increases.

Of course, presidents have the strongest incentives for unilateralism during divided government, from which they expect worse statutory outcomes. Whether they will be able to exploit these opportunities, however, depends on congressional capacity. High-capacity congresses grant less discretion to presidents who do not share their preferences. These presidents, moreover, will likewise eschew unilateral actions that disfavor well-resourced legislative majorities, since threats of ex post retaliation are more credible. Because presidents and Congress disagree most over the direction of policy movement during divided government, it is difficult for presidents to unilaterally change the status quo in mutually beneficial ways. Under unified government, however, Congress affords presidents broader discretion because of their shared preferences. Consequently, there are more opportunities to unilaterally move policies in ways preferred by both branches of government. Altogether, then, we expect more unilateral actions under unified government, relative to divided, when congressional capacity is high.

These patterns will reverse under low-capacity conditions, however. When Congress has relatively few resources, restricting discretion and imposing ex post costs becomes challenging, regardless of presidential preferences. Consequently, presidents can press their advantage and unilaterally bypass these congresses, particularly during divided government, when the benefits of unilateralism are greatest relative to potential statutory outcomes.

These arguments lead to our second prediction:

Prediction 6.2: Conditional on high policymaking capacity, when Congress is low in resource capacity, presidents issue more executive orders under divided government relative to unified government. This effect is reversed when Congress has high levels of resource capacity.

Data and Measurement

Measuring Presidential Executive Orders

To test these predictions, we collected all numbered and unnumbered presidential executive orders issued between 1905 and 2019 from the CIS Index to Presidential Executive Orders and Proclamations (maintained by ProQuest Congressional). The CIS contains many types of unilateral directives, but we only count those it identifies as an executive order. In addition to the numbered series, this includes unnumbered orders related to the Panama Canal, public lands, and Native American reservations.[9] Our analysis begins in 1905, since it is the first year the Department of State systematically collected executive orders. Prior to 1905, serious questions exist as to the volume of missing orders never retrieved (Dodds 2013; Mayer 2002).

We isolate nonceremonial executive orders given the political dynamics discussed previously should manifest when orders substantively influence policy. In particular, we omit ones used for ceremonial purposes related to flags, medals, seals, commemorations, deaths, and other similar categories. Previous studies have also recognized the importance of identifying policy-relevant executive orders, proposing several alternative methods for determining their significance.

One class of measures codes an order as "significant" if it is mentioned in a prominent national newspaper or the *Congressional Record* (see Howell

2003; Mayer 2002). One difficuty with these measures is that identification of significant orders by these actors may be subjective or uncorrelated
with the concept of significance advanced by political scientists (Chiou and
Rothenberg 2014). Furthermore, they may not be appropriate indicators of
significance for executive orders issued before their publication was mandated
by the Federal Register Act, given that legislators and reporters can only men-
tion ones they know about at the time. Thus, unnumbered executive orders or
those signed prior to the Federal Register Act may go unnoticed for years and
are largely not identified by conventional significance measures. Similar problems exist for measures based on sources such as court cases and law reviews
(Mayer 2002).

Chiou and Rothenberg (2014) developed a significance measure for executive orders issued between 1947 and 2003 based on an item response theory
model accounting for biases in varied sources, including prominent news-
papers and news magazines; law reviews; and congressional, presidential,
and judicial mentions of executive orders. Regardless, it still faces the same
challenge as others in extending the analysis backward in time.

Alternatively, Warber (2006) hand-coded executive orders in the modern
era, categorizing them according to whether they deal with symbolic, routine,
or policy-related matters. This method bypasses the flaws inherent in outside
source evaluations of significance. Parallels do exist between his symbolic category and the ceremonial ones we eliminated. Yet we include many of the
orders viewed as "routine" by Warber in our analyses, particularly ones related
to civil service matters—a historical source of contestation between presidents and Congress.[10] Finally, both the Chiou and Rothenberg (2014) and
Warber (2006) significance data exclusively consider modern presidencies,
and thus cannot be used for historical analyses.

Given the drawbacks of existing significance measures and that our theory
should apply to all policy-related executive orders, we simply analyze nonceremonial ones.[11] Overall, we identify 16,654 non-ceremonial executive orders
issued in the 115 years between 1905 and 2019, averaging 145 orders per year. Of
these orders, 14,970 are numbered and an additional 1,684 are unnumbered.

As an initial test of our ideas, and following the discussion in chapter 3,
we first characterize years prior to the end of World War II as a period of
low congressional capacity and the postwar era as high capacity. We select
1945 as the cutoff year given many capacity-related reforms passed around this
time, including the Federal Register Act of 1935, the Legislative Reorganization Act of 1946, the Administrative Procedure Act of 1946, and the creation

of the GAO.[12] Furthermore, the presidency literature broadly views 1945 as the beginning of the modern presidency, following important developments in its administrative scope and expansion (e.g., Neustadt 1990 [1960]). Many of the empirical studies of executive orders, consequently, begin here.[13] This periodization, however, is just a first test of our hypotheses, and we conduct tests over the full time period later in the chapter. Thus, our conclusions are not driven in any consequential way by this choice.

During low-capacity periods (1905–44), presidents issued a mean of 310 orders annually. Those facing high-capacity congresses (1945–2019), on the other hand, deployed fewer orders on average, at 56 per year. These differences are statistically significant. Moreover, bivariate negative binomial regression analysis reveals 82 percent fewer executive orders were signed under high-capacity congresses, as compared to the earlier period.[14] Overall, these statistics provide preliminary support for prediction 6.1.

The key question for discerning constraint or evasion is not how much presidents invoke these powers generally, as indicated by the volume of executive orders, but whether their use is influenced by congressional preferences (prediction 6.2). If presidents issue orders more frequently when legislative majorities oppose them, then evasion prevails. Here, their power is less restrained and can be used to change policies in ways countering the desires of Congress. If they forbear from unilateralism when confronting opposed congressional majorities, then executive power is constrained. To test this contention, we employ negative binomial regression models to analyze executive order counts.[15]

Independent Variables

Our main independent variable is an indicator for *Divided* government, measured as "1" if the majority of either the Senate or House is controlled by the opposite party of the president and "0" otherwise. We also account for other covariates identified in previous work that could confound our relationships of interest.

Given deference to presidents on foreign policy and in times of international conflict (Canes-Wrone, Howell and Lewis 2008; Cooper 2002; Howell, Jackman, and Rogowski 2013; Marshall and Pacelle 2005; Wildavsky 1969), we include an indicator for instances of *War*.[16] Scholars argue presidents use more executive orders at the beginning and end of their terms (e.g., Mayer 2002), particularly if preceded or succeeded by an opposing party (Howell

2003). As such, *Administration Change* is coded as "1" in the first year of a president's term following a partisan administration change and "0" otherwise. Comparably, *Lame Duck* is coded as "1" in the final year preceding an opposing administration and "0" otherwise.

We include the yearly inflation rate to account for economic effects.[17] Presidents may rely more heavily on executive orders in response to economic distress (Krause and Cohen 1997; 2000), as under Nixon and Carter. Additionally, we use two variables capturing the growth of the federal government, to approximate the scope of federal activity and demand for executive action over time. First, we measure yearly federal spending as a percentage of GDP (*Spending as % GDP*). Presidents should rely more on unilateralism when government activity is more expansive, relative to the size of the economy. Second, we employ an absolute measure of the resources available to cabinet departments with logged *Ln(Exec. Exp.)*, collected from the *Statistical Abstracts of the United States* and the OMB.[18]

We also include linear time trends to account for over-time changes in executive order usage not accounted for in the previously described variables.[19] All models include presidential fixed effects to capture idiosyncratic shocks to executive order issuance that are constant within presidencies, such as the size of the policy agenda or individual presidents' proclivities for unilateralism. Finally, the reported standard errors are clustered by Congress.

Empirical Analysis by Periods of Legislative Capacity

For our initial analysis, we compare periods of low and high congressional capacity: period 1 (1905–44) and period 2 (1945–2019). According to our theory, we expect divided government to be associated with increases in order usage during the former and decreases during the latter. And that is what we find.

The first column of table 6.1 shows the analysis during Period 1, revealing a positive and statistically significant effect of divided government. When confronting a Congress controlled by the opposition party, executive orders increase by 38 percent. Yet this result only holds during periods of low legislative capacity. Following substantial developments in congressional resources, the estimated effect of divided government is negative in period 2—decreasing annual order usage by 10 percent relative to unified government. Taken together, the analysis provides firm initial support for prediction 6.2. Presidents are more restrained when encountering oppositional

TABLE 6.1. The Effects of Divided Government on Presidential Executive Orders, by Periods of Capacity

	Period 1	Period 2
Divided	0.324***	−0.103**
	(0.0956)	(0.0452)
Inflation	0.0156**	0.0254***
	(0.00723)	(0.00620)
Spending as % GDP	−0.0237***	0.0084**
	(0.00867)	(0.004)
War	0.164	0.143***
	(0.153)	(0.0534)
Lame Duck	0.208**	0.114
	(0.0879)	(0.0738)
Administration Change	0.443**	−0.0347
	(0.193)	(0.085)
Ln(Exec. Exp.)	−0.389***	−0.0804
	(0.136)	(0.0613)
Period	1	2
Years	1905–1944	1945–2019
N	40	75
President FEs	✓	✓

Negative binomial regression coefficients reported, with standard errors clustered by Congress in parentheses. Presidential fixed effects, time trend, and constant not shown. Significance codes: $^*p < 0.1$, $^{**}p < 0.05$, $^{***}p < 0.01$, two-tailed tests.

congresses with ample resources, but are freer to pursue unilateralism to evade low-capacity legislative opponents.[20] These results persist even when controlling for factors that might impact government activity, such as inflation, spending, and war. Finally, we conduct analyses using other indicators of executive order significance in the online appendix and find the results are robust across these alternative measures.

The Moderating Effects of Legislative Capacity

While the previous analysis offers evidence for prediction 6.2, it does not directly examine how changes in congressional capacity influence unilateralism. In this section, we consider the entire time period to evaluate the role of resources in moderating the effect of divided government on executive order activity. Following our analysis in chapter 3, we operationalize resource capacity in two ways.

First, we use logged inflation-adjusted legislative expenditures (*Ln.[Leg. Exp.]*). This data is collected from the *Statistical Abstracts of the United States*, maintained by the United States Census Bureau from 1905 to 2003,[21] and from the Office of Management and Budget from 2004 to 2019.[22] Second, we use the logged annual number of committee staffers (*Ln(Leg. Staff)*), assembled from the Brookings Institution's *Vital Statistics on Congress*.

To test prediction 6.2, we interact both *Ln(Leg. Staff)* (column 1) and *Ln(Leg. Exp)* (column 2) with *Divided* in table 6.2. In addition to the previous control variables, we also include an indicator for the periods following the LRA of 1946, which was crucial for augmenting both legislative expenditures and staff sizes. With this variable, we can estimate the effects of capacity within the periods before and after the LRA's passage.[23]

For clarity of interpretation, the substantive effects of the interactions are presented in figure 6.2. As shown, resource capacity moderates the effect of divided government on executive order use over time. When legislative expenditures or committee staffing is at its lowest (about $146 million or 221 staffers), presidents issue significantly more executive orders under divided government as compared to unified: 11–12 additional orders. At higher levels of resources, however, this positive effect dampens and then reverses. That is, when resources are at their peak (about $5 billion or 3,300 staffers), presidents deploy 16 and 21 fewer executive orders, respectively, under divided government. Overall, these analyses offer further support for prediction 6.2, by directly examining the effects of resources and relaxing assumptions about what years correspond to high or low capacity. Presidents evade partisan opponents in resource-impaired congresses, but exercise restraint when legislative capacity is enhanced.

Testing Our Assumptions about Presidential Capacity

One potential concern is that we do not directly measure presidents' capacity to issue executive orders, particularly given the associated internal costs of authoring them. In chapter 2, we assumed presidents maintain sufficient capacity to develop and deploy executive orders throughout our period of study. As head of the executive branch, they control the information, personnel, and resources produced by agencies necessary for crafting orders. Even before major developments in the 1930s and 1940s that institutionalized the

TABLE 6.2. The Effect of Divided Government on Presidential Executive Orders, Conditional on Legislative Capacity

	Model 1	Model 2
Divided	1.192***	2.905**
	(0.427)	(0.927)
Ln(Leg. Staff)	0.451**	
	(0.223)	
Ln(Leg. Exp.)		0.291*
		(0.155)
Divided x Ln(Leg. Staff)	−0.168***	
	(0.0611)	
Divided x Ln(Leg. Exp.)		−0.110**
		(0.0438)
Inflation	0.00867*	0.0125**
	(0.00525)	(0.00567)
Spending as % GDP	−0.0215**	−0.0209**
	(0.00867)	(0.00821)
War	0.179**	0.186**
	(0.0793)	(0.0767)
Lame Duck	0.193***	0.234***
	(0.0518)	(0.0631)
Administration Change	0.117	0.126
	(0.0967)	(0.0897)
Ln(Exec. Exp.)	−0.237*	−0.248*
	(0.131)	(0.127)
Post LRA	−0.535	−0.514
	(0.332)	(0.324)
Years	1905–2015	1905–2019
N	111	115
President Fixed Effects	✓	✓

Negative binomial regression coefficients reported, with standard errors clustered by Congress in parentheses. Presidential fixed effects, time trend, and constant not shown. Significance codes: $^*p < 0.1$, $^{**}p < 0.05$, $^{***}p < 0.01$, two-tailed tests.

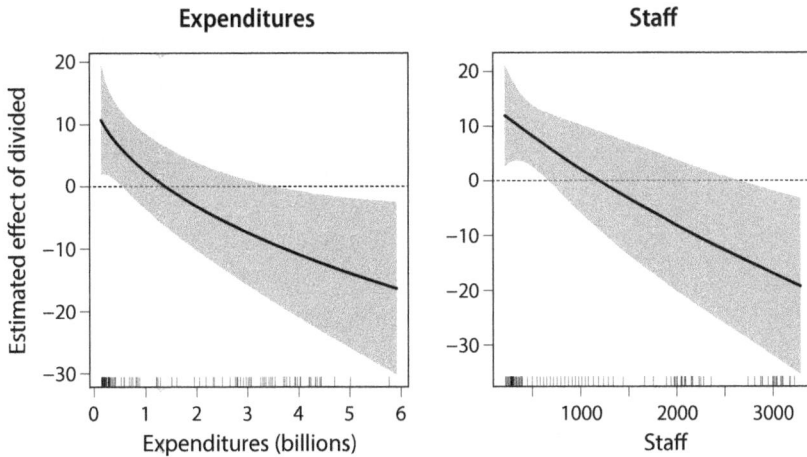

FIGURE 6.2. The marginal effect of divided government on executive orders, while varying legislative capacity.

presidency, notably the EOP's creation in 1939, we argue presidents still had broad capacity to employ this unilateral tool. Indeed, the most active period of unilateral activity occurred prior to 1939 (see figure 6.1). Of course, before the Reorganization Act of 1939, executive capacity was mostly located within agencies themselves. Even in the modern era, however, many executive orders originate outside the White House (Rudalevige 2012).

One might still question whether changes in presidents' capacity could influence the unilateral pursuit of their policy goals, in a similar manner as legislative capacity inhibits congressional constraints. In other words, are presidents with relatively lower capacity less able to increase or decrease unilateralism during divided government? Do the organizational developments in the presidency over time influence these dynamics? If so, then the underlying assumptions of our theory and the empirical results could be incomplete or flawed. To investigate this question, we measure presidential capacity as: (1) the logged presidential and executive office expenditures prior to 1939; and (2) the logged EOP expenditures after its creation in 1939 (*Presidential Capacity*). The EOP is an important indicator of presidential capacity given its role in coordinating executive branch activities, notably policy development and implementation. With this measure, we rerun our analysis from table 6.2 with a variable interacting *Presidential Capacity* and *Divided Government* in table 6.3.

TABLE 6.3. The Effect of Divided Government on Presidential Executive Orders, Conditional on Presidential Capacity

	Model 1	Model 2
Divided	1.092**	2.241**
	(0.442)	(0.928)
Ln(Leg. Staff)	0.464**	
	(0.232)	
Ln(Leg. Exp.)		0.300*
		(0.166)
Presidential Capacity	0.00726	0.00989
	(0.0489)	(0.0490)
Divided x Ln(Leg. Staff)	−0.181*	
	(0.0999)	
Divided x Ln(Leg. Exp).		−0.111*
		(0.0652)
Divided x Presidential Capacity	0.0102	0.00489
	(0.0432)	(0.0389)
Inflation	0.00818	0.0123**
	(0.00554)	(0.00577)
Spending as % GDP	−0.0216**	−0.0209**
	(0.00879)	(0.00827)
War	0.187**	0.192**
	(0.0874)	(0.0827)
Lame Duck	0.195***	0.238***
	(0.0589)	(0.0683)
Administration Change	0.112	0.122
	(0.0950)	(0.0887)
Ln(Exec. Exp.)	−0.251	−0.260*
	(0.155)	(0.149)
Post LRA	−0.512	−0.496
	(0.351)	(0.336)
Years	1905–2015	1905–2019
N	111	115
President Fixed Effects	✓	✓

Negative binomial regression coefficients reported, with standard errors clustered by Congress in parentheses. Presidential fixed effects, time trend, and constant not shown. Significance codes: $^*p < 0.1$, $^{**}p < 0.05$, $^{***}p < 0.01$, two-tailed tests.

Overall, the interaction term is positive, but statistically insignificant, while the estimated coefficients are substantially smaller than the ones for legislative capacity. Changes in presidential capacity do not motivate executive order usage during unified or divided government. These results substantiate our assumptions that presidential capacity is sufficiently elevated throughout this time period, and its inclusion does not materially alter unilateral activity. Moreover, the interactions between divided government and both measures of legislative capacity remain negative, statistically significant, and substantively meaningful. In other words, executive capacity does not influence our theoretically predicted relationships.

Presidential Memoranda

Though our analyses so far are centered on executive orders given the regularity of their use and legal validity, presidents have increasingly relied on memoranda for similar purposes and use both types of directives to achieve their policy goals (Cooper 2002; Lowande 2014). Accordingly, in this section, we include presidential memoranda in our measure of unilateralism as a robustness check.

Collecting the universe of memoranda presents some challenges. Unlike executive orders, there is no legal requirement to publish memoranda in the *Federal Register*. Thus, presidents can select which ones to publish and which to omit. To ensure we are gathering memoranda not in the *Federal Register*, we searched through the American Presidency Project (APP) database, which includes several sources of presidential documents, communications, and speeches.[24] We identified all memoranda providing instructions to federal agencies from these searches.[25] Using the same criteria as for executive orders, we discard memoranda used for ceremonial purposes. Next, we combed the *Federal Register* to locate additional memoranda not found in the APP database. Of the 3,059 memoranda we identified between 1862 and 2016, 470 (15 percent) were found in the *Federal Register* and did not appear in the APP. There were 963 memoranda (32 percent) that were *not* published in the *Federal Register*, but surfaced in other presidential papers. These figures reveal the importance of relying on multiple sources when identifying memoranda and the challenges of establishing a complete accounting of these directives.

To measure our new dependent variable of total directives, we sum nonceremonial executive orders and memoranda per year.[26] Often, presidents use memoranda to make determinations, which are statutorily required findings they must report to Congress concerning a specific foreign policy activity. Although some determinations can be controversial, most are routine (Cooper 2002). We thus also exclude them in our count as an alternative dependent variable, to ensure they are not unduly influencing our results.[27] We use the same set of independent variables as in the previous analyses.

Table 6.4 reports the results for both dependent variables. Our argument and previous results are once again confirmed when examining the conditional effects between divided government and legislative capacity on all unilateral directives (table 6.4), as evidenced by the negative and significant coefficients on the interaction terms. This result holds for the staffing and expenditure measures, across both dependent variables. Together, these findings give us confidence our conclusions are not driven by decisions to omit or include memoranda.[28]

Discretion and Executive Order Use by Issue Area

The findings in the previous sections provide evidence that changes in congressional capacity impact executive unilateralism. However, we have not yet demonstrated a direct link between legislative and executive actions. We assume this task in the remainder of the chapter by incorporating discretion into the analysis.

When Congress enjoys abundant resources, it can constrain unilateral action by decreasing the discretion upon which these actions seemingly rely. In this way the discretion presidents enjoy is central for their calculations about the potential policy benefits from unilateralism. This argument, however, is predicated on the assumption presidents actually need discretionary authority to act unilaterally and are therefore constrained by its limits. This assumption is central to our argument and others in the literature more generally. However, it has yet to be empirically tested. To do so, we first shift away from the legal conceptions of discretion highlighted in previous work to a more political definition, which we term the *discretionary attitude* of Congress toward the president in any given policy area and point in time. We then describe its importance for presidents' strategic calculations.

Why Discretion Matters for Unilateral Action

In *Youngstown v. Sawyer* (1952), the Supreme Court struck down a Truman executive order directing the secretary of commerce to seize control of steel mills, by declaring it lacked statutory or constitutional authorization. In his

TABLE 6.4. The Effect of Divided Government on Presidential Executive Orders and Memoranda, Conditional on Legislative Capacity

	Model 1	Model 2	Model 3	Model 4
Divided	1.661***	1.494***	3.416***	3.051***
	(0.446)	(0.415)	(0.909)	(0.851)
Ln(Leg. Staff)	0.221	0.0854		
	(0.265)	(0.240)		
(Leg. Exp.)			0.256	0.239
			(0.159)	(0.147)
Divided x Ln(Leg. Staff)	−0.251***	−0.224***		
	(0.0627)	(0.0576)		
Divided x Ln(Leg. Exp.)			−0.167***	−0.148***
			(0.0439)	(0.0396)
Inflation	0.00598	0.00785	0.00903	0.0114**
	(0.00534)	(0.00524)	(0.00573)	(0.00545)
Spending as % GDP	−0.0233***	−0.0231***	−0.0227***	−0.0223***
	(0.00891)	(0.00888)	(0.00846)	(0.00847)
War	0.194***	0.169**	0.203***	0.180**
	(0.0752)	(0.0786)	(0.0721)	(0.0747)
Lame Duck	0.200***	0.204***	0.200***	0.217***
	(0.0528)	(0.0484)	(0.0449)	(0.0479)
Administration Change	0.114	0.172**	0.121*	0.176**
	(0.0806)	(0.0835)	(0.0771)	(0.0752)
Ln(Exec. Exp.)	−0.253**	−0.272**	−0.266**	−0.286**
	(0.129)	(0.126)	(0.126)	(0.121)
Post LRA	−0.519	−0.459	−0.529	−0.483
	(0.338)	(0.335)	(0.330)	(0.327)
N	111	111	115	115
President Fixed Effects	✓	✓	✓	✓
Determinations Included	Yes	No	Yes	No

Negative binomial regression coefficients reported, with standard errors clustered by Congress in parentheses. Presidential fixed effects, time trend, and constant not shown. Significance codes: *$p < 0.1$, **$p < 0.05$, ***$p < 0.01$, two-tailed tests.

concurring opinion, Justice Robert H. Jackson famously posited that presidential authority to act is greatest when directly authorized by Congress and weakest when explicitly forbidden by statute. When the law is silent, however, Jackson argued there is a "zone of twilight" wherein the constitutionality of presidential action may not be absolutely clear, but more circumstantial.

Presidents thus need to draw on some statutory or constitutional discretion, either implicit or explicit, to affect policy unilaterally. Indeed, the process of writing orders appears conscious of this need for legal justification. Most notably, President Kennedy issued an executive order in 1962 mandating the attorney general review proposed orders to examine their "form and legality," thus embedding legal analysis directly into the process of developing orders. Such scrutiny, on its face, implicates a substantial degree of concern for the law in executive calculations about unilateralism.

Typically, presidents cite both statutory and constitutional sources in executive orders, but with varying degrees of specificity (Mayer 2002). In some cases, Congress directly authorizes presidential actions—for example, by requiring proclamations for adjusting tariffs or determinations on foreign policy. In other situations there is no room for executive innovation, as in establishing statutorily specified income tax rates. Mostly, however, presidential action falls within the nebulous "zone of twilight," where its legality depends on subjective judgments about whether an action lies within discretionary boundaries.

Indeed, presidents often cite broad statutory authorities to justify their actions. For instance, Title 5, Section 3301, of the US Code has been cited in countless executive orders pertaining to federal employees, such as rules for appointing members of the Foreign Service (EO 13749), ethics standards for executive branch employees (EO 12834, EO 13490, EO 13770), and reducing the size of the federal workforce (EO 12839).[29] Other times, they invoke vague clauses from Article II of the Constitution to justify commanding agency actions as head of the executive branch, despite the fact that most policymaking authority is delegated specifically to agencies rather than the president (Cooper 2002). Throughout the post–World War II era, presidents have frequently relied on this constitutional authority without reference to any other sources (Belco and Rottinghaus 2017). For example, many executive orders begin with the phrase "By the authority vested in me as President by the Constitution and the laws of the United States of America, it is hereby ordered as follows."

Yet, at the same time, the legal authority invoked in executive orders may simply be rhetorical. Presidents, in reality, have wide latitude in selecting which laws to cite when justifying these orders without having to materially change their content. This flexibility is enhanced by vague constitutional provisions and broad legislative delegations to the executive branch common throughout the twentieth century (Lowi 1969). Indeed, Belco and Rottinghaus (2017) find presidents strategically alternate between statutory and constitutional citations of authority based on the likelihood of congressional retaliation.

Though the federal courts impose costly punishments on presidents by overturning executive orders that violate legal boundaries, as in the Youngstown case as well as recent examples related to Obama's immigration orders and George W. Bush's national security ones, executive orders are difficult to challenge in court. They are not reviewable under the APA, and it is arduous to obtain standing to challenge them (Thrower 2017). Given their reliance on the executive branch to enforce judicial rulings, courts may also be reticent to strike at the heart of presidential power and choose instead to avoid these cases (Moe and Howell 1999).

Congress, on the other hand, may provide a more meaningful constraint to ensure presidents act within their discretionary boundaries. It can inflict costly punishments onto the executive branch for violations of discretion, including active oversight, delaying or rejecting presidential nominees, defunding agencies or programs, and passing laws that decrease executive power or debilitate presidential policy goals. Though presidents ostensibly have flexibility in identifying nebulous constitutional and statutory provisions as bases of executive authority, Congress still maintains its own beliefs about how much discretion presidents hold to change policy in any given area.

Importantly, these preferences for executive discretion may be different than those expressed directly in statutes, vary by policy area, and shift over time based on factors such as ideological disagreement, economic or international crises, and natural disasters. For instance, a financial meltdown might incur an expanded discretionary attitude toward the president in the area of macroeconomics even if no laws change, but it may be less influential on beliefs about presidential power over federal lands.

Consequently, discretion for unilateralism might also be understood in a political, rather than legal, sense. This conceptualization differs from that in previous work, which tends to center on whether presidential actions can be justified by the content of laws cited therein. Here, we argue presidents are more likely to act unilaterally at times when Congress indicates they have more discretion in a particular policy area. When presidents perceive less congressional leeway, they also expect diminished policy gains from uni- lateralism and issue fewer executive orders. In this way, discretion is not a fixed quantity throughout time, even if the Constitution and laws are rela- tively stationary. Executive opportunities are instead ever-changing, depend- ing upon the discretionary attitude of Congress at any given time and the threat of ex post sanction for using this discretion in ways legislative majorities oppose.

Despite its separation from the texts of laws, this discretionary attitude may likewise politically empower the judiciary to strike against orders, secure in the knowledge of congressional reinforcement. Indeed, Howell (2003) finds that courts are more likely to overturn executive orders when Congress is at odds with the president. Thus, presidents concerned about judicial review may not just worry about whether they can cobble together fragments of the US Code or the Constitution to justify their actions, but instead also assess congressional beliefs about the amount of discretion they should currently have in a particular policy area.

Taken together, costly congressional punishments and judicial interven- tions galvanized by legislative opponents lead us to expect presidents will be attentive to the discretionary attitudes of Congress when crafting unilateral directives. When they encounter diminished discretionary support from the current legislative majority in a particular policy area, they will be less likely to issue executive orders. As discretion increases, however, presidents enjoy greater opportunities for unilateralism.

Discretion and Executive Order Data by Issue Area

We test this argument by directly examining the connection between discre- tion and unilateralism. To do so, we divide executive orders by issue areas and use our measure from chapter 4 to characterize executive discretion in these corresponding areas for every year. Because our discretion measure only encompasses 1960 to 2015, the analysis is limited to those years. Accordingly, our specific unit of analysis is the policy area-year, as detailed in the following paragraphs.

Dependent Variable: Executive Orders by Policy Area. To measure our dependent variable, we code executive orders by policy area based on the twenty-one major topic codes developed by the Comparative Agendas Project (CAP).[30] Some topics contain few assigned orders, in part due to the similarities between many of CAP's categories. As such, we combine these categories based on natural groupings of policy areas. For instance, because commerce and technology issues are often linked in the executive and Congress (e.g., the Department of Commerce and Commerce, Justice, and Science appropriations subcommittee), we couple CAP's *Domestic Commerce* topic category with its *Technology* category to produce our own *Commerce* grouping. We also merge the *Civil Rights, Immigration,* and *Law and Crime* categories into one *Law and Crime* category. Finally, we collapse the *Foreign Trade* and *International Affairs* topic codes into an *International Affairs* category. In total, we construct seventeen policy area categories.

Next, we assign issue categories to each executive order. We recognize that these groupings are not mutually exclusive, since executive orders often deal with multiple policy areas at a time. As such, each order was assigned one or more policy areas. Coders were instructed to assign executive orders to as many categories as were appropriate for that order. For instance, several executive orders were used to create emergency boards settling labor disputes within transportation companies. We classified such orders into three categories: labor (because of the dispute), transportation (given the nature of the companies), and government operations (since the order creates an administrative entity). Based on this coding, we then count the number of nonceremonial executive orders by each category in every year. Presidents issued an average of 4.68 executive orders per policy-year, with a standard deviation of 7.59 and ranging from 0 to 53 (Government Operations in 1962).[31]

Independent Variable: Discretion by Policy Area. We use our appropriations-based measure of discretion developed in chapter 4 as the main independent variable. This measure produces an observation of discretion given to an agency, for each appropriations subcommittee of both chambers in every year between 1960 and 2015. We aggregate our discretion measure up to the policy-year level by assigning every agency observation one or more issue categories based on its mission statement. Similar to our procedure for coding executive orders, we allow agencies to be designated multiple categories when appropriate. We then summed the total spending and report pages in each policy category and year. The logged ratio of these two factors forms our measure of discretion for each policy-year observation (*Discretion*). The average level of discretion across policy areas between 1960 and 2015 is 6.13, with a standard

TABLE 6.5. The Effect of Discretion on Presidential Executive Orders

	(1)	(2)	(3)	(4)	(5)	(6)
Discretion	0.0913*	0.0941***	0.0698***	0.0885***	0.0602***	0.0769***
	(0.0497)	(0.0229)	(0.0202)	(0.0247)	(0.0229)	(0.0234)
Leg. Production			0.253***	0.156**	0.124**	0.0904
			(0.0708)	(0.0711)	(0.0631)	(0.0715)
Salience			0.639*	0.995**	1.118***	1.052***
			(0.366)	(0.391)	(0.382)	(0.393)
N	922	922	867	867	867	867
Topic FE		✓	✓	✓	✓	✓
Subcommittee FE			✓	✓	✓	✓
Presidential FE					✓	✓
Year FE						✓

Negative binomial coefficients reported, with standard errors clustered by Congress in parentheses. Subcommittee, presidential, and year fixed effects and constant not shown. Significance codes: $*p < 0.1, **p < 0.05, ***p < 0.01$, two-tailed tests.

deviation of 1.67. Substantively, this corresponds to $459 million in spending per appropriations report page.

Issue Area Analysis

We report the results using negative binomial regression analyses in table 6.5. Model 1 regresses the count of executive orders in a given policy-year on the observed level of discretion, yielding a positive correlation. In particular, a standard deviation increase in discretion is associated with a 16.5 percent increase in executive orders in a given policy area. The estimated coefficient is on par with the effects of other political variables discussed earlier in the chapter. Model 2 adds fixed effects for each policy category to control for time-invariant differences that may impact both discretion and presidential unilateralism. While the coefficient barely shifts, its precision increases considerably when accounting for policy areas.

Model 3 estimates the regressions with additional policy-year control variables, which could capture the underlying demand or policy activity in a particular area in a given year. First, we account for the current level of legislative production in a policy area to control for the possible effects of the authorizations process.[32] To construct this variable (*Leg. Production*), we take the natural logarithm of the number of laws passed in a particular policy area plus one. Second, we include the salience of the policy area (*Salience*). Public interest may compel Congress to grant less discretion to the administration in areas of constituent attention. On the other hand, presidents may seek to unilaterally respond to public concerns. This variable corresponds to the proportion of responses in a given policy-year identifying a related issue as the most important problem facing the country, using the CAP coding of Gallup Poll's Most Important Problem question.[33]

The results of the analysis are largely unchanged when adding these control variables. The estimated relationship between discretion and executive order usage remains positive and statistically significant, though the effect size is somewhat smaller. Here, a standard deviation increase in discretion is associated with a 12.4 percent increase in executive orders. As expected, both legislative production and salience yield significant and positive relationships with executive order issuance.

Model 4 includes additional fixed effects for the House and Senate appropriations subcommittees that oversee agencies within given policy areas, and our results remain robust. Finally, models 5 and 6 control for time in two different ways. First, model 5 employs fixed effects for presidents. Given variation in our key independent variable within years in this analysis, we include year fixed effects in model 6, which is our preferred specification. These fixed effects account for year-level variables that affect all policy areas, including ideological division between the president and Congress, congressional capacity, war, and economic conditions. Once again, discretion is positively and significantly associated with executive orders in both models. Specifically, a standard deviation increase in discretion yields a 13.7 percent spike in unilateral activity (model 6).

Overall, these results heartily affirm the idea that discretionary grants limit executive unilateralism. While most theories treat discretion as exogenous and empirical analyses ignore it, we directly estimate its impact on unilateralism and confirm its importance as a mechanism of constraint. Our measure differs from previous theoretical conceptions by capturing the discretionary attitude of Congress toward the executive branch. These findings produce more reliable insights into the influence of discretion than measures involving statutory citations of authority, which can be more easily manipulated by presidents. These results, along with those provided in chapter 4, give further credence to our theoretical claims that high-capacity congresses can deter executive action through decreased discretionary levels. They also provide a strong link between congressional and executive behavior, demonstrating the centrality of Congress in limiting presidential power.

Summary and Conclusion

The effects of legislative capacity are not simply confined to the actions of Congress, but instead ripple throughout the separation of powers systems. Presidential views of unilateral policy opportunities are in part determined by legislative majorities' capacity to constrain their behavior. First, legislative capacity impacts presidents' discretion to alter policies, which is intrinsically linked with congressional resources. Through its effect on discretion, capacity fundamentally delimits the policy benefits presidents can reap from unilateralism.

Second, resource capacity impacts presidents' calculations about the likelihood of ex post sanctions for using their discretion in ways that disfavor legislative majorities. Low-capacity congresses face severe resource restrictions that raise the costs of imposing such sanctions. When congressional resources are depleted, presidents unilaterally evade congresses that do not share their goals. On the other hand, when Congress possesses abundant resources, these opportunities for evasion are curtailed and we observe patterns of constraint. Thus, the power of presidential pens and phones is determined fundamentally by the capacity of Congress. Presidential action can be restrained, but it is by no means guaranteed to be.

To illustrate this argument empirically, we leverage the substantial over-time variation in congressional resources to determine whether they moderate the effects of divided government on executive unilateralism. Because Congress was relatively low in resource capacity through World War II, we examine whether the impact of divided government varies before and after 1945. As expected, presidents pursue evasive unilateral strategies prior to 1945, but are relatively constrained under divided government in the postwar period. Of course, other differences in US politics before and after 1945 might plausibly explain these results. To more directly examine the consequences of capacity, we analyze the entire executive order time series from 1905 through 2019. Indeed, the effect of divided government is decreasing in levels of both committee staff sizes and overall legislative expenditures. Furthermore, we provide evidence that discretion directly bears on executive order use, providing an important and new empirical link between legislative and executive action. These results provide a powerful affirmation of Congress's role in checking executive power in the United States, even in the contemporary era when other scholars see little role for it.

Overall, we shed light on a long-standing, unresolved question about executive unilateralism: Why are modern presidents restrained in their use of unilateral powers during divided government, when the policy incentives to bypass Congress are seemingly the greatest? In our account, the answer lies in legislative capacity. With a clear view of what Congress needs for executive constraint, we illuminate not only the mechanisms underlying presidential deference in the contemporary era, but also how and why we identify the opposite patterns in earlier periods.

While these findings offer firm evidence in favor of our theory, the analysis is limited in notable ways. First, the attention to one particular (albeit important) time series—executive orders at the federal level—is not ideal. There are many reasons to expect it is not representative, which may obscure broader inferences about separation of powers politics. Second, policymaking capacity has remained sufficiently high at the federal level, narrowing our ability to fully empirically evaluate our arguments in this context. To resolve these issues, we leverage variation in another context: the separation of powers systems across the fifty US states.

7

Calling Their Own Shots?

UNILATERAL POLICYMAKING IN THE US STATES

Early federal responses to the COVID-19 pandemic were widely criticized as disorganized and anemic. President Trump regularly downplayed the disease's severity, touted unproven treatments (e.g., hydroxychloroquine) or fabricated ones entirely (e.g., exposing patients to large doses of UV light or disinfectants), and publicly undermined federal agencies' health guidance (most notably, the use of masks). In contrast to his once claim of "total authority" over state governmental responses, Trump later indicated to governors they should "call your own shots" when it comes to critical public health guidelines that he made clear would not be coming from the White House.[1]

State governors accordingly filled this policy and leadership vacuum, drawing on their own vast unilateral authorities to mitigate the effects of the pandemic in their states. Governors spearheaded initial efforts to enforce social distancing guidelines and buttress overwhelmed state medical systems. Roy Cooper (D-NC), for instance, was one of many governors to ban large gatherings, while closing public schools and "non-essential" businesses (Executive Order 120).[2] Governor Mike DeWine (R-OH) waived eligibility requirements for state unemployment benefits amid rampant job loss (EO 2020-03D).[3] Governor Tim Walz (D-MN) ordered all medical and veterinary practices to create an inventory of medical supplies that could be used for COVID-19 treatment. As detailed in chapter 1, these unilateral actions became flash points of national and statewide controversy, as many decried gubernatorial abuses of power, and others bemoaned gubernatorial timidity in combating a worsening global pandemic.

The use of state executive orders extends beyond responses to public health emergencies. Following the February 2018 high school shooting in

Parkland, Florida, governors adopted high-profile unilateral actions increasing state regulation of firearms. Governor Gina Raimondo (D-RI) penned an executive order directing law enforcement agencies to consider the "red flag reports" of potentially dangerous individuals with guns and take the necessary legal steps to disarm them. This order was not the first time governors acted unilaterally on gun control. On October 15, 2015, Governor Terry McAuliffe (D-VA) signed an executive order banning firearms from executive branch agency offices. Soon after, the Republican-controlled legislature passed a bill to overturn parts of this order. McAuliffe vetoed the bill, but Republican legislators did not have the necessary supermajority support to override it. In the end, the governor's unilateral order prevailed.

These examples provide several insights into legislative constraint and executive power in US states. First, and perhaps unfamiliar to some readers, state governors issue executive orders with substantial policy consequences. While most studies of unilateralism primarily spotlight presidents, less is known about these political dynamics in subnational contexts.[4] Second, as for presidents, governors too face constraints from other political actors when contemplating unilateral strategies. Like Congress, state legislatures can overturn executive orders by passing new statutes. As the Virginia gun control example demonstrates, however, they may be limited by institutional rules, such as supermajority veto override requirements. Some state legislatures also have nonstatutory tools at their disposal to punish the executive branch and enhance their ability to constrain governors, such as regulatory review, legislative vetoes, and budgetary powers. Even differences in the time legislatures spend in session can affect the opportunities they hold for tempering gubernatorial power.

We leverage this variation to better understand the mechanisms of constraint underlying separation of powers politics in the United States. We examine how policymaking and resource capacities interact to shape governors' strategies for deploying unilateral actions. As hypothesized, both domains of capacity are necessary conditions for inducing executive restraint, and neither alone is sufficient. Rather, their interaction is critical in structuring the distribution of power across the branches. Using the most comprehensive dataset of nearly 25,000 gubernatorial executive orders issued between 1993 and 2013 across fifty states, we find strong support for our theoretical arguments. When *either* policymaking opportunities or resources is lacking, we observe patterns consistent with executive evasion; when legislatures maintain both domains of capacity, governors are more constrained. Our approach to capacity is in stark contrast to previous ones, which examine only one domain or their additive relationships. These alternative approaches, we show, mischaracterize legislative power.

Although the previous chapter's findings on presidential executive orders lend support to our arguments, the portion of our theory concerning policymaking capacity is thus far unexamined since it has remained sufficiently high in Congress (as highlighted in chapter 3). Fortunately, the fifty US states provide another context in which these strategies can manifest given greater variation in policymaking and resource capacities. Thus, by turning to the states, we are not seeking to merely confirm or replicate our findings from the federal level; rather, they allow us to test a central element of our theoretical framework. In doing so, we can better illuminate the dynamics of unilateralism at both levels of government.

The Evolution of Legislative Capacity in the US States

In 1945, the American Political Science Association's (APSA) Committee on American Legislatures released a report on the decline of state legislatures, writing:

> The most important function of state legislatures today is to exercise broad control over state executive departments. . . . The legislature nevertheless needs adequate information concerning the work of the executive departments to pass upon legislative policies, to determine the amount of funds to be appropriated, and to be able to take action to correct or improve administration when necessary. In short, the legislature cannot perform its legislative functions unless it exercises effective legislative oversight over administration. (Zeller 1954, 172)

But how do legislatures maintain such control? We argue the answer lies in policymaking and resource capacities, both required for executive restraint. In this section, we review how each domain varies across states and over time.

Policymaking Capacity

Following the American Revolution, states were charged with designing their own constitutions and governing institutions. The majority of these setups featured legislative supremacy at the expense of governors. Wary of the excesses of executive power from their colonial experiences, state constitutions generally endowed governors with few powers, many of which could be easily checked by the legislature. In some states, legislatures even appointed governors and other executive officials, who often served for terms as short as a year, ensuring their dependence on the legislature (Keefe 1966; Williams 1989; Wood 1993).

State legislatures were at the height of institutional and political authority, surpassing even the US Congress in formal power and influence over policy during this time period (Clucas 2019; Novak 2008). As Clucas (2019, 2) writes of these early legislative bodies, "There simply was no other political body at either the national level or in the states that was in a position to challenge state assemblies." By the end of the nineteenth century, however, public opinion of forceful state legislatures soured. With the rise of powerful party machines and widespread political corruption, citizens came to view legislatures as ineffective, unproductive, and unrepresentative. One proposed solution was to narrow the power disparity between the legislative and executive branches of government in state constitutions. Accordingly, constitutional reforms swept through the states giving governors the power to veto legislation. Though few constitutions initially endowed chief executives with veto power, most states granted it by the beginning of the twentieth century (Fairlie 1917; Watson 1987).

Many powerful legislatures, however, attached policy riders to appropriations bills. Because of the "must-pass" status of these bills, legislatures could maintain their advantage over the executive branch by obstructing gubernatorial policy goals. As Dinan (2006, 116) notes, "The increasing resort to legislative riders and omnibus bills gave the legislature the upper hand and made it much less likely the governor could accomplish these goals. . . . The challenge for [state constitutional reformers] was to settle on a particular reform that would restore the balance between the legislative and executive branches." In response, many governors were given line item veto powers in the appropriations process, allowing them to selectively reject some provisions of these bills while accepting others. First enacted in 1865 by the Georgia constitution, many states readily adopted the item veto throughout the nineteenth and twentieth centuries. By 2017, only five state governors (Indiana, Nevada, North Carolina, Rhode Island, and Vermont) did not possess any line item veto power, according to the Council of State Governments. Initially, states beginning with Pennsylvania in 1885 allowed governors to only reduce or nullify the amount appropriated. By the turn of the twentieth century, some states such as Alabama and Virginia permitted amendatory vetoes, authorizing governors to formally recommend other modifications to the bill (de Figueiredo 2003).

Other constitutional reforms also strengthened chief executives at the expense of legislatures. For instance, state constitutions during the nineteenth century were amended to allow for the popular election of governors, ensuring their independence from legislatures. Some also granted governors greater control over the executive branch through appointments and reorganization powers (Conant 1988). Other states empowered their chief executives to call special sessions and direct budgetary processes (Keefe 1966).

State reforms in the nineteenth century likewise reduced the amount of time legislatures were in session as another solution to perceptions of widespread corruption. Most states shifted from annual legislative sessions to biennial ones over the course of the nineteenth century. In 1832, 88 percent of state legislatures met every year. But by 1889, this figure was down to 16 percent, with the remaining legislatures meeting every other year (Squire 2012). Reformers viewed the reduction of legislatures' session lengths as a way to decrease their influence in the policymaking process. As Teaford (2002, 13) notes, "These restrictions reflected a prevailing concern that legislatures produced too many laws and would commit manifold mischief if allowed to meet too often or too long." Some states even debated implementing quadrennial sessions, with Mississippi and Alabama briefly adopting them in the early twentieth century. Furthermore, many state constitutions limited the number of days legislatures could meet in regular and special sessions (Zeller 1954).

Though the public wanted to temper legislative power in the nineteenth century, their views on the matter reversed in the decades to follow. Social, technological, and economic changes generated greater public demand for government services, as these changes had done on the federal level. Most legislatures were ineffective in bringing about desired policy change, largely due to the institutional constraints placed on their policymaking capacity. Former president of the American Bar Association Charles S. Rhyne noted in 1965 that "[state legislatures] continue to try to solve jet-age problems with horse-and-buggy methods" (Miller 1965).

As at the federal level, these changes created power imbalances between the executive and legislative branches of government. Growing governmental responsibilities led to the expansion of administrative power, as well as the consolidation of gubernatorial power to control executive branch agencies. As Keefe (1966, 59–60) wrote of these disparities in 1966, "the legislature's loss of parity with the governor may be identified as the outstanding fact of twentieth century state politics." He further described the enormous advantages of governors:

> Superior visibility, superior constitutional position, superior staff assistance, superior claim to representation of statewide interests, superior position in the state party, and superior access to political resources (jobs, publicity, credit, wealth, prestige, information, etc) give the governor the opportunity to make his office about what he chooses. (Keefe 1966, 60)

Beginning in the late nineteenth and early twentieth centuries, a nationwide movement to reform legislatures and increase their effectiveness as institutions arose in an effort to bring about greater responsiveness to public demands. As Lynton K. Caldwell of the Council of State Governments wrote in 1947:

> Dissatisfaction with the traditional organization and procedure of state legislatures has grown among legislators, who undertake the perplexities of present-day law-making with inadequate assistance and ineffective machinery. Legislation was seldom a problem, but it is today more difficult than at any time in our national history. As the responsibilities thrust upon legislatures are increased, so must the tools and processes of legislation be improved if the quality of legislation is to meet the needs which call it forth. (Caldwell 1947, 281)

In response to reform movements, state legislatures started to meet more frequently, increasing their opportunities to confront executives. Only six state legislatures met on a yearly basis in 1947 (Caldwell 1947). Today, only Montana, Nevada, North Dakota, and Texas meet biennially. Legislatures who met every other year faced difficulties in writing legislation, particularly budgets, that could structure effective governance in an increasingly complex era for two years at a time. It became apparent that more frequent sessions were needed to manage the changing social and economic landscapes throughout the states, while grappling with a burgeoning executive branch.

Such changes also yielded increasingly unmanageable workloads for many legislatures. The Committee on American Legislatures described this problem in their 1954 report, writing, "The state legislature has not kept pace with these developments . . . to cope adequately with the greatly increased volume of legislation" (Zeller 1954). Accordingly, many states adopted rules to accelerate the legislative process, like permitting prefiling of legislation prior to the beginning of the session, time limitations for bill introductions, and a consent calendar to expedite certain noncontroversial issues. They also reduced the number of standing committees, which, along with other changes in committee assignments and leadership structures, helped consolidate power in the majority party.

Though policymaking capacity has undoubtedly increased in most state legislatures since the end of the nineteenth century, these gains have not been monotonic or equivalent across states. While all subnational governments now allow governors to veto legislation, for instance, the number of legislators required for an override differs from state to state, leading to differences in the ability of partisan majorities to legislate alone. In some states, like Pennsylvania, legislatures need two-thirds of their members to override a veto. Thirteen states, including Delaware and North Carolina, require a slightly lower majority for overrides (three-fifths). Still, others only call for a simple majority to reject a veto, creating a scenario in six states where majority parties can seemingly act more freely. The debates over the adoption of override requirements self-consciously centered on the relative powers of these two branches in states' politics. In fact, a long-standing distrust of the executive branch was the reason why North Carolina did not adopt the executive veto until 1997 (McGrath, Rogowski, and Ryan 2015).

While states generally authorize governors to deploy the line item veto for appropriations-related activities, the potency of this power varies depending on numerous state-specific provisions surrounding it. According to the 2018 Book of the States, some states only allow governors to veto the amount in appropriations bills, while others also permit the rejection of their legislative content. Nine states give governors line item veto power for appropriations and nonappropriations bills, while five states make no provision for it of any kind. Beyond item vetoes, states differ in the degree to which governors are empowered to alter, review, or reject budgetary proposals. Gubernatorial power in the budgetary process has implications for how many opportunities legislatures have to temper executive prerogatives.

Although many states shifted toward annual legislative sessions during the twentieth century, a number reverted back to biennial sessions, such as Montana and Nevada. Reporters Megan Messerly and Michelle Rindels describe the challenges Nevada legislators face today with brief biennial sessions, particularly as it relates to combating gubernatorial power: "The short session, coupled with the facts that lawmakers are relatively inexperienced compared to those in decades past and have limited staff, pushes off a significant amount of power to Nevada's full time governor."[5] Other states have faced similar problems constraining the executive in light of abbreviated legislative sessions. For instance, one journalist noted the difficulties of Texas legislators in retaliating against Governor Rick Perry's executive orders, given the limited amount of time they sit in session:

> The legislative branch can try to fight back. It can pass a law overturning an executive order. It can cut appropriations for the governor or for his pet projects. It can investigate whether he should have acted sooner in the scandal concerning sexual abuse of offenders in Texas Youth Commission facilities. The Senate can refuse to confirm gubernatorial appointments. . . . But the bottom line is that the Legislature can take action for 20 weeks every two years, and the governor can take action for 52 weeks every year. The governor has the advantage if he wants it, and Perry clearly wants it.[6]

Furthermore, many states have imposed limitations on the number of days legislatures can meet within a calendar year. Some, such as Idaho and Michigan, have none. Others specify short meeting periods, such as the forty-five day limits in South Dakota and New Hampshire. Provisions for convening special sessions also differ across states and over time based on whether the legislature or governor can call a special session, whether the legislature can determine the subject of the special session, and the number of legislators required to agree to a special session (whether with or without gubernatorial consent).

There are likewise differences in the availability of other nonstatutory powers granted to legislatures to constrain the executive branch. For instance, some states allow them to review regulations promulgated by executive branch agencies (Huber and Shipan 2002; Woods 2004). These chambers can review either proposed or enacted rules, both, or neither. Some states give legislatures only advisory powers (e.g., Washington), while others, such as Nevada, permit them to formally suspend a regulation. Many states place time limits on when legislatures raise objections before the regulation automatically goes into effect. These are important checks on a key policymaking power of the executive branch.

Finally, there is abundant variation concerning legislatures' involvement in the selection of executive officials. Gubernatorial appointments to executive branch agencies require legislative confirmation in some states, but not in others. Sometimes, legislatures actually hold the power to appoint certain executive branch officials themselves without governors' input. According to the 2018 Book of the States, for instance, legislatures are solely responsible for selecting the state auditor in seven states.

Resource Capacity in the US States

The development of resource capacity in the US states follows similar trends, particularly in response to shifting attitudes toward legislative power and performance. Its evolution has likewise not been unidirectional, but has waxed and waned across states and over time.

One major challenge for early state legislatures was low compensation. In lieu of a salary, every state in 1832 paid their legislators a per diem, ranging from $1.50 in Rhode Island to $4.00 in Alabama, with many imposing additional limitations on how many days they could collect these rates (Squire 2012). Because legislative pay was not enough to even cover travel and living expenses in many states, it was difficult to attract and retain qualified candidates for office.

Predictably, paltry salaries led to high turnover rates during the first half of the nineteenth century, reaching a high of 70 to 100 percent in some legislatures such as Connecticut, Georgia, and New York. At the end of the century, turnover was nearly 100 percent in Iowa, Illinois, Wisconsin, Indiana, and Ohio. These trends persisted into the twentieth century, and in 1954, the Committee on American Legislatures reported that more than half of all state legislators at the beginning of each session were new to the seat (Zeller 1954). These frequent changes in membership were debilitating for the functioning of state legislatures, which were filled with inexperienced members struggling to learn on the job (Lockard 1966; Ray 1974; Squire 2012). Furthermore, legislators who knew they would not be employed in the capital for long had little incentive to invest in their representative and legislative tasks (Keefe 1966). As political scientist Charles S. Hyneman stated in his 1938 study on legislative turnover, "A state legislature will not function effectively unless a substantial number of its members have acquired several sessions of experience in the lawmaking process" (1938, 21).

Insufficient salaries also contributed to corruption. On the milder end, legislatures were notorious for expediting legislation with implications for their own salaries. Other practices were less benign. For instance, cash-strapped members accepted passes from railroad companies for transportation, leading to accusations about the undue influence of the industry on legislative policymaking. Conflicts of interest were also pervasive among these part-time legislators, who were motivated to protect the interests of their private sector jobs and employers (Keefe 1966). On the more extreme end, members solicited bribes and extorted money from businesses and industries over whom they had power (Butler 1985; Squire 2012; White 2003). In 1964, Illinois state senator (later US senator) Paul Simon surmised that "one-third of the members accept pay-offs" (Keefe 1966).

Legislators also lacked effective staff assistance. In the early nineteenth century, legislatures employed few staffers, most of whom had clerical duties or served the entire chamber in positions such as the sergeant at arms. In 1966, John C. Wahlke reported that few state legislatures had dedicated administrative staff for their members and instead borrowed clerical employees such as stenographers from executive agencies. Because of these staffing deficits, legislators faced difficulties in writing legislation, researching policy, overseeing the executive branch, and even responding to constituent concerns. Duane Lockard remembered the day to day struggles he faced as a state legislator with insufficient staffing to meet his needs:

> I recall that a constituent once wrote asking me to help him obtain an automobile license plate with his initials on it; he apologized for bothering me, but he wondered if my office staff could take care of it for me. A corner in my hallway at home, piled high with bills, reports, and propaganda, was as near as I had come to an office; and for staff I had a part-time secretary who could barely manage to keep up with the duties assigned her by the committee of which I was chairman. (1966, 114)

The number of staff available to the chamber, committees, and legislators did significantly increase over the course of the twentieth century. However, many of these positions were temporary ones created while the legislature was in session. Most staff roles were clerical in nature and did not directly assist legislators in developing legislation. Moreover, staffers were rarely policy experts. Many had other jobs or earned their positions due to nepotism or patronage. Thus, although legislative staffing resources grew during this time, human capital development did not necessarily follow (Lattimer 1985; Squire 2012). As a consequence, many legislatures relied on executive branch agency personnel for policy information, which was not always unbiased. As Wahlke (1966, 32) put it, "Some 'counsel' may be highly colored by the political preferences of the agency giving the advice."

Finally, over the course of the nineteenth and early twentieth centuries, many states commenced the construction of capitol buildings for the dedicated use of conducting legislative business. Such facilities increase or reflect the prestige of legislatures and facilitate their work, in and out of sessions. Many of these buildings, however, were poorly constructed and fell victim to fires and floods. For instance, in 1921, the grand Victorian-style capitol building in Charleston, West Virginia, burned to the ground. Almost the entire state government had been housed in the building, and scores of important public records were destroyed. Ammunition that was being stored in the attic compounded the effects of the fire, making it all the more destructive. It proved utterly devastating to the operation of state government. The temporary capitol building erected to replace the old one was made of wood and nicknamed "the Pasteboard Capitol." Predictably, it also suffered the same fate, falling to ashes in 1927 (Wallace 2012). Consequently, legislatures often lacked permanent office space and were forced to move to temporary locations, often in different cities. Writing in 1966, John C. Wahlke reported that only four states provided office space for their legislators in the state capital. Instead, many legislators and committees worked from hotel rooms, their private businesses, or even at their desks in the chamber. The absence of physical space further strained a legislature's ability to fulfill its duties. Wahlke (1966, 136) writes, "The physical facilities in which all but a very few American state legislatures undertake their tasks are limited or even primitive. A modern business attempting to carry on under comparable circumstances would be thought hopelessly out of date."

Though legislatures largely lacked adequate resources and human capital in the 1800s, their resource capacity grew after the turn of the century, once again due to heightened public demand for governmental services. Legislative salaries increased over this time period, motivated by the prospect of recruiting and retaining quality members (Rosenthal 1996; Squire 2007). Indeed, turnover rates in legislatures declined until the 1990s, providing members with new levels of experience in the tasks of governance, oversight, and crafting legislation (Moncrief, Niemi, and Powell 2004; Shin and Jackson 1979).

New capitol infrastructure during this time further reinforced the prestige of legislative work (Rosenthal 1996).

States also created support agencies to provide policy information to legislatures. Legislative reference services were first established in New York and Massachusetts in the 1890s and eventually spread throughout the states (Wahlke 1966). Many governments created offices of legislative counsel to assist in writing bills and advising members of their policy effects. Other legislative agencies were formed to independently analyze fiscal and administrative government operations (Zeller 1954).

Despite these initial increases in resource capacity, there was a considerable movement among political scientists, policy groups, the public, and legislators themselves in the latter half of the twentieth century to expand on these gains (Moncrief 2019; Rothstein 1990). In their 1954 report on state legislatures, the Committee on American Legislatures made numerous recommendations, such as raising member pay, lengthening legislative terms to match the governor, instituting annual sessions without time or pay limitations, augmenting staff sizes, and creating more legislative support agencies. The Committee on Legislative Processes and Procedures, established by the Council of State Governments, also produced similar suggestions (Zeller 1954).

In an edited volume on these issues, Alexander Heard proclaimed in the introduction, "State legislatures may be our most extreme example of institutional lag" (1983, 3). Journalist James Nathan wrote in a 1965 article in the *National Civic Review* that state legislatures faced difficulties in keeping pace with rising governmental responsibilities, recommending increases in legislators' salaries, staffers, and session lengths (Miller 1965). Lockard (1966) lamented that legislators were overworked, underpaid, and under staffed amateurs who struggled to grapple with the demands of office. He argued legislative resources were crucial in restoring parity with the executive branch, writing that "by not providing desperately needed help to the legislature is assuredly undermining its own foundation. Legislators, as a result, are dominated by governors, bureaucracies, and lobbyists, in part because they cannot provide any alternative sources of information for substantiating their independent judgement" (1966, 114–15).

Among lawmakers, California General Assembly speaker Jesse Unruh was a particularly forceful advocate in the 1960s for improving state legislative capacity. In addition to promoting full-time legislative sessions and pay increases, he also advanced investments in staff resources as a way to combat the informational disparity between the legislative and executive branches.

These reforms spread beyond California, and staff sizes and quality, support agencies, legislative sessions, and salaries were all on the rise by the 1980s. However, the pendulum swung in the other direction in the 1990s, as legislatures once again faced charges of ineffectiveness and corruption. Consequently, growth in salaries and staff resources tapered off and, in some cases, reversed. Squire (2012) reports that legislators in twenty-seven states made less (in constant dollars) in 2009 relative to 1979.

Perhaps most notably, there was also a wave of reforms imposing term limits on state legislators beginning in the 1990s, with twenty-one states adopting them. These newly imposed term limits yielded an uptick in legislative turnover, which was detrimental to these legislatures' human capital given subsequent decreases in overall expertise and experience. Research demonstrates such term limits subsequently enhanced executive branch influence in policymaking, thus sabotaging legislatures attempts to rein in gubernatorial power (Carey, Niemi, and Powell 1998; Kousser 2005). Despite their widespread adoption, some were also later repealed (see figure 1.2), producing even more variation in human capital within states.

The Implications of Undulating Legislative Capacity

What are the implications of changes in state legislative capacity for executive power? On the legislative side, scholars have studied many indicators of capacity. The most prominent of these measures is the Squire Index, an additive index of legislative professionalization, capturing some elements of policymaking capacity (the length of legislative sessions) and resources (legislative salaries and staff). With this index, scholars have linked higher levels of legislative professionalism to better constituent representation, less party control, higher legislative productivity, more resistance to gubenatorial budgetary and policy agendas, and greater statutory control over agencies (Huber, Shipan, and Pfahler 2001; Kousser and Phillips 2012; Lax and Phillips 2009; Maestas 2003; Squire 1993). As noted in chapter 2, however, combining measures of policymaking and resource capacities into a single additive index elides interactive relationships among the two domains and may lead to mistaken inferences.

Less is known about the connection between state legislative professionalism and gubernatorial unilateral action. Notably, Cockerham and Crew Jr. (2017) find governors issue more executive orders when facing full-time legislatures rather than part-time ones. Barber, Bolton, and Thrower (2019) show other aspects of policymaking capacity, such as veto-proof majorities and rule review powers, constrain executive order use during divided government. Bolton and Thrower (forthcoming) demonstrate that the timing of legislative sessions also moderates the influence of interbranch conflict on executive unilateralism. Most studies on executive policymaking in the states, however, only consider professionalism or other individual aspects of capacity. They do not theoretically examine the interactive effects between different domains of capacity and other variables of interest.

Theoretical Underpinnings of Legislative Capacity and Gubernatorial Unilateralism

With these considerations in mind, we now explore how state legislative capacity influences the exercise of unilateral power. We test our theory with gubernatorial executive orders, which we discuss in detail in the next section. For now, we assert that they serve much the same function as presidential executive orders. As such, we start with the same assumptions delineated in the previous chapter. Governors, like presidents, use executive orders to pursue their policy goals, but are limited by internal and external costs as well as statutory and constitutional discretion in doing so.

Executive orders require time, internal coordination, and resources in their development. There can also be externally imposed costs from the public, interest groups, and political actors if opposition is mobilized against these actions. Consequently, governors are reticent to issue orders that yield few policy benefits or that are likely to be overturned or provoke negative reactions from other political actors. Whether governors can expect sanctions for using discretion in ways that are unfavorable to legislative preferences depends fundamentally on policymaking and resource capacities. Some legislatures may find ample opportunities for such retaliation because they can easily pass statutes or maintain enough powers to punish executives outside of the statutory process, such as oversight, budgets, and appointments. When these opportunities are scarce, the potential for legislative sanction should be of little consequence for executive strategies.

Policymaking capacity is thus a necessary, but not sufficient, condition for legislatures seeking to punish the executive branch through statutory and nonstatutory processes. Legislatures likewise require resources to act on these opportunities. As in Congress, mechanisms for controlling and sanctioning the executive are costly for state legislatures in terms of time, money, and other resources. These costs are less binding for legislatures high in resource capacity. For instance, numerous and experienced staff can continually oversee the executive branch or write constraining legislation. Large budgets allow legislatures to hire and retain more qualified staff and members. In sum, policymaking capacity provides legislatures with the levers to regulate the executive branch, while resources facilitate the operation of these controls. Both are necessary for legislatures to impose constraints on the executive branch.

High-capacity legislatures can thus more credibly retaliate against excessive unilateral action and limit executive discretion. Accordingly, governors tread more carefully overall when exercising unilateralism. This leads to our first prediction:

> **Prediction 7.1:** When both legislative policymaking and resource capacities are high, governors issue fewer executive orders overall. If either legislative policymaking or resource capacity is low, governors issue more executive orders overall.

As discussed in chapter 2, executives have the greatest incentives to use unilateral power when legislatures do not share their policy and political goals. Here, unilateralism can deliver outcomes more favorable to the governor than what would result from the legislative process alone. Legislatures, however, can deter such gubernatorial behavior through statutory and nonstatutory means. Of course, whether governors can expect these sanctions for unfavorable policymaking depends on whether legislatures retain sufficient policymaking *and* resource capacities.

If either is lacking, governors will perceive greater opportunities for unilateralism in the face of legislative opposition, with less fear of reprisal. Executive evasion is thus expected. If legislatures are high in both domains of capacity, however, governors will forbear from issuing directives making legislative majorities worse off relative to the status quo. During divided government, governors have fewer opportunities for unilateral actions that will simultaneously benefit them and the legislative majority. Thus, they will exercise restraint and issue fewer executive orders. This logic leads to our second prediction:

Prediction 7.2: When both legislative policymaking and resource capacities are high, governors issue fewer executive orders during divided government. If either legislative policymaking or resource capacity is low, governors issue more executive orders under divided government.

Executive Orders in the US States

Like presidents, governors have numerous unilateral tools at their disposal to direct executive policymaking. Some states allow governors to issue proclamations, for purposes such as calling special sessions and making commemorations (as in West Virginia) or declaring disaster emergencies (Texas). In other states (e.g., Alaska and Illinois), governors issue administrative orders to manage routine executive branch functions. Though not all governors have the power to issue proclamations, administrative orders, signing statements, or other unilateral tools, every governor issues executive orders, which is why we study them here.

As at the federal level, executive orders are written directives issued by governors to executive branch agencies and officials providing instructions on implementing the law. Some governors draw their authority to issue them from implied or inherent powers derived from constitutions, statutes, and by nature of the executive office or common practice. Others are explicitly authorized by statute or state constitution. Some states dictate specific purposes for executive order usage, like reorganizing the executive branch (see Alaska Constitution, Article III, Section 23).

Most states have procedures for filing and publishing executive orders, similar to the requirements under the Federal Register Act. Like presidential executive orders, gubernatorial orders are generally not subject to a state's administrative procedure act. As such, there are no clearly stated procedures for judicial review of executive orders. Nine states, however, do require specific procedures for the issuance of executive orders. Some states, such as Missouri and North Carolina, allow legislatures to review executive orders, but these reviews are often limited in scope and context.

Some gubernatorial orders are employed for ceremonial purposes or routine administrative tasks. With respect to the former, governors can issue executive orders to lower flags in response to a tragedy, as New Jersey governor Chris Christie did on February 15, 2012, following the death of popular singer Whitney Houston. Orders are likewise commonly adopted to declare holidays, commemorate anniversaries, name highways, and create or design agency flags and seals. Many executive orders serve routine administrative purposes, like calling special elections, acknowledging court vacancies, or managing state attorney case loads in Florida. They can also prescribe personnel policies such as sick leave, days off, holidays, and pay increases.

More interestingly, governors often employ executive orders for more consequential administrative purposes. In states like Georgia, they are used to make appointments or issue suspensions, pardons, or removals of important executive branch officials. Governors can also set broad policies dictating executive branch activities like agency operations, nondiscrimination policies, codes of ethics, property management, and policies for government contractors. Other orders structure the executive branch through agency and program creation, termination, continuation, and reorganization.

Governors frequently use executive orders to initiate new policies or give instructions on how to implement existing ones. One common strategy is to create a new governing executive body to manage a newly announced policy initiative, both of which can be done with the same executive order. For instance, Governor Ben Nelson created the Nebraska Transportation Industry Task Force to oversee the newly created Transportation Efficiency Project (EO 95-3; February 8, 1995). Governors also commonly sign executive orders to allocate funds to certain projects and delegate authority to various agencies for particular actions.

Overall, gubernatorial executive orders operate in much the same way as presidential ones. They are deployed for a variety of functions with substantive policy implications. As such, they can further the governor's policy goals—potentially to the detriment of legislatures' own goals. Despite their importance for state policymaking, there are only a handful of studies examining the determinants of gubernatorial executive order use, with somewhat limited data in terms of state and year coverage (e.g., Barber, Bolton, and Thrower 2019; Ferguson and Bowling 2008; Cockerham and Crew Jr. 2017; Sellers 2017).

Data and Measurement

Measuring Executive Orders

To test our theoretical predictions, we first gathered gubernatorial executive orders from online state registers, governmental websites, and historical archives. To supplement this data, we used LexisNexis to search available state registers, administrative codes, or analogous publications for executive orders. In total, we collected 24,232 executive orders from all fifty states between 1993 and 2013.[7]

Next, we isolate orders related to substantive policy, where we believe our theory should most apply. To do so, we omit orders related to ceremonial functions and routine administrative functions. As previously mentioned, ceremonial executive orders can include naming a highway, lowering flags to half mast, declaring a holiday, or commemorating a historical event or tragedy. Routine administrative orders might encompass extending the life or expanding the membership of an advisory committee, scheduling a special election, closing state offices for a holiday, declaring a disaster emergency, instituting state employee pay raises and other employee benefit policies, as well as issuing administrative leaves, pardons, and technical corrections of previous orders. With the omission of these categories, our dataset numbers 17,553 executive orders.

Our dependent variable is the number of executive orders issued in a state-year. Overall, governors employ about thirteen orders per year. In comparison, presidents signed thirty-seven orders per year during this same period. In the online appendix, we report summary statistics for executive order usage by state in the time period of our study.

As mentioned in chapter 6, executive power should not just be measured by the overall volume of executive orders, but must be evaluated by whether and how these counts are responsive to legislative preferences. If governors use more orders to bypass legislative opponents, then the observed patterns are consistent with evasion, and executive power is at its zenith. However, if governors use fewer executive orders under conditions of ideological dissonance with the legislature, then we can infer executive power is more constrained. Our theory, of course, contends that evasion and constraint is dependent upon legislative capacity. We describe the operationalization of these additional variables in the following section.

Independent Variables

Divided. To measure executive-legislative conflict, *Divided* is coded as "1" if the governor is from the opposing party of the legislative majority in either chamber and "0" otherwise.

Resource Capacity. While measuring partisan division is relatively straightforward, capturing resource and policymaking capacities is not. Since our conceptualization is new, the extant literature provides little guidance. Here, we present two reasonable ways of operationalizing these concepts and consider their robustness. We recognize there may be other indicators worthy of inclusion and hope future research continues to improve upon their measurement.

For our primary measure of resource capacity, we collect data from the National Conference of State Legislatures (NCSL) on total staff employed by each state legislature (*Staff Per Member*), based on surveys conducted in 1979, 1988, 1996, 2003, 2009, and 2015. We use linear interpolation between these data points to estimate the staff numbers in the remaining years. To account for differences across chambers and over time in their membership, we divide staff by the number of legislators and take the natural logarithm. Staffing is useful as an indicator of resource capacity because it is measured consistently across time and states, and it is likewise essential for legislative functioning. It has also fluctuated within states over time, providing important variation we can leverage in our analysis.

We acknowledge, however, that there are other potentially important indicators of resources. As such, we create an alternative resource capacity scale combining the staff measure described above, legislative expenditures per member (logged), and state term limits (*RC*). The expenditures data is drawn from Bowen and Greene's (2014) study of state legislative professionalism.[8] To measure human capital, we use an indicator for whether the state lacks term limits for its legislators in any given year (i.e., coded "1" in the absence of term limits and "0" otherwise). In the absence of term limits, legislators gain experience and expertise in office, inducing higher resource capacity via human capital. When legislators are term limited, they do not have the same opportunity to acquire such human capital and resource capacity should therefore be lower. Given two of these variables are continuous and the other is binary, we use factor analysis to create a scale of resource capacity for each state-year in our dataset. The resulting factor score ranges from −2.27 to 2.25 with a mean of 0 and a median of 0.01. To the extent that the staffing and index measures produce similar results, it will give greater confidence our choices about operationalizing resources are not unduly driving our conclusions.

Policymaking Capacity. We create a policymaking capacity scale for each state-year using the sum of five distinct binary indicators (*PC*). First, one of the most straightforward ways legislatures can retaliate against executives is through new legislation. These laws may serve to overturn a governor's order or otherwise impose disciplinary costs in other ways. Since governors can and will veto these laws, legislatures need a large enough majority to override such vetoes for their sanctions to endure. Accordingly, if a state legislature has a veto-proof majority in a given year, then its receives one point on the index.[9] In our dataset, 27 percent of state-years feature a legislature with a veto-proof majority, which can occur during either divided or unified government. Veto-proof majorities arise much more frequently in the states than at the federal level, where it last occurred in the 89th Congress (1965–66).

Second, as previously argued, the amount of time legislatures are in session can also influence their policymaking capacity by affording them opportunities to carry out their legislative functions. In particular, a legislature's ability to call or determine the agenda of special sessions can extend its working time and allow it to shape the agenda, both of which are helpful in constraining the executive branch. As such, state-years receive a point on the policymaking capacity index if the legislature is permitted by law to either call a special session or determine its agenda and 0 if it possesses neither of these powers. These variables are collected from *The Book of States*.[10] Legislatures possess one of these special session powers in 78 percent of the state-years in our dataset.

We also seek to capture nonstatutory powers available to legislators to sanction the executive branch. Including both nonstatutory and statutory powers in the same index can be rationalized due to the results from Barber, Bolton, and Thrower (2019) demonstrating that either type of policymaking opportunity alone can be sufficient for executive restraint. Of course, these powers vary across and within states, manifesting in a variety of formal and informal tools, norms, practices, and rules. As such, it is nearly impossible to observe and measure the full range of these mechanisms available to legislatures. Instead, we focus on three factors measured consistently across states and time.

Accordingly, the third component of our policymaking capacity scale is regulatory review—that is, the ability of the legislature to review either proposed or existing rules promulgated by executive branch agencies. This power is one of the most important formal mechanisms legislatures have to check the executive branch and has been a focal point in other state policymaking research (e.g., Huber, Shipan, and Pfahler 2001). It is directly linked to retaliation against executive orders, which are often used to initiate rulemaking (Cooper 2002). If state legislatures possess rule review powers, then they receive one point on the policymaking capacity index. They are relatively common in our dataset, occurring in 87 percent of state-years, though there is over time variation within seven states.

Fourth, legislatures may be unable to respond to adverse executive orders through the budget process (e.g., by defunding a new program) when governors can line item veto provisions in funding bills. Conversely, legislatures can more credibly sanction governors who do not have these means to alter, and in some cases essentially rewrite, the budget. Accordingly, if governors do not hold the line item veto power specifically in the context of appropriations in a given state-year, that state receives another point on the policymaking capacity index (occurring in 17 percent of state-years).

Finally, given our theoretical framework is centered on the ability of majorities to respond to gubernatorial unilateralism, it is important to account for their actual legislative power. Legislative majorities exert more influence in the policymaking process when they have greater control over the agenda (Anzia and Jackman 2012; Cox and McCubbins 2005). These majorities should be best positioned to retaliate against a governor who has issued an executive order counter to their policy preferences. To capture these dynamics, we use the measure created by Anzia and Jackman (2012) that indicates whether a committee appointed by the majority party in either chamber has gatekeeping powers. If majority-appointed committees have the power to set the agenda in this way, the legislature receives a point on our policymaking capacity index. Eleven states grant committees this power.[11]

The total policymaking scale ranges from zero to five. In the modal state-year, legislatures possess two of these components (44 percent of observations). The second most common category is states with three indicators (30 percent of observations). On the low end of the scale, 14 percent of observations only have one or zero of the policymaking capacity indicators, while just 12 percent possess four or five indicators. Overall though, more than 70 percent of legislatures exhibit some variation on the policymaking capacity scale during the period of our study. The maximum a state changes along the scale is by two points (Connecticut, Indiana, Maine, South Dakota, and Utah). The remaining states shift at least one point on the scale during the duration of our study. These statistics are not surprising given many of these powers are fairly fixed. It also gives us confidence that the results from the within-state analyses are not being driven by wild changes in one state or another. However, readers should keep this distribution in mind when examining the results we present later in the chapter.

As in the previous chapters, we include interaction terms between our variables of interest as key tests of our predictions. To evaluate prediction 7.1, we include an interaction between the policymaking capacity scale and logged staff per member measure ($PC \times Staff$).[12] We use a triple interaction between divided government, resource capacity, and policymaking capacity (*Divided x PC x Staff*) to test prediction 7.2.

Controls. We include numerous control variables that could confound our relationships of interest. First, there is a long-standing literature arguing executives with public support have bargaining advantages over legislatures (Neustadt 1990 [1960]), with evidence on the federal and state levels showing a positive correlation between legislative success and public approval (Kousser and Phillips 2012; Rivers and Rose 1985). Given the difficulties in measuring gubernatorial approval over time for every state in our dataset, we use the governor's vote share in the previous election (*Govn'r Previous Vote Share*) as a proxy. However, voters are often more responsive to national politics and can reward or punish their state officials based on their own opinions of the current president and her party (Atkeson and Partin 1995; King and Cohen 2005; Rogers 2016). Accordingly, we include a variable measuring the percentage of the presidential vote won by the governor's party (*Presidential Vote for Govn'r Party*).

Second, we include an indicator for governors in their final term in office (*Term Limited*) to account for the possibility executives are motivated by preserving their own legacies or seeking higher political office (Kousser and Phillips 2012) and thus face different incentives for unilateralism. Likewise, governors encountering reelection for themselves or their parties could alter their use of unilateral actions based on increased public scrutiny. *Election Year* is thus coded as 1 in gubernatorial election years and 0 otherwise.[13]

Like presidents, governors use executive orders in response to economic crises (Bolton and Thrower 2016; Krause and Cohen 1997; 2000). Fiscal conditions can also affect capacity levels. Accordingly, we use the annual percentage change in per capita income obtained from the Bureau of Economic Analysis (*State Income Growth*). We likewise include a measure of the state unemployment rate in a given year collected from the Bureau of Labor Statistics (*Unemployment*). Finally, we control for governors' institutional resources by using a modified version of the Beyle index (Beyle and Ferguson 2008), excluding factors in this index that were not consistently collected over time—notably, reorganization power and election procedures. Thus, the index encompasses gubernatorial tenure potential, budgetary powers, veto powers, and appointment powers (*Governor Power*).[14] Formal gubernatorial power may free executives deploying unilateral actions and could also be associated with lower levels of legislative capacity, particularly policymaking opportunities.

Finally, the analyses include state fixed effects to account for unobserved differences between states that might influence capacity and unilateralism, such as states' political contexts, practices related to gubernatorial executive orders, or views on legislative capacity. We also use year fixed effects to control for changes in the overall US political or economic climate impacting every state in a given year. Taken together, the state and year fixed effects are the crux of our identification strategy, eliminating numerous potentially confounding variables. The inclusion of these fixed effects also assures the estimated effects of our variables of interest on executive unilateralism occur due to within-state changes in these variables over time rather than cross-state differences.[15]

State-Level Analysis

Table 7.1 displays the results from negative binomial regression analyses. Model 1 includes state and year fixed effects as well as our three key independent variables of interest, uninteracted: *Divided*, *PC*, and *Staff Per Member*. Model 2 adds in the control variables. All three of the estimated coefficients for our key variables are negative in this model, though only the policymaking capacity scale is statistically significant. Of course, as we noted in the theoretical discussion, this analysis does not account for the interdependencies among these three variables. For instance, it is not surprising to us that the effect of divided government is insignificant in these models. The estimates are obtained from combining situations of low and high legislative capacity, each of which have opposite predicted effects.

The only way to evaluate these interdependencies is through the interactions discussed above. Model 3 represents our key test of prediction 7.1, where we anticipate executive unilateralism will decrease when legislatures are relatively high in *both* domains of capacity. Neither domain alone, however, is sufficient for constraint. The results strongly support this hypothesis. Here, we estimate a negative and statistically significant coefficient on the interaction term *PC x Staff*. Notably, the main effects of *PC* and *Staff Per Member* are each statistically insignificant, indicating they have no significant impact unless the other is relatively high. Together, these coefficients suggest the

TABLE 7.1. The Effect of Resource Capacity, Policymaking Capacity, and Divided Government on Gubernatorial Executive Orders

	Model 1	Model 2	Model 3	Model 4	Model 5
Divided	−0.089	−0.013	−0.014	−0.085	0.227*
	(0.059)	(0.050)	(0.050)	(0.240)	(0.123)
PC	−0.156***	−0.219***	−0.011	−0.093	−0.135**
	(0.054)	(0.053)	(0.123)	(0.125)	(0.064)
Staff Per Member	−0.177	−0.072	0.276	0.117	
	(0.159)	(0.122)	(0.222)	(0.233)	
Resource Capacity Index					0.277
					(0.286)
Divided x PC				0.059	−0.109*
				(0.109)	(0.057)
Divided x Staff				0.227**	
				(0.112)	
PC x Staff			−0.140*	−0.035	
			(0.077)	(0.080)	
Divided x PC x Staff				−0.122**	
				(0.060)	
Divided x RC					0.121*
					(0.072)
PC x RC					−0.017
					(0.072)
Divided x PC x RC					−0.093**
					(0.045)
Govn'r Power		−0.385***	−0.359***	−0.404***	−0.502***
		(0.086)	(0.103)	(0.108)	(0.096)
Presidential Vote for Govn'r Party		1.334***	1.258***	1.213***	0.970***
		(0.360)	(0.358)	(0.312)	(0.300)
Govn'r Previous Vote Share		−0.914**	−0.928***	−0.970***	−0.792**
		(0.357)	(0.357)	(0.347)	(0.387)
Election Year		−0.116**	−0.116**	−0.109**	
		(0.049)	(0.049)	(0.050)	
Term Limited		−0.232***	−0.233***	−0.239***	−0.195***
		(0.055)	(0.055)	(0.053)	(0.063)

(Continued on next page)

TABLE 7.1. (*continued*)

	Model 1	Model 2	Model 3	Model 4	Model 5
Unemployment		0.030	0.035	0.030	0.031
		(0.028)	(0.029)	(0.028)	(0.030)
State Income Growth		−0.025*	−0.026**	−0.025*	−0.028**
		(0.013)	(0.013)	(0.013)	(0.013)
N	840	836	836	836	674
State FEs	✓	✓	✓	✓	✓
Year FEs	✓	✓	✓	✓	✓

Negative binomial coefficients reported, with standard errors clustered by governor in parentheses. State and year fixed effects and constant not shown. Significance codes: *$p < 0.10$, **$p < 0.05$, ***$p < 0.01$, two-tailed tests.

effect of each domain of capacity is decreasing in the other. Both resource and policymaking capacities are necessary to decrease executive unilateralism, as expected.

To more easily interpret these interactive effects, we calculated the predicted number of executive orders at different levels of policymaking and resource capacities, as depicted in figure 7.1. Each cell of the grid displays the predicted number of orders under different conditions. The columns depict increasing policymaking capacity ranging from 0 to 5, while the rows feature predictions at different levels of resource capacity (in particular, the 5th, 25th, 50th, 75th, and 95th percentiles). As discussed above, most observations fall into the central squares of the figure. The lower left-hand quadrant represents scenarios where policymaking and resource capacities are at their lowest levels, while the upper right-hand quadrant corresponds to observations where both domains of capacity are at their peak. Consistent with our argument, the predicted number of executive orders issued by governors is smallest in the upper right quadrant of the grid, where resource and policymaking capacities are relatively high. The numbers are substantially larger in the other three quadrants of the grid. Taken together, these results offer support for prediction 7.1.

Model 4 of table 7.1 provides the key test of prediction 7.2: a triple interaction between *Staff Per Member*, *PC*, and *Divided*. Governors should have the greatest policy incentives for unilateralism during divided government. However, whether they can act on these impulses or will be inhibited by the preferences of legislative majorities depends fundamentally on capacity. When resource and policymaking capacities are relatively high,

Predicted Executive Orders at Different Levels of Capacity

Staff Capacity	0	1	2	3	4	5
95%	44.45	30.39	20.78	14.21	9.72	6.64
75%	36.52	27.59	20.84	15.75	11.90	8.99
50%	32.50	26.05	20.88	16.74	13.42	10.75
25%	29.60	24.88	20.91	17.57	14.77	12.41
5%	24.77	22.79	20.97	19.29	17.74	16.32

Policymaking Capacity

FIGURE 7.1. The predicted number of executive orders, while varying policymaking and resource capacities. The policymaking scale is discrete, running from zero to five. *Staff Per Member* is continuous, and we present estimates from the 5th, 25th, 50th, 75th, and 95th percentiles of the distribution. Overall, we find strong support for prediction 7.1.

we expect negative and significant effects of divided government (implying constraint). However, when either is lacking, we should uncover positive or insignificant impacts of divided government (implying evasion). Overall, our argument predicts the estimated coefficient for the triple interaction term should be negative and statistically significant. And that is exactly what we find. The effect of divided government is decreasing in both types of capacity.

Figure 7.2 displays the marginal effects of divided government at different levels of policymaking and resource capacities based on the results reported in model 4. The results broadly confirm our hypotheses. First, the cells in the upper right quadrant reveal a negative and significant effect of divided

Marginal Effect of Divided Government at Different Levels of Capacity

Staff Capacity	0	1	2	3	4	5
95%	20.66***	7.31**	−0.23	−4.22	−6.08*	−6.70*
75%	11.94***	4.65***	0.02	−2.80*	−4.40**	−5.19**
50%	7.85**	3.28*	0.16	−1.91*	−3.22**	−3.97**
25%	5.08	2.29	0.26	−1.17	−2.15	−2.78
5%	0.79	0.61	0.46	0.34	0.24	0.15

Policymaking Capacity

FIGURE 7.2. The marginal effect of divided government, while varying policymaking and resource capacities. The policymaking scale is discrete, running from zero to five. *Staff Per Member* is continuous, and we present estimates from the 5th, 25th, 50th, 75th, and 95th percentiles of the distribution. At high levels of both resource and policymaking capacities, we observe a negative and statistically significant effect of divided government, consistent with the idea that high-capacity legislatures constrain executives. When either is lacking, we estimate positive effects, suggesting room for executive evasion when capacity levels are relatively low. Overall, we find strong support for prediction 7.2. Significance codes: *$p < 0.10$, **$p < 0.05$, ***$p < 0.01$, two-tailed tests.

government. When policymaking and resource capacities are relatively high, executives are effectively restrained by legislatures with opposed policy and political goals. At the 75th percentile of resource capacity and in a state-year where three out of the five indicators of policymaking capacity are present, we estimate governors will sign approximately 2.8 fewer executive orders per year. The unconditional mean number of state-year orders is 13.1, representing a roughly 21 percent decrease. At the highest levels of both capacity domains, the effect of divided government is more than doubled, with an estimated 6.7 decline in the number of executive orders issued (or a roughly 51 percent decrease relative to the unconditional mean).

On the other hand, these patterns of constraint dissipate and reverse as both policymaking and resource capacities decrease. In particular, we estimate positive, and, in many cases, statistically significant effects of divided government when resource and/or policymaking capacity is low. For instance, when only one indicator of policymaking capacity is present, and resource capacity is at the 25th percentile of the distribution, the estimated marginal effect of divided government is an *additional* 2.29 executive orders in a given state-year. This figure corresponds to a 17 percent increase in uni-lateralism over the unconditional mean number of executive orders. Notably, the results of the analysis remain the same when using the resource capacity index as an alternative measure in model 5.

In the online appendix, we evaluate where historical and contemporary congresses would be placed in figure 7.2, based on its levels of resource and policymaking capacities over time. We find that its location in this grid, both when it is has low and high resource capacity, corresponds to the patterns of constraint and evasion in unilateralism we observe in chapter 6. This exercise further validates the capacity measures used in this chapter and the empirical results from the previous one.

The regression analysis also reveals other factors that might influence exec-utive unilateralism. First, governors issue fewer executive orders if they are endowed with other institutional powers, as evidenced by the negative and statistically significant coefficient on *Govn'r Power*. Though this effect might suggest a trade-off between unilateralism and other formal powers, future researchers might examine separate components of this measure to inves-tigate which ones are complements or substitutes to unilateralism. Second, governors deploy fewer orders during election years, when public scrutiny and gubernatorial electoral incentives are the greatest. Relatedly, governors in their final terms in office also rely less on unilateral powers. This finding might suggest term limited governors, perhaps with an eye for higher public office, are wary of relying on unilateral power due to the possibility of public backlash (see, e.g., Reeves and Rogowski 2015). While gubernatorial popular-ity, as proxied by vote share in previous election, corresponds to depressed unilateralism, higher levels of presidential vote share appear to increase the governor's use of executive orders. This result implies state residents might be paying greater attention to national politics, and thus presidential popular-ity is more helpful to governors. Alternatively, governors could be using their own political capital to pursue other means of policymaking. Finally, gover-nors deploy fewer orders as state income growth increases, providing some support for the notion that executives rely more greatly on unilateralism in response to economic turmoil.

As in chapter 6, we gauge whether the capacity of governors plays a meaningful role in producing our results. Our theoretical argument assumes gubernatorial capacity is consistently high enough to carry out unilateral strategies. Whether or not governors issue these orders instead depends more on external, rather than internal, constraints and costs. To evaluate whether this assumption is valid, we relax it empirically in the online appendix and interact measures of gubernatorial capacity with divided government. We find that executive capacity does not moderate the impact of divided government on executive order use, nor does it diminish our main interactive effects with legislative capacity.

Finally, in the preceding chapters, we provided evidence demonstrating no discernible relationship between ideological or partisan division and congres-sional capacity. We examine whether this relationship might manifest in states by regressing *Staff Per Member* and *PC* on *Divided Government*, while includ-ing the other control variables. In both cases, the estimated effect of divided government is negative—the opposite of what one would expect if legisla-tures were increasing their capacity to confront the executive. Furthermore, the coefficients are small and statistically insignificant.[16] Thus, as at the fed-eral level, capacity in state legislatures does not appear systematically affected by partisan disagreement. These results give us confidence that our estimates are not being driven by any potentially confounding relationship between divided government and legislative capacity.

Summary and Conclusion

Though presidential unilateralism often captures national headlines, gov-ernors too wield the power of the pen to shape some of the most vital policies regulating our daily lives. Even so, they confront distinct political environments from presidents, particularly in terms of the capacities of the legislatures they face. These differences in subnational political contexts have implications for policymaking that are not necessarily observed in Congress, providing researchers opportunities to evaluate and elaborate upon previously untested theories at both the state and federal levels.

As we highlight throughout this chapter, state legislatures vary in policymaking and resource capacities, implicating executive constraint. They differ in the opportunities they have to confront governors due to factors such as veto override thresholds, budgetary powers, regulatory review abilities, control over special sessions, and countless other characteristics. States also vary in the resources legislatures possess, such as staffing, funding, and expertise, that provide the means for capitalizing on policymaking opportunities. Taken together, we argue policymaking and resource capacities are both necessary conditions for executive restraint.

We uncover support for these theoretical arguments, using the most comprehensive dataset of over twenty-five thousand gubernatorial executive orders in all fifty states between 1993 and 2013. In cases where both capacities are high, we find patterns of executive constraint. Governors issue fewer executive orders, particularly during divided government when they have the greatest incentives to go it alone.

When either policymaking or resource capacity is absent, however, legislatures are unable to respond. Here, chief executives discover greater opportunities for unilateralism, especially when legislative outcomes are likely to be relatively worse from their perspective. Indeed, we reveal patterns consistent with evasion under low legislative capacity. This result stands in contrast to those uncovered for the "modern," post–World War II era for presidents, which is the predominant subject of analysis for studies of unilateralism. Yet it is consistent with our findings from historical periods at the federal level, when congressional resources were scarce. Overall, then, the empirical analyses in this chapter further reinforce our theory.

These findings also have methodological implications for the study of state politics, particularly with respect to the measurement of professionalism. The most prominent of such measures is the Squire index, which is an additive scale of legislator salary, staff resources, and session lengths (Squire 2007). The first two components, we argue, correspond to resource capacity and the latter to policymaking capacity. Such additive measures ignore the interactive elements of capacity. For instance, a state legislature may be high in professionalism on this index because of generous salaries and staffing, but if it lacks relatively long sessions, then it will be unlikely to effectively challenge executive power. To be clear, we are not simply recommending separating components of the index and including them independently in a regression. Instead, they should be considered in an interactive fashion, both when developing and empirically evaluating theories about legislative capacity.

Overall, this chapter critically advances the theoretical argument of this book. Only when we turn to the states can we understand how resource and policymaking capacities unite to affect the activities of executives. While capacity directly empowers legislatures, we show here and in the previous chapter that it also has important incentive effects for chief executives—even in the realm of unilateralism, where executive power can, at least in theory, exist in its most unbridled form. Whether executive power will flourish or languish fundamentally depends on legislative resource and policymaking capacities. This fact has important implications for the distribution of powers in separated systems and for evaluating contemporary policy debates on legislative reform. We grapple with these questions in our concluding chapter.

8

The Future of Legislative Capacity and Executive Power

But the great security against a gradual concentration of the several powers in the same department, consists in giving to those who administer each department the necessary constitutional means and personal motives to resist encroachments of the others. The provision for defense must in this, as in all other cases, be made commensurate to the danger of attack. Ambition must be made to counteract ambition.

—JAMES MADISON, *FEDERALIST* 51

Addressing a nascent nation wary of both monarchial presidents and tyrannical legislatures, James Madison and the other constitutional framers advocated for a system dividing power among three independent branches of government. This design, he hoped, would check rapacious political ambitions and prevent the aggrandizement of power in any one person or institution. Over the last century, however, deep and persistent reservations have emerged about whether the separation of powers system adequately limits executive power. Contemporary political observers lament Congress's unwillingness or inability to confront an increasingly puissant presidency. Is the US separation of powers system actually enough to "counteract" executive ambition as intended? Can legislatures check executive power? What do they need to do so?

Political scientists have uncovered substantial evidence of apparent presidential constraint, at least in the modern era (e.g., Chiou and Rothenberg 2014; Epstein and O'Halloran 1999; Howell and Pevehouse 2007). While these findings might indicate that Madison's intuition was correct, they are also limited in important regards. First, they almost exclusively examine the contemporary federal government and thus only provide an incomplete account of US political systems. Contrary to public perception, presidential executive orders were deployed much more vigorously before World War II. Governors too flex power to varying degrees, across states and time. Second, existing scholarship often leaves the mechanisms underlying executive constraint opaque, leading some to question whether it is really Congress producing these patterns at all, or if it is the result of checks from the public or another institution.

The pertinent question, then, is not merely *whether* a separation of powers system can effectively restrain executive ambition, but rather *when* and *why* it is able to do so. Scholarly and media discourse largely spotlights partisan or ideological disagreements as the primary impetus for institutional behavior. While such conflict may lead legislatures to check executives, we contend it is far from sufficient for curbing executive power. Instead, legislatures must possess the *will* and the *ability* for executive constraint.

But what does it actually mean to have the ability to check executive power? In chapter 2, we introduced a new concept of legislative capacity and delineated its two domains. A legislature needs adequate resources (*resource capacity*) and opportunities for influence in the policymaking process (*policymaking capacity*) to be a high-capacity institution. *Both* domains of capacity are necessary, but not alone sufficient, for legislatures to curb executive power. Given its wide array of formal and informal powers, we contend Congress maintains sufficiently high policymaking capacity for constraint. Yet, as discussed in chapter 3, congressional resource capacity has varied substantially throughout the twentieth century. Resources and opportunities each fluctuate in the US states over time.

Legislative capacity has profound consequences for the distribution of power in US policymaking. Our theory considers how it affects legislative activities *and* executive power. When legislatures lack policymaking opportunities or the requisite resources for action, they are less able to impose constraints on executive branch actors. Legislatures with both capacities, on the other hand, are more empowered to temper executive ambitions. Our empirical analyses of discretion (chapter 4) and oversight (chapter 5) in the US Congress reinforce these claims.

Importantly, legislative capacity is likewise influential in shaping executive incentives as well, a key contribution of our work. This relationship should manifest even in the case of *unilateral* powers, where legislative assent is not directly required. Threats of constraint are less potent from low-capacity legislatures, who impose fewer ex ante discretionary limitations and encounter difficulties punishing chief executives for acting against the majority's interests. Here, executive power thrives; presidents and governors can exercise greater unilateralism to bypass unfriendly legislatures. Retaliatory actions and diminished discretion are credible threats from high-capacity legislatures, however, urging executive self-restraint.

These theoretical arguments withstand empirical scrutiny when examining presidential and gubernatorial unilateralism in chapters 6 and 7. With regard to the former, we explain why modern presidents are constricted by contemporary congresses, while their predecessors were relatively unfettered when issuing executive orders. These findings suggest the answer to the long-standing puzzle in the separation of powers literature about presidential constraint is due, in large part, to the development of critical resources that transformed Congress from a low- to high-capacity institution. By extending the scope of our analysis and leveraging these changes we gain a better sense of unilateralism in historical eras, along with vital insights into what underlies patterns of constraint in contemporary politics. In chapter 7, we leverage disparities in resource and policymaking capacities across the US states, with the most comprehensive dataset on gubernatorial executive orders, to bolster our key theoretical claim that both domains are necessary conditions for executive restraint.

By bringing legislative capacity to the forefront and examining executive power through the lens of legislatures, we achieve new and important understandings about how, when, and why the tides of power shift between Congress and the president—or legislatures and executives, more generally—in separated systems. Ambition is not sufficient to counteract ambition. Legislative capacity is a critical condition for our separation of powers system to operate as Madison and the constitutional framers intended.

Although not yet central in the scholarly study of executive branch behavior, some political observers and even politicians have highlighted the necessity of reforming Congress as an institution to fix the ails of governance. With our theoretical and empirical insights in mind, the remainder of this chapter probes whether the presidency today is actually overpowered and then considers several proposed congressional reforms aimed at rebalancing American government.

Evaluating Presidential Constraint

Contemporary observers of American politics tend to offer bleaker assessments than our own of the present Congress and its position in the separation of powers system. In a 2020 report, the Presidential Task Force on Congressional Reform of the American Political Science Association (APSA), declared, "Congress today is overwhelmed. After decades of self-imposed disinvestment in expertise and staffing, Congress lacks the resources and knowledge to stand on an equal footing either with the executive branch, or with the tens of thousands of lobbyists employed in Washington." (Presidential Task Force on Congressional Reform 2020, 8). Clearly, in the view of many political scientists, Congress is weak and inadequately resourced; as a result, presidential power can dominate.

The basis of this conclusion emanates from the precipitous decline in staffing resources and spending during the 1990s. If one takes a long view of congressional capacity, as we do in this book, the claim is perhaps overstated. Compared to the mid-twentieth century, Congress currently retains fairly high levels of resources. Neither the APSA report nor many other writings lamenting congressional weakness vis-à-vis presidents systematically scrutinize executive behavior to evaluate the merits of this claim. Our results indicate contemporary legislative capacity is sufficient for at least some degree of executive constraint. At 2019 spending levels, for instance, we show presidents can be expected to issue twelve fewer executive orders during divided government relative to unified. Similar patterns manifest for contemporary levels of committee staff capacity. Thus, we do not agree with the strong version of the argument that Congress today is *incapable* of constraining executive power.

It is possible, though, that this relatively binary notion of restraint (i.e., are there more or less executive orders during divided government?) is too simplistic. Instead, normative debates over executive power might hinge on the *degree* of constraint observed. For instance, our results reveal the 2015 levels of congressional staffing are associated with about eight fewer executive orders during divided government relative to unified, implying some degree of presidential constraint. It is also clear from these findings, however, that increasing staff resources will substantially bolster this restraint. For instance, at 1994 levels of staffing, we find the impact of interbranch conflict more than doubles, to about seventeen fewer orders during divided government relative to unified. Thus, in either case, these effects are consistent with a binary notion of presidential constraint, but whether it is "enough" constraint in either scenario is unclear. What is the correct benchmark? There are obviously no clear or easy answers to this question, and it will ultimately be adjudicated by the political system itself. By clearly linking capacity and executive unilateral behavior, we hope our work can clarify debates about whether presidents and governors are constrained, what legislatures need to cabin executive power, and how legislative capacity affects the broader distribution of power in a separated system.

Continuity or Change? The Trump Administration and Beyond

Our general findings that presidents are constrained might seem like a puzzling conclusion as we write this chapter at the end of the Trump presidency. After all, many political observers view the last four years as further evidence for congressional abdication in the face of ever-expanding presidential power. Reflecting on Trump's term, political scientists Steven Levitsky and Daniel Ziblatt condemned Congress's failure to sufficiently rein in the president. Even during the two years of divided government that did feature some constraint, Congress, they write, "did not deliver anything resembling a well-functioning system of checks and balances."[1]

Nothing better epitomizes the concerns many had about Trump's determination to exercise unbridled power than his declaration of "total" authority during the 2020 coronavirus pandemic.[2] Uttered in the context of congressional dysfunction and genuine confusion about the relative powers the federal and state governments had to address the pandemic, the statement seemed to encapsulate the erosion of checks and balances during the Trump presidency. We must be careful, however, not to conflate Trump's rhetorical bluster with an actual expansion of the institution's power.

Many of Trump's policy actions during the COVID-19 pandemic reflected the constraints on his office rather than some new expansive understanding of presidential power. After many provisions of the initial coronavirus legislative economic response package expired in the summer of 2020 and a renewal was stalemated in Congress, Trump took up his pen (or, rather, his Sharpie) to deploy unilateral actions addressing the crisis. These directives were met with negative reactions from Democrats and even some Republicans, who decried them as being beyond the scope of his power. As Senator Ben Sasse (R-NE) put it, "The pen-and-phone theory of executive lawmaking is unconstitutional slop."[3]

Yet by any objective measure, Trump's directives were limited. His August executive order (EO 13945) is illustrative. Designed to backstop legislation passed earlier in the year that prohibited the evictions of renters receiving federal housing assistance or those in buildings with a federally backed mortgage, the order simply decreed:

> The Secretary of Health and Human Services and the Director of CDC shall consider whether any measures temporarily halting residential evictions of any tenants for failure to pay rent are reasonably necessary to prevent the further spread of COVID-19 from one State or possession into any other State or possession.

This directive, prodding other actors, is not one of a president with "total authority." Instead, it reflects the real limits on a president's discretion to make policy. Chief executives must still rely on agencies, acting within the bounds of their authorities, to carry out presidential policy goals. In the weeks following the order, the CDC devised a program in response, whereby renters could avoid evictions upon completion of a form attesting to their job or income loss.

Interestingly, this program was not designed to evade an unfriendly legislature, but instead shifted policy towards the preferences of the congressional Democratic majority in the House. At the time, Speaker Nancy Pelosi's expressed dissatisfaction with these and other orders, calling them "meager, weak and unconstitutional actions." Her and other Democrats' criticisms were more rooted in the fact that the orders did not do enough, rather than them stretching policy too far. Indeed, the CDC program was originally scheduled to end on December 31, 2020, but Congress acted to extend it for an additional month, essentially codifying the fruits of the president's order into law.[4] Outside the pandemic response, the early evidence from his administration suggests Trump's overall patterns of unilateralism and regulatory behavior largely reflect the continuation of, rather than a departure from, previous presidential practices (Potter et al. 2019).

How has Congress performed during the Trump presidency? In the estimates of some observers, terribly. Historian Douglas Brinkley bemoaned the "shrinkage" of Congress, claiming, "It's created this massive void in our democracy."[5] We do not entirely agree with this assessment. Certainly during the first two years of the Trump administration, Congress appeared relatively accommodating to the president's unilateral actions, such as the Muslim ban and withdrawing from the Paris climate accords. Yet the Republicans who controlled both chambers of Congress were not necessarily opposed to those polices, consistent with the idea that presidents often use unilateralism to shift policies in ways that legislative majorities favor. Even still, there were notable instances of Republican opposition to Trump's actions, such as the concurrent House and Senate investigations into his campaign's involvement with Russia during the 2016 election. When Democrats retook the House in 2019, Trump's legislative agenda ground to a halt, oversight and investigations surged, and he was ultimately impeached twice. These events do not to us clearly reflect "shrinkage" or "abdication."

The courts also served to check Trump's policy ambitions, even on issues central to his agenda. Though the Supreme Court ultimately upheld the Muslim ban in its final iteration, it was a significantly watered-down version from what Trump originally intended following several court-ordered revisions. Likewise, policies such as the US Census's citizenship question and the effort to end the Deferred Action for Childhood Arrivals program ultimately failed, in large part due to procedural challenges in court. Republican and Democratic judges rebuffed the Trump campaign's baseless legal challenges to the 2020 election results. Thus, in both Congress and the courts, among Democrats and even some Republicans, there were real efforts to curtail the Trump administration.

Institutional or Personal Power?

Despite these institutional barriers, there were still noteworthy developments in presidential power under Trump. In general, however, these shifts were not particularly innovative for extending the power of the presidency. Most enhanced Trump's *personal* power, rather than the *institutional* power of the office. In our estimation, the latter was only marginally expanded at best.

The development that could most implicate interbranch relations was the Trump administration's refusal to comply, and in some cases its interference, with congressional subpoenas for testimony and documents, including the president's tax returns. The latter issue was adjudicated by the Supreme Court in the spring of 2020, ruling that Congress must demonstrate a "valid legislative purpose" to issue subpoenas and tailor them to prevent possibly unconstitutional burdens. This decision ostensibly limited legislators' ability to command information from executive branch actors. The long-term impact of this decision will depend on future court interpretations and applications of the precedent as well as legislative and executive practices.

In another dramatic episode from his term, Trump declared a national emergency to transfer otherwise-appropriated funds to the construction of a US-Mexico border wall. Such reallocation strategies, however, were not pioneered by Trump. President Obama, for example, used legally questionable transfers to fund cost-sharing reduction payments to support the Affordable Care Act (Reynolds and Wallach 2020). Either way, these types of actions land in a legal and political gray area, but it is one of Congress's own creation. To accommodate unexpected contingencies, Congress has long provided transfer and reprogramming authorities to agencies, both on a regular basis and through extraordinary means like Trump's invocation of a national emergency (Schick 2008). Though Congress has the power to reject such emergency declarations, it has failed to do so. Congress did, however, reject Trump's requests to "backfill" the funds reallocated to the border wall.[6] Whether this behavior represents a true expansion of presidential power depends on whether President Joe Biden and other future presidents continue to broadly reallocate budgetary authority. Further, the nature of subsequent congressional responses to this evolving presidential administrative strategy may likewise prove determinative.

Trump more vigorously pushed the boundaries of the *personal prerogatives* of the presidency. These efforts mostly reflected his desire to preserve the health of his businesses and to win reelection, rather than the pursuit of any clear policy objective. On the (relatively) minor end, there were unanswered questions throughout his presidency about his business dealings, obligations to foreign creditors, and tax status. He likewise fought several lawsuits during his administration over alleged violations of the Emoluments Clause, given his continued business income from foreign interests. These lawsuits never gained much traction in the courts, however. It is unclear whether future presidents will face similar financial conflicts of interest or follow Trump's precedents of minimal transparency.

Trump and his associates' activities in both the 2016 and 2020 election campaigns continually pressed the boundaries of propriety and legality. While the Justice Department's long-standing position is that sitting presidents cannot be charged with crimes, close Trump affiliates, including Michael Cohen, have faced legal repercussions for various campaign-related scandals. Trump himself could be subject to criminal or civil charges related to his involvement in directing the illegal campaign finance activities Cohen executed. Notably,

Trump was first impeached by the House for leveraging foreign policy decisions to extract personal campaign favors from Ukranian officials, though, of course, he was not convicted by the Senate.

Perhaps the greatest manifestation of Trump's willingness to seize power for personal gain was his conduct after the 2020 presidential election. Facing a decisive defeat in the Electoral College and popular vote, Trump refused to concede for months. Instead, he and his supporters falsely claimed the election was "stolen" and rife with voter fraud. This claim was rejected by state Republican and Democratic election officials alike, and no court across the country found the allegations credible. This campaign of disinformation culminated on January 6, 2021, when a violent mob of Trump supporters (apparently goaded on by his exhortations at a rally earlier that day) overran the Capitol building as legislators sat to count the electoral votes. It is difficult to imagine a graver threat to separation of powers than the president unleashing insurrectionists to violently disrupt official proceedings of the Congress he opposes. Fortunately, after control of the Capitol was restored, legislators continued tallying the electoral votes into the evening and Trump became the unequivocal loser of the 2020 election.[7]

One week after the attack, the House of Representatives impeached Trump for the second time for "inciting violence against the Government of the United States."[8] Ten House Republicans joined every Democrat to support impeachment, with House Republican conference chair, Liz Cheney (R-WY) lamenting, "There has never been a greater betrayal by a President of the United States of his office and his oath to the Constitution." The following month, the Senate again failed to convict President Trump, though an unprecedented seven Republican senators joined every Democrat in voting guilty. At the very least, it seems clear the events of January 6, 2021, will be abhorred for generations to come and serve as a stain on Trump's legacy. The question of whether these consequences will be enough to deter future presidents from similar actions remains to be seen. It will be a grim watch for scholars of American institutions, to be sure.

There is no doubt Trump's actions are troubling, representing a quantum leap in presidential corruption. His conduct after the 2020 election, in particular, represent a desperation for power unseen in previous presidencies. However, it appears in many cases the main cause Trump sought to advance was his own, rather than a vision of public policy or an expanded presidency per se. On the latter terms, he did rather little relative to his predecessors to expand the power of his office vis-à-vis Congress. Even so, the full impact of his tenure will only become clear as future presidents decide whether to emulate or eschew his example.

Reforming Congressional Capacity

While we might be rather sanguine about the prospects for contemporary congressional constraint over executive branch policymaking, even in the aftermath of the Trump administration, contemporary reformers still see areas for improvement. We end with a discussion of numerous ongoing reform efforts to bolster the capacity of Congress.

The Committee on the Modernization of Congress

After assuming majority power in 2019, House Democrats created the Select Committee on the Modernization of Congress, tasked with making recommendations on topics including rules and procedures for considering legislation, technology, and "staff recruitment, retention, and compensation and benefits."[9] In arguing for establishing the committee, Representative Lipinski (D-IL), a primary proponent, highlighted the separation of powers concerns underlying his efforts: "Congressional dysfunction increasingly turns more power, however, over to the President and to the courts, which takes power away from the American people. So Congress needs reform so it can function as it was intended and return power to the American people."[10] The committee was reauthorized at the beginning of the 117th Congress.

A number of the committee's features might facilitate its success (see chapter 3). First, in 2019, it was established by a bipartisan vote of 418–12, a stark contrast to the typical party-line rules votes.[11] Second, the rules resolutions further ensured bipartisan consensus by mandating that the committee consist of an equal number of Democrats and Republicans, and its reports must pass with eight of twelve members approving.

On March 10, 2020, the committee's first resolution passed the House by a vote of 395–13 (H. Res. 756). While an impressive margin, there is little in the resolution that will, in our view, improve Congress's capacity to constrain the executive branch in the near term. It does not authorize new spending and largely consists of instructions for administrative units to produce reports on capacity-related issues. The parts of the resolution that most implicate capacity simply require a report on increasing the personal office staffing cap, a study on staff benefits, and "rapid response" reports from CRS.

It is unclear how removing the personal office staffing cap will improve Congress's institutional power. Some studies indicate the cap is typically not binding for most offices. Instead, the size of the Members' Representational Allowance (MRA), which is the budget given to congressional members for staffing and other purposes like travel, appears to place greater downward pressure on staff sizes, though some members do not even use the full MRA (McCrain 2020). Further, it is not guaranteed members would use new staff resources for policy purposes rather than constituency service. As documented in chapter 3, communications and similar staff have increased substantially over the last few decades.

Of all the proposals, augmenting staffers' benefits would likely have the greatest impact on capacity. This change could potentially mitigate turnover and increase experience, which, as shown in chapters 4 and 5, influences legislative outputs. Finally, the "rapid response" reports should ostensibly be capacity-enhancing, but the provision does not allocate resources for these purposes. As such, it is not clear yet what, if anything, will materialize from this provision. While this initial resolution was perhaps underwhelming from a separation of powers standpoint, there is still the possibility that more will emerge. The contents and consequences of the committee's future reports will ultimately determine the enduring effects of its work on congressional capacity.

Technology Assessment and Reviving the OTA

Another area championed by the Select Committee and outside reformers is the need to revitalize the Office of Technology Assessment (OTA). Created in the 1970s to report on the nexus of technology and policy, its funding was ultimately terminated in 1995 by new Republican majorities. Since its abolition, individuals, groups, and politicians themselves have advocated for reinstating its funding. Former Rep. Rush Holt (D-NJ) tried unsuccessfully to reinitiate appropriations for the agency several times. Most recently, he introduced a 2014 amendment to the Legislative Branch Appropriations Bill (H. Amdt. 649 to H.R. 4487, 113th Congress) to allocate $2.5 million to the OTA. The amendment was defeated along a party-line vote: 83 percent of Democrats (minority party) in support and 96 percent of Republicans (majority party) opposed.

Recent endeavors to revive the OTA have similarly languished. Representative Mark Takano (D-CA) attempted to amend the FY 2019 legislative branch appropriations bill to restore $2.5 million in funding. The amendment failed 195–217, again along party lines, with only fifteen Republicans voting in support. The Democratic majority once again included $6 million for reopening the agency for two fiscal years in the initial draft of the FY 2020 Legislative Branch Appropriations bill, but it was ultimately stripped from the final version.

Though expertise can certainly increase congressional capacity, we are somewhat skeptical a new OTA would have any more staying power than the old one. First, the motivation of limiting congressional spending remains strong. Creating a new agency to directly benefit Congress would likely inspire broadsides against legislative excess. Indeed, in arguing against the Takano amendment, then Representative Frelinghuysen, the Republican Chair of the House Appropriations Committee, asserted that the new OTA would be redundant given the GAO's authority; others cited general fiscal concerns (see 164 Cong. Rec. H4971).

Economy is not the only motivation for OTA opposition, particularly since these amendments only requested paltry funding amounts relative to annual federal spending. Indeed, Republicans have not aspired to abolish other legislative support institutions. While the $2.5 million OTA funding amendment to the FY 2019 Legislative Branch appropriations bill was being rejected, legislators also recommended an additional eighty full-time equivalent employees for GAO and $6.4 million in CRS funding (H. Rpt. 115-696). Instead, the same perception of a liberal-leaning OTA that motivated Republicans to eliminate the agency in 1995, as detailed in chapter 3, likely sustains their skepticism through today.

Consequently, what are the prospects for increasing congressional capacity through technical expertise? We see two potential paths forward. First, to resurrect a OTA with any degree of durability, advocates need broad-based support from both parties. The mantle of restoring the agency has been carried primarily by liberal Democrats in Congress. Such efforts can only be successful if there is also support among Republicans, which requires overcoming their preconceptions of the OTA and concerns about public skepticism of congressional spending. Such impartiality might be made credible, for instance, through the OTA's structure and leadership. Support from the conservative- and libertarian-leaning R Street Institute or perhaps the bipartisan consensus from the Select Committee might be additional avenues for the OTA to gain credibility with Republicans.

The second, and perhaps more pragmatic, option may be to abandon its revival and instead buttress existing technology assessment capabilities, by empowering other support agencies like the GAO. Though Congress mandated the GAO engage in technology assessment beginning in the early 2000s, this effort has been described as understaffed and has produced few reports (Graves and Kosar 2018). Yet further equipping this agency has several advantages. The GAO has long enjoyed a reputation as an impartial resource to legislators. This pedigree affords some legitimacy to the conclusions that it reports, a key problem of earlier OTA incarnations. Indeed, Republicans have not sought to deauthorize the GAO's technology assessment activities. Of course, there are drawbacks to this approach. The GAO's primary competencies are auditing and program evaluation, which differ substantially from technology assessment. Conceivably, these parts of GAO's mission could consume resources meant for technology assessment or overshadow a technology assessment mission. Ensuring this scenario does not arise would require congressional oversight. Nonetheless, this approach is perhaps more promising in the long term, barring a significant change in Republican attitudes.

Staffing Resources

Technology assessment is just one area in which to improve congressional capacity. Another would be expanding funds to hire member and committee staff for policy development and analyses. Since legislators select staffers themselves, they are a particularly useful resource and do not face the same skepticism or concerns about bias.

Enlarging committee staff may have ambiguous effects for members, since committee chairs often control these resources rather than rank-and-file or minority members (e.g., Presidential Task Force on Congressional Reform 2020; Curry 2015). One possible solution would be to increase associate staff available to members. For instance, some committees, such as the House Rules and Appropriations Committees, have at times footed the bill for staffers who work directly for a member in the policy portfolio of that committee. Increasing associate staff also helps to ensure new staff resources are more likely to be focused on policy rather than on other activities, such as communications or constituent services. Additional associate staff may not automatically induce greater involvement in policymaking, if these powers remain centralized among leadership. However, more staff may produce greater deliberation and diffuse power, since rank-and-file members would gain access to information and policy analysis.

Another important component of resource capacity is staff and member experience. There are numerous barriers to cultivating the latter. Committee turnover is driven primarily by electoral outcomes and changes in the majority party. Moreover, the House and Senate Republican caucuses impose six-year term limits on committee chairmanships, which diffuses opportunities for leadership but reduces chair experience. Abolishing these restrictions will certainly increase capacity in our estimation, but will also run headlong into intracaucus politics and the desires of rank-and-file members to ascend to leadership positions.

Staff experience might be easier to enhance. Salary hikes and additional benefits like those recommended by the Select Committee could extend staffers' tenures by lessening the appeal of lucrative outside opportunities on K Street and elsewhere (Cain and Drutman 2014). Indeed, 51 percent of staffers cited low pay as a key reason for leaving their position in a 2013 survey by the Congressional Management Foundation and the Society for Human Resource Management (Congresional Management Foundation 2017). However, these types of reforms might be politically controversial since they entail additional spending on Congress itself. From the 1940s "pension grab" to the 1990s Contract with America, lawmakers have long sought to avoid perceptions of wasting taxpayer dollars on themselves. Though such a charge would be unfounded in this case, facts have never stopped an anti-Washington narrative from capturing the public imagination. Indeed, citizens largely prefer cutting congressional resources. In a 1993 Americans Talk Issues poll, 63 percent of respondents favorably rated reductions in congressional members' staff of 25 percent. And, 74 percent of respondents in a Gallup Poll survey disapproved of the $4000 pay raise Congress imposed in 1999.

Reformers might frame investments in legislative capacity in ways that engender public support, if the costs are perceived to be offset by potential benefits. For example, a majority of respondents (53 percent) in a 1999 Americans Talk Issues Survey supported buttressing congressional resources when framed as a solution to Y2K-related issues. It is not clear, however, how such a message would fare in the wild, particularly amid widespread perceptions of congressional waste and corruption. If the past is any guide, skittish legislators might be reluctant to bolster capacity in these ways without the political cover of a large, bipartisan coalition, similar to the ones backing the previous Legislative Reorganization Acts. As obvious as reforms might be for increasing congressional capacity, clarion calls for enriching resources that do not grapple with the perceived associated political costs will go unheeded.

Alternatively, political scientists Lee Drutman and Steven Teles advocate that congressional staffers and executive branch employees rotate between their different institutions. In their words, "This would also have the benefit of increasing the networks of congressional staff that allow them to engage in serious oversight, and also increase the belief in executive branch agencies that their counterparts in Congress are trust-worthy and knowledgeable" (2015). Yet the implications for separation of powers are unclear. Allowing executive branch employees to serve legislators would lead to a situation where laws were written and implemented by the same actors, thereby undermining the separation of powers. Such a proposal would not necessarily support the independent power of Congress. Indeed, Mills and Selin (2017) find that highly productive congressional committees actually employ *fewer* detailees (i.e., temporary employees borrowed from the executive branch), highlighting a staffer who commented that the "committee worried that detailees would convey sensitive legislative information to the executive branch." Even given the extra labor, detailees may not be the most effective avenue for enhancing congressional capacity.

Conclusion

Despite the evidence of contemporary executive branch constraint we uncover in this book, there are still several ways to invigorate congressional capacity that would likely further limit executive power. Investments in staffing and support agencies such as the GAO are particularly fruitful avenues. Such reforms will, in our view, further enhance congressional control over executive branch actors. But analogous transformations across the fifty states may prove to be even more consequential, given pervasive deficits in state legislatures' capacities. Across all levels of government, broad bipartisan support will be needed to overcome partisan policymakers' skepticism and public disapproval of legislative self-spending. In an increasingly polarized time, that is no small feat. Yet all is not lost.

Historical congresses and state legislatures were once ill equipped to confront expanding executive power but instituted reforms throughout the twentieth century to acquire the necessary resources for effective checks and balances. Indeed, we find evidence that contemporary congresses maintain sufficient capacity to constrain presidential power, though sympathetic copartisan legislators often remain passive. State legislatures are far more variable in their ability to curb gubernatorial actions. In some states, evasion thrives as it did for pre-World War II presidents; in others, executive unilateralism is effectively contained. Legislatures can strengthen their capacity and play a meaningful role in separated systems, even in this current polarized era.

But capacity is not simply a one-way ratchet. There are continuing political challenges to its durability, as legislators sacrifice their own tools on the altars of economy and reelection. The future of legislatures' power depends not only on their will to restrain the executive branch, but likewise on whether they nurture their capacity in the face of strong political headwinds. Without capacity, the promise of separation of powers will wither. Indeed, checks are in the balance.

NOTES

Chapter 1. Executive Power in the Shadow of Legislative Capacity

1. DC Circuit Court of Appeals, *Committee on the Judiciary of the House of Representatives v. Donald F. McGahn, II,* decided February 28, 2020, https://www.cadc.uscourts.gov/internet /opinions.nsf/29F7900862BA6CD68525851C00784758/$file/19-5331-1831001.pdf.

2. Quoted in Schlesinger (1973, 377).

3. Peter Baker and Maggie Haberman, "Trump Leaps to Call Shots on Reopening Nation, Setting Up Standoff With Governors," *New York Times,* April 13, 2020, https://www.nytimes .com/2020/04/13/us/politics/trump-coronavirus-governors.html.

4. Tamara Keith, "Wielding a Pen and Phone Obama Goes It Alone," NPR, January 20, 2014, www.npr.org/2014/01/20/263766043/wielding-a-pen-and-a-phone-obama-goes-it-alone.

5. Ashbook Center at Ashland University, "Transcript of David Frost's Interview with Richard Nixon," Teaching American History, https://teachingamericanhistory.org/library /document/transcript-of-david-frosts-interview-with-richard-nixon/.

6. Art Carden, "Presidential Power is a Powerful Problem," *Forbes,* August 28, 2018, www .forbes.com/sites/artcarden/2018/08/28/presidential-power-is-a-powerful-problem/?sh=413 3cf011d9c.

7. Quoted in Marc Fisher, "Donald Trump and the Expanding Power of the Presidency," *Washington Post,* July 30, 2016, www.washingtonpost.com/politics/donald-trump-and-the -dangers-of-a-strong-presidency/2016/07/30/69cfc686-55be-11e6-b7de-dfe509430c39_ story.html?utm_term=.b7de476e1a16.

8. Kenneth Lovett, "Andrew Cuomo Defends His Use of Executive Power: 'I run the government,'" *New York Daily News,* July 22, 2015, www.nydailynews.com/news/politics/cuomo -executive-power-run-government-article-1.2301086.

9. Vickie Aldous, "Jackson County Commissioners Want Limits on Governor's Emergency Powers," Ashland Tidings, June 13, 2020, https://www.ashlandtidings.com/top-stories/news /2020/06/13/jackson-county-commissioners-want-limits-on-governors-emergency-powers/.

10. Legislative Branch Capacity Working Group, "About LegBranch #MakeCongress-GreatAgain." LegBranch, accessed April 14, 2021, https://www.legbranch.org/about-leg branch/. Accessed February 17, 2020.

11. Moreover, moving away from divided government, Chiou and Rothenberg (2014) show there is no correlation between gridlock and unilateralism.

12. Note that unless otherwise noted, all monetary figures we report in this book are in real 2009 dollars.

Chapter 2. Legislative Capacity, Executive Action, and Separation of Powers

1. Senate Commerce, Science, and Transportation Committee and Senate Judiciary Committee Joint Hearing on Facebook, April 10, 2018.

2. Laura Bradley, "Was Mark Zuckerberg's Senate Hearing the 'Worst Punisment of All'?," *Vanity Fair*, April 11, 2018, www.vanityfair.com/hollywood/2018/04/mark-zuckerberg-facebooktestimony-congress-cambridge-analytica-late-night.

3. Numerous strands of conceptual and theoretical literatures are linked to policymaking capacity as we conceive it here. One connection is to Mezey's notions of "policymaking power" and "support" (Mezey 1979), based on the degree to which legislatures can reject or alter executive proposals. He also argues legislatures require support from the larger political system to operate in a somewhat autonomous manner. Similarly, Polsby (1975) distinguishes between "arenas" and "transformative legislatures"—two ends of a spectrum describing the independent power of legislatures. The latter can craft legislation in any way they see fit, drawing upon any information and ideas they want. In systems featuring arena legislatures, such as Westminster parliaments, the power that underlies legislative acts may originate elsewhere, such as in the executive. These arena legislatures are akin to what Cox and Morgenstern (2001) identify as "reactive assemblies" in Latin America, where legislative initiatives often originate outside the legislature. Our idea of policymaking capacity is distinct from and somewhat more capacious than these previous ones. Huber and Shipan (2002) note the importance of the "bargaining environment" for structuring the ability of legislatures to pass laws. They operationalize this idea in terms of whether chambers in bicameral legislatures are led by the same party. Our concept of policymaking capacity is broader than this, importantly encompassing the nonstatutory powers legislatures possess to direct policymaking and impose costs on the executive.

4. Particularly, if the legislature has repeated interactions with executive/bureaucratic actors as well as nonstatutory means of imposing costs for noncompliance, these nonstatutory mechanisms may be a powerful means of policy direction. See, e.g., Bolton (2021).

5. Bill Carey, "A Throwback from the Days of All-Powerful Governors," *Nashville Post*, June 29, 2000, www.nashvillepost.com/home/article/20446286/a-throwback-from-the-days-of-allpowerful-governors.

6. Of course, the degree of partisan control has varied in Congress over time, with some periods featuring less power for party leaders. In robustness checks, we do examine total staff, with almost identical results. Both staff measures are, unsurprisingly, highly correlated over time given most are associated with the majority.

7. For an analysis of research in this area, see Crook et al. (2011).

8. Thom Tillis, "I Support Trump's Vision on Border Security. But I Would Vote against the Emergency," *Washington Post*, February 25, 2019, www.washingtonpost.com/opinions/2019/02/25/i-support-trumps-vision-border-security-i-would-vote-against-emergency/?utm_term=.43218ca22bee. Accessed May 16, 2019.

9. Furthermore, Esterling (2007) finds evidence that members of Congress have incentives to engage in oversight activity and invest in their own expertise to do so, in order to attract campaign contributions.

10. Note that unified government does *not* imply that the legislative outcome will be as beneficial to the executive as the unilateral outcome. Supermajoritarian requirements may

necessitate accommodating the preferences of pivotal actors with ideal points relatively far from that of the executive (Krehbiel 1998). All we are claiming is that the relative policy benefits of unilateralism will be higher on average in divided relative to unified government.

11. This is a departure from other formal models in the legislative-executive literature. Typically, discretion is modeled as a restriction on the magnitude of policy change an executive actor can affect with no constraint on the direction. Despite the idiosyncrasy of this assumption, when directional constraints are removed and executives can use discretion however they wish, the predictions of the model do not match the data nearly as well as when the directional assumption is maintained (Chiou and Rothenberg 2014; 2017).

12. Executive calculations about whether to adhere to discretionary bounds in the Huber and Shipan (2002) model are conditioned by the possibility that what they term "non-statutory factors" intervene and move the executive's policy choice directly to the legislature's ideal point. These factors are unrelated to legislative capacity in the theoretical setup and are not explicitly defined in the model (though they are meant to capture features of the political system impacting the implementation of policies after agencies act). The legislature does not take action or pay costs to execute these "non-statutory factors"; instead, their implementation is exogenous. One might be tempted to view "non-statutory factors" as akin to policymaking capacity because Huber and Shipan (2002) measure the concept in their empirical tests using an indicator for whether a legislature can veto executive regulations. We believe, however, that legislative veto powers more clearly align with our understanding of policymaking capacity than with how "non-statutory factors" operate in their model. Legislative vetoes require direct legislative action (and resources) and would revert policy back to the status quo rather than to the legislature's ideal point. To clarify, when we refer to non-statutory mechanisms of constraint, we are referring generally to a legislature's opportunities to impose costs and constraints on executives ex ante or ex post (through, e.g., oversight, committee reports). Moreover, we expect the presence of these opportunities to *interact* with resources to produce high levels of legislative capacity, a relationship not considered in Huber and Shipan (2002).

Chapter 3. "Outmanned and Outgunned": The Historical Development of Congressional Capacity

1. Marian Currinder, "Letter in Support of Increased Funding for the Legislative Branch in FY2020," LegBranch, March 21, 2019, https://www.legbranch.org/letter-in-support-of -increased-funding-for-the-legislative-branch-in-fy2020/.

2. Casey Burgat, "Crippled Congress = Expanded Executive Powers," R Street Institute, February 20, 2018, https://www.rstreet.org/2018/02/20/crippled-congress-expanded-execu tive-powers/. Accessed December 29, 2020.

3. Though, for a recent revisionist view, see Mashaw (2012).

4. The subpoena power has been the subject of legal challenges during the Trump administration, which we discuss in the conclusion.

5. For example, see 63 H. Rpt. 1227, where the House Committee on the Library unanimously endorsed the creation of a Legislative Research Division in the Library of Congress.

6. See Lee (2006) for a detailed treatment of the BOE.

7. See Gene L. Dodaro, "Fiscal Year 2018 Budget Request, U.S. Government Accountability Office, Statement of Gene L. Dodaro, Comptroller General of the United States," Government Accountability Office, June 21, 2017, https://www.gao.gov/assets/gao-17-604t.pdf.

8. See Christopher Chantrill, "US Federal Government Spending," US Government Spending, accessed April 14, 2021, www.usgovernmentspending.com/spending_chart_1900 _2020USk_20s2lio11tcn_Fof_US_Federal_Government_Spending.

9. See Galloway (1951) for a thorough accounting or PL 79-601.

10. These figures come from our dataset of committee staffers, which we introduce more fully in chapter 5.

11. In subsequent amendments the number of agencies covered expanded considerably. See Ginsberg and Greene (2016) for an overview.

12. H. Con. Res. 192 (1992).

13. Following Krause (2007), we opt against regressions in logged levels given the trended nature of the time series and evidence of non-stationarity.

14. Since data prior to 1947 is sporadic (collected in 1891, 1914, 1930, and 1935), we use linear interpolation for the missing years. The results are materially unaltered when examining only 1947 to 2015, when the staffing data is more consistently available. We begin in 1905 because this is the starting year for our later empirical work.

15. DW-NOMINATE scores are estimated using the votes of members of Congress to determine their relative ideological positions through time and within congresses. Examining either the House or the Senate median alone does not change our conclusions.

16. We lag these and the control variables by one year for models 1–3 given appropriations decisions are typically made in the prior calendar year.

17. For years prior to 1939, we use expenditures attributed to the presidential office.

18. Inflation data is collected from the Bureau of Labor Statistics.

19. Following previous scholars (e.g., Cohen 2012), war is coded as 1 in the following periods: American combat involvement in World War I (1917–18) and World War II (1941–45), the Korean War (1950–52), the Vietnam War (1964–75), the Gulf War (1990–91), and the heaviest fighting in Iraq and Afghanistan (2001–3).

20. The results do not appear to be driven by any of these choices. Excluding the fixed effects or using simple robust standard errors does not affect the results. We also explored vector error correction models to account for cointegration, following Krause (2007). Our conclusions are unaltered in those models. Finally, in alternative specifications we test interactions between our measures of executive branch size and ideological divergence, since it is possible that the variables moderate one another. We do not find any statistically or substantively significant interactive effects.

Chapter 4. Pulling the Purse Strings: Legislative Capacity and Discretion

1. See *Hawaii v. Trump*, 878 F.3d 662 (9th Cir. 2017).

2. See S. Rpt. 1400, 79th Congress.

3. Our measure only includes discretionary funding and therefore omits mandatory spending. While mandatory programs constitute a large proportion of federal spending, levels are

also largely fixed by formulas determined outside the appropriations process and are less readily manipulated by political actors. As such, we do not claim that our measure characterizes the sum total of an agency's discretion. Instead, it represents one specific (but important) discretionary decision congressional actors make annually for an agency that we can use to study the political dynamics of discretion.

4. We take the natural logarithm of this measure to reduce the influence of outliers in the analyses.

5. In the online appendix, we show that the logged budget authority portion of the measure behaves differently from the report length portion in validation tests, further supporting the idea it is tapping into is a concept distinct from constraint.

6. We conduct additional analyses using full committee staff rather than subcommittee staff, given greater centralized leadership control over the appropriations committees over time (Hanson 2014). While the results generally accord with the theoretical framework, they are not consistently statistically significant, in contrast to those reported below that are focused on subcommittee resources. The combination of these findings suggests the effects of resources in the appropriations process inhere largely at the subcommittee level, which is one reason we focus on this context in the analyses.

7. We also conduct analyses using minority and majority party subcommittee staff combined. The substantive conclusions of these analyses remain unchanged from those reported here, likely because the overwhelming proportion of subcommittee staff are majority staffers across our time period. We find null results when we using only minority staff in the analysis, giving us further confidence that we are measuring the effects of substantive changes in capacity rather than some other broader trend driving staffing and outcomes.

8. Unlike other committees in Congress, the Appropriations committees have typically been exempt from caps on staffing levels. The absence of a cap, however, does not mean staff resources are unlimited. Less direct constraints likely bind the staffing levels on the committee, such as overall budgets and norms of universality.

9. We were unable to locate some directories prior to 1967, and those years are thus omitted from our analysis. Additionally, for some years in the 1970s, the directories did not distinguish staff by subcommittees for the Senate Appropriations Committee. Where that is the case, those subcommittee-years are omitted from the analysis.

10. Other seasonal issues only commenced publication later in the time period we examine.

11. Other proprietary sources, such as Legistorm, are available only for short time periods during our study (e.g., post-2000). The House and the Senate also publish summaries of their disbursements; however, these are unavailable for some earlier time periods. Even still, our measure is highly correlated with alternatives ones based on the official disbursement data. The *Vital Statistics on Congress* publishes standing committee staff counts based on annual disbursement data from 1994 to 2015. Happily, the correlation between our counts and those is 0.85.

12. This distinction is usually indicated based on their position title (e.g., it contains the word "Minority" or the abbreviation "Min.") or in the case of associate staff is based on the member for whom they work. We do not include the District of Columbia or the Legislative Branch Subcommittees, because their operations do not align with our theory centered on constraint of executive branch actors.

13. As a robustness check, we distinguish between policy-oriented staffers and administrative staffers. As expected, the former exhibits stronger effects on changes in discretion than the latter, likely due to the fact that staffers with policy positions are the ones dealing more directly with decisions impacting executive branch discretion. However, given the difficulties in assigning staff as "policy" or "nonpolicy" discussed in chapter 3, we focus here on the majority versus minority distinction.

14. Note that these measures of experience naturally overlap with seniority, which could be another important aspect of staff or member capacity.

15. For those who began their service in or before 1959, this source alone will not produce an accurate measure of their experience. Existing datasets, such as Charles Stewart's historical committee data, do not divide rosters into subcommittees. To determine the starting date of chair and member subcommittee service, we rely on publications of the House and Senate Appropriations Committees detailing their historical rosters. For the Senate, the committee produced the report *Committee on Appropriations, 1867–2008* (110 S. Doc. 7, 2nd session). The House committee produced a similar report in *A Concise History of the House of Representatives Committee on Appropriations* in December 2010.

16. Unlike the historical rosters of members and chairs released by the committees, there is no such publication for committee staffers. To determine their start dates, we searched for their names on Congressional Proquest to locate sources where they appear on a congressional document associated with the Appropriations Committee in their respective chamber. Three types of documents include staffers' names in this era. First, the Legislative Reorganization Act of 1946 mandated that committees semiannually report the names, positions, and salaries of their staffers in the *Congressional Record*. Second, committee and subcommittee documents often include staff names. Finally, congressional directories published in the 1930s and 1940s include the names of key professional staffers on some committees. Overall, we found clear references to 73 percent of staffers serving in 1959 prior to that year. For those staffers, we recorded the earliest year they appear in some document as their beginning year. The key risk of this measure is that it may understate the levels of staff experience on these committees, which would only bias against our results.

17. We ran analogous models using DW-NOMINATE Common Space scores to calculate the absolute ideological distance between the president and the Appropriations subcommittee chair, yielding substantively identical results. We prefer the partisan measures, however, given that presidential DW-NOMINATE scores from the earlier eras of our time period are estimated using very little data.

18. We also examined models with less restrictive time fixed effects (e.g., president fixed effects) and find similar results.

19. We also run analyses combining these measures into a single scale using factor analysis. We still find strong evidence in favor of the conditional ally principle effect.

Chapter 5. Continuous Watchfulness? Legislative Capacity and Oversight

1. Eugene Kiely and D'Angelo Gore, "In His Own Words: Trump on Russian Meddling," FactCheck, February 19, 2018, www.factcheck.org/2018/02/words-trump-russian-meddling/.

2. US House of Representatives Permanent Select Committee on Intelligence, "Schiff Statement on House Republicans' Premature Shutdown of Russia Investigation," US House of Representatives Permanent Select Committee on Intelligence, March 12, 2018, https://intelligence .house.gov/news/documentsingle.aspx?DocumentID=361.

3. Tim Mak, "Senate Trump-Russia Probe Has No Full-Time State, No Key Witnesses," *Daily Beast*, May 5, 2017, www.thedailybeast.com/senate-trump-russia-probe-has-no-full-time -staff-no-key-witnesses.

4. Matthew Weber, "U.S. Senate's Russia Investigation Smaller Than Previous Enquiries," Reuters, fingfx.thomsonreuters.com/gfx/rngs/USA-RUSSIA-SENATE-INVESTIGATION /010040SF1Q6/index.html.

5. US Senate Select Committee on Intelligence, "Report on Russian Active Measures Campaigns and Interference in the 2016. U.S. Election—Volume 5: Counterintelligence Threats and Vulnerabilities," US Senate, https://www.intelligence.senate.gov/sites/default /files/documents/report_volume5.pdf.

6. See, for example, *McGrain, v. Daughtery* (1927), *Sinclair v. United States* (1929) and *Watkins v. United States* (1957).

7. In short, they searched LexisNexis and ProQuest databases using key words to isolate hearings related to "alleged misconduct within the executive branch" (68) and validated the search results with hand coders. The authors generously provided us a list of the validated CIS investigations, which we used to generate three distinct dependent variables we then combine into a single index.

8. In their replication materials, Kriner and Schickler (2014) note that the CIS mistakenly recorded each witness for an investigation related to the Federal Housing Authority (FHA) in 1954 as its own investigation. To redress this error, they identify the correct number of days associated with the FHA investigation (378) and subtract that number from the total days and investigations to produce a corrected version of those dependent variables. We follow this same procedure here.

9. All of the relationships we report are replicated when examining each element of the index separately, reflecting the high degrees of correlation among the factors.

10. To identify the starting year of the 1,955 committee staffers that appear in the first year of our dataset (1967), we searched their names on Congressional Proquest to locate the year in which their name first appears in a document related to that specific committee.

11. The results of our analyses hold when using total staff (majority and minority) as well as when isolating staffers with "policy" positions.

12. *Committees in the U.S. Congress, 1947–1992* (Nelson) and *Congressional Committee Assignments, 103rd to 114th Congresses, 1993–2017* (Stewart and Woon). Both are available at web.mit .edu/17.251/www/data_page.html#0.

13. We determine the start date of chairs and committee members who were already serving in 1967 by using the aforementioned Nelson, Stewart, and Woon datasets (which extend back until 1947) as well as resolutions at the beginning of congresses that assign members to committees for the few seated prior to 1947.

14. The results of those analyses are substantively identical when using ideology-based measures of preference divergence with DW-NOMINATE.

15. The results remain unchanged when coding this variable to include the duration of these wars in our dataset.

16. We also examine models subsetted by the House and Senate, finding results consistent with the pooled analysis. The chamber and committee fixed effects, in those respective analyses, control for any time invariant features of chambers that might confound our results.

17. Because some of our control variables are not available until the 1940s, these models begin in 1947. Factors such as presidential approval are crucial in explaining congressional incentives for oversight and thus should be accounted for in our analysis. However, models without these controls over the longer time series produce largely similar results.

18. Because Fowler's data extends back to 1947, we focus here on overall staffing since she collects that variable for the entire time period. Given that this is a placebo test, we do not want to limit its power to detect significant effects by using our other measures, which would result in the loss of one third of the observations.

Chapter 6. The Pendulum of Power: Unilateral Policymaking

1. "Obama on Executive Actions: 'I've Got a Pen and I've Got a Phone," CBS DC, January 14, 2014, washington.cbslocal.com/2014/01/14/obama-on-executive-actions-ive-got -a-pen-and-ive-got-a-phone/.

2. Barack Obama, "Remarks in Las Vegas," October 24, 2011, American Presidency Project, www.presidency.ucsb.edu/ws/index.php?pid=96941.

3. This act authorizes the president to "prescribe policies and directives that the President considers necessary" to "provide the Federal Government with an economical and efficient system" for procurement and supply.

4. A related earlier version of this analysis appears in Bolton and Thrower (2016).

5. Section 1, Clause 1: "Executive power shall be vested in a President of the United States."

6. Section 1, Clause 8: "Before he enters on the Execution of his Office, he shall take the following Oath or Affirmation 'I do solemnly swear (or affirm) that I will faithfully execute the Office of the President of the United States, and will to the best of my Ability, preserve, protect and defend the Constitution of the United States.'"

7. Section 3, Clause 5: "He shall take Care that the Laws be faithfully executed."

8. Recall from chapter 3 that congressional policymaking capacity has been sufficiently high during the time period of our study, so we focus on resources here.

9. The CIS uses the following identification numbers to identify classes of directives used in this analysis: EO, Numbered Executive Orders; 23, Executive Orders Relating to the Panama Canal (1902–1934); 33, Executive Orders Relating to Public Land (1841–1935); 38, Executive Orders Relating to Indian Reservations (1850–1892); 41, Executive Orders Relating to Public Land (1820–1913). We exclude attachments, such as maps or related correspondences, and orders not signed by the president.

10. In previous work, we show that the inclusion or exclusion of civil service orders has little effect on the overall statistical patterns we report here (Bolton and Thrower 2016).

11. We conduct several robustness checks in the online appendix using various significance measures and find none of our conclusions are altered.

12. See chapter 3 for more details.

13. The results of the analysis below remain unchanged when selecting any year in the 1940s (including 1947, when the LRA took effect) as the dividing point of the analysis. These findings, combined with our later analyses that consider the whole time period, give us confidence our empirical results are not driven by an arbitrarily chosen cut point.

14. These results also hold when including presidential fixed effects.

15. We opt for negative binomial regressions given overdispersion in the data. An examination of chi-square and likelihood ratio statistics also suggests that the negative binomial is the most appropriate model.

16. Following previous scholars (e.g., Cohen 2012), war is coded as "1" in the following periods: American combat involvement in World War I (1917–18) and World War II (1941–45), the Korean War (1950–52), the Vietnam War (1964–75), the Gulf War (1990–91), and the years of heaviest fighting during the wars in Iraq and Afghanistan (2001–3). We also used a broader definition of the Afghanistan/Iraq conflicts extending through the end of our time series and find that the conclusions we report here are unaltered.

17. This variable is collected from the Bureau of Labor Statistics.

18. We isolate nondefense expenditures to disentangle changes in the demand for domestic services from changes in defense spending caused by other noninstitutional factors such as sudden military conflict.

19. In the models examining the whole time period, we employ a quadratic time trend given the underlying pattern of the executive order time series. The inclusion or exclusion of these time trend variables does not affect our empirical results.

20. One potential concern with the analysis is that there are only six years of divided government during period 1 (1911–12, 1919–20, 1931–32), which might not provide enough variation for meaningful analysis. As a robustness check we use ideological distance measures using DW-NOMINATE scores, which provide greater variation in interbranch conflict, and find that the results are robust. Finally, one might argue that the nature and impact of divided government has changed over time. As such, we interact divided government with the time trend variable as another robustness check and find an insignificant effect. Instead, the effect of divided government is consistent over time within each of these different time periods, respectively.

21. See US Census Bureau, "Statistical Abstracts Series," United States Census Bureau, December 19, 2018, www.census.gov/library/publications/time-series/statistical_abstracts .html.

22. Office of Management and Budget, "Historical Tables," White House, accessed May 21, 2019, https://www.whitehouse.gov/omb/historical-tables/.

23. The results are robust when excluding this post-LRA variable.

24. Specifically, the APP includes: the Messages and Papers of the President, 1789–1929; the Public Papers of the President, 1929–present; the Weekly Compilation of Presidential Documents, 1977–2009; and the Daily Compilation of Presidential Documents, 2009–present.

25. We omit those used to make individual appointments. Additionally, we omit memoranda of disapproval, which are used as public statements of vetoes rather than instructions to agencies.

26. We use an analogous procedure to identify nonceremonial memoranda as we did for executive orders.

27. About 45 percent of memorandum make a presidential determination.

28. We find our results likewise hold when replicating the period analysis from table 6.1.

29. These provisions from a 1966 law provide the president with broad authority to "prescribe such regulations for the admission of individuals into the civil service in the executive branch as will best promote the efficiency of that service."

30. See "CAP Topics," Comparative Agendas Project, www.comparativeagendas.net/pages/master-codebook.

31. See the online appendix for more summary statistics of executive orders by policy area and year.

32. We also consider lags of this variable and the results are substantively identical to those we report below.

33. CAP does not record laws or salience data for the culture policy area, thereby decreasing the number of observations in models 3-6.

Chapter 7. Unilateral Policymaking in the US States

1. Kevin Liptak, Kristen Holmes, and Ryan Nobles, "Trump Completes Reversal, Telling Govs 'You are going to call your own shots' and Distributes New Guidelines," CNN, April 16, 2020, https://www.cnn.com/2020/04/16/politics/donald-trump-reopening-guidelines-coronavirus/index.html.

2. Roy Cooper, "Executive Order No. 120," State of North Carolina, March 23, 2020, https://files.nc.gov/governor/documents/files/EO120.pdf.

3. Mike DeWine, "Executive Order 2020-03D," State of Ohio, March 16, 2020, https://governor.ohio.gov/wps/portal/gov/governor/media/executive-orders/executive-order-2020-03-d.

4. See Barber, Bolton, and Thrower (2019), Cockerham and Crew Jr. (2017), and Sellers (2017) for important exceptions.

5. Megan Messerly and Michelle Rindels, "Public Careers, Private Lives: Part-Time Lawmakers Must Navigate Inevitable Conflicts," *Nevada Independent*, February 3, 2019, www.thenevadaindependent.com/article/public-careers-private-lives-part-time-lawmakers-must-navigate-inevitable-conflicts.

6. Paul Burka, "More Power to Him?," *Texas Monthly*, April 2007, www.texasmonthly.com/politics/more-power-to-him-2/. Accessed April 19, 2019.

7. We begin our analysis in 1993 due to limitations in the data availability of executive orders across states and of some of our independent variables.

8. The Bowen and Greene measure is not available for the entire 1993–2013 time period.

9. Note that this measure captures the threshold at which legislatures can overturn a veto, which is a fundamental component of policymaking capacity through the statutory process. Some state legislatures might have an easier time meeting their threshold depending on the size of their majority party.

10. One may wonder if a more appropriate measure would be the total days a legislature is in session. In other work (Bolton and Thrower forthcoming), we show the degree to which session lengths impact gubernatorial activities depends on whether legislatures have the ability to dictate their own sessions. Furthermore, the number of days spent in session may be endogenous to underlying political conflict in the system, reflecting the conflation

of capacity (which refers to the ability of the legislature to do something) with what they actually do.

11. This indicator only varies by state, not year. But the results are unchanged if it is omitted from the index. The results also remain robust when omitting any one of the other components of the index.

12. Interestingly, *Staff Per Member* and the policymaking capacity scale are actually negatively correlated ($\rho = -0.18$), highlighting the importance of considering these two domains of legislative capacity separately and casting doubt on previous measures that seek to combine them into a single index.

13. See Carl Klarner, "Governors Dataset", Harvard Dataverse, February 23, 2013, https://doi.org/10.7910/DVN/PQoY1N.

14. Krupnikov and Shipan (2012) argue that budgetary factors in the Beyle index may be inconsistent over time as well. The results we report here are robust to excluding this measure, excluding the suspect years of the measure (pre-1994), and using alternative measures of gubernatorial power and prestige, such as the salary of the governor.

15. Of course, the estimation of a triple interaction with these sets of fixed effects is a difficult task due to limited power. The results of the analysis are substantively identical when using random intercepts for each state instead of fixed effects, which leverages cross-state variation in estimating the effects as well. The combination of these results gives us greater confidence in our estimates.

16. In the model examining *PC*, the estimated coefficient for divided government is -0.06 with a standard error of 0.05. In the model examining *Staff Per Member*, the estimated coefficient for divided government is -0.01 with a standard error of 0.01.

Chapter 8. The Future of Legislative Capacity and Executive Power

1. Steven Levitsky and Daniel Ziblatt, "The Crisis of American Democracy," American Federation of Teachers, https://www.aft.org/hc/fall2020/levitsky_ziblatt.

2. Peter Baker and Maggie Haberman, "Trump Leaps to Call Shots on Reopening Nation, Setting Up Standoff With Governors," *New York Times*, April 13, 2020, https://www.nytimes.com/2020/04/13/us/politics/trump-coronavirus-governors.html.

3. Mairead McArdle, "Trump Slams Sasse for 'Foolishness' In Response to Criticism of Covid Executive Orders," *National Review*, August 10, 2020, https://www.nationalreview.com/news/trump-slams-sasse-for-foolishness-in-response-to-criticism-of-covid-executive-orders/.

4. See P.L. 116-260, Division N, Title 5, Section 503.

5. Lisa Mascaro, "It's Not Just the Presidency: Trump Is Changing the Congress," Associated Press, July 11, 2020, https://apnews.com/article/3e1b0fc5f17ad40b242a9555b2ac412e.

6. See Jennifer Shutt, "Appropriators Reach Spending Agreement, Fend Off Possibility of Government Shutdown," Roll Call, December 12, 2019, https://www.rollcall.com/2019/12/12/appropriators-reach-spending-agreement-fend-off-possibility-of-government-shutdown/.

7. During this harrowing affair, quick-thinking staffers escaped with the Electoral College ballots just moments before agitated mobsters, who likely would have destroyed them, barreled

into the Senate chambers. As Senator Jeff Merkley (D-OR) extolled, "If our capable floor staff hadn't grabbed them, they would have been burned by the mob." This tale further reinforces the importance of quality staff for legislative functioning, as we have repeatedly emphasized throughout this book. Jacob Pramuk, "Senate Salvages Electoral College Ballots before Rioters Break into the Chamber," CNBC, January 6, 2021, https://www.cnbc.com/2021/01/06/electoral-college-ballots-saved-during-capitol-riots.html.

8. H. Res. 24, 117th Congress.

9. See H. Res. 6, 116th Congress, Title II.

10. *Congressional Record*, January 4, 2019, Page H223.

11. The margins on the other titles in the rules package were far narrower. Title I passed 234–197, and the final tally for Title III was 235–192.

BIBLIOGRAPHY

Aberbach, Joel D. 1990. *Keeping a Watchful Eye: The Politics of Legislative Oversight.* Washington, DC: Brookings Institution.

Acs, Alex. 2019. "Congress and Administrative Policymaking: Identifying Congressional Veto Power." *American Journal of Political Science* 63(3):513–529.

Aldrich, John H., and David W. Rohde. 2000. "The Republican Revolution and the House Appropriations Committeee." *Journal of Politics* 62(1):1–33.

Anzia, Sarah F., and Molly C. Jackman. 2012. "Legislative Organization and the Second Face of Power: Evidence from U.S. State Legislatures." *Journal of Politics* 75(1):210–24.

Arnold, R. Douglas. 1990. *The Logic of Congressional Action.* New Haven, CT: Yale University Press.

Arter, David. 2006. "Comparing the Legislative Performance of Legislatures." *Journal of Legislative Studies* 12(3-4):245–57.

Atkeson, Lonna Rae, and Randall W. Partin. 1995. "Economic and Referendum Voting: A Comparison of Gubernatorial and Senatorial Elections." *American Political Science Review* 89(1):99–107.

Bailey, Jeremy D., and Brandon Rottinghaus. 2014. "Reexamining the Use of Unilateral Orders: Source of Authority and the Power to Act Alone." *American Politics Research* 42(3):472–502.

Barber, Michael, Alexander Bolton, and Sharece Thrower. 2019. "Legislative Constraints on Executive Unilateralism in Separation of Powers Systems." *Legislative Studies Quarterly* 44(3):515–48.

Barber, Michael, and Nolan McCarty. 2015. "Causes and Consequences of Polarization." In *Solutions to Political Polarization in America,* ed. Nathaniel Persily, 15–58. New York, NY: Cambridge University Press.

Bawn, Kathleen. 1995. "Political Control Versus Expertise: Congressional Choices about Administrative Procedures." *American Political Science Review* 89(1):62–73.

Beckmann, Matthew N. 2010. *Pushing the Agenda: Presidential Leadership in US Lawmaking, 1953–2004.* New York: Cambridge University Press.

Belco, Michelle, and Brandon Rottinghaus. 2017. *The Dual Executive: Unilateral Orders in a Separated and Shared Power System.* Palo Alto, CA: Stanford University Press.

Bendor, Jonathan, and Adam Meirowitz. 2004. "Spatial Models of Delegation." *American Political Science Review* 98(2):293–310.

Beyle, Thad, and Margaret Ferguson. 2008. "Governors and the Executive Branch." In *Politics in the American States,* 9th ed., Virginia Gray and Russell L. Hanson, 192–228. Washington, DC: CQ.

Bimber, Bruce. 1996. *The Politics of Expertise in Congress*. Albany: SUNY Press.

Binder, Sarah A. 1999. "The Dynamics of Legislative Gridlock, 1947–96." *American Political Science Review* 93(3):519–33.

Bloch Rubin, Ruth. 2020. "Lessons from the History of Reform." In *Congress Overwhelmed: The Decline in Congressional Capacity and Prospects for Reform*, ed. Timothy M. LaPira, Lee Drutman and Kevin R. Kosar, 255–67. Chicago, IL: University of Chicago Press.

Blum, James L. 1992. "The Congressional Budget Office: On the One Hand, On the Other." In *Organizations for Policy Analysis: Helping Government Think*, ed. Carol H. Weiss 218–35. Newbury Park, CA: Sage.

Bolton, Alexander. Forthcoming. "Gridlock, Bureaucratic Control, and Non-Statutory Policy-making in Congress." *American Journal of Political Science*.

Bolton, Alexander, and Sharece Thrower. 2016. "Legislative Capacity and Executive Unilateralism." *American Journal of Political Science* 60(3):649–63.

Bolton, Alexander, and Sharece Thrower. 2019. "The Constraining Power of the Purse: Legislative Appropriations and Executive Discretion." *Journal of Politics* 81(4):1266–81.

Bolton, Alexander, and Sharece Thrower. Forthcoming. "Legislative Constraints, Ideological Conflict, and the Timing of Executive Unilateralism." *Legislative Studies Quarterly*.

Bowen, Daniel C., and Zachary Greene. 2014. "Should We Measure Professionalism with an Index? A Note on Theory and Practice in State Legislative Professionalism Research." *State Politics & Policy Quarterly* 14(3):277–96.

Brown, Robert L. 2010. "Measuring Delegation." *Review of International Organizations* 5: 141–75.

Brudnick, Ida. 2011. "The Congressional Research Service and the American Legislative Process." Technical report, Congressional Research Service.

Bryce, Lord. 1995 [1888]. *The American Commonwealth: Volume I*. Indianapolis: Liberty Fund.

Butler, Henry N. 1985. "Nineteenth-Century Jurisdictional Competition in the Granting of Corporate Privileges." *Journal of Legal Studies* 14 (January):129–66.

Byrd, Robert C. 1989. *The Senate, 1789-1989: Addresses on the History of the United States Senate*. Washington, DC: US Government Printing Office.

Cain, Bruce E., and Lee Drutman. 2014. "Congressional Staff and the Revolving Door: The Impact of Regulatory Change." *Election Law Journal: Rules, Politics, and Policy* 13(1):27–44.

Calabresi, Steven G., and Christopher S Yoo. 2008. *The Unitary Executive: Presidential Power from Washington to Bush*. New Haven, CT: Yale University Press.

Caldwell, Lynton K. 1947. "Strengthening State Legislatures." *American Political Science Review* 41(2):281–89.

Calvert, Randall L., Mathew D. McCubbins, and Barry R. Weingast. 1989. "A Theory of Political Control and Agency Discretion." *American Journal of Political Science* 33(3):588–611.

Cameron, Charles M. 2000. *Veto Bargaining: Presidents and the Politics of Negative Power*. New York: Cambridge University Press.

Canes-Wrone, Brandice. 2010. *Who Leads Whom? Presidents, Policy, and the Public*. Chicago: University of Chicago Press.

Canes-Wrone, Brandice, William G. Howell, and David E. Lewis. 2008. "Toward a Broader Understanding of Presidential Power: A Reevaluation of the Two Presidencies Thesis." *Journal of Politics* 70(1):1–16.

Carey, John M., Richard G. Niemi, and Lynda W. Powell. 1998. "The Effects of Term Limits on State Legislatures." *Legislative Studies Quarterly* 23(2):271–300.

Carey, John M., Richard G. Niemi, Lynda W. Powell, and Gary F. Moncrief. 2006. "The Effects of Term Limits on State Legislatures: A New Survey of the 50 States." *Legislative Studies Quarterly* 31(1):105–34.

Carson, Nancy. 1992. "Process, Prescience, and Pragmatism: The Office of Technology Assessment." In *Organizations for Policy Analysis: Helping Government Think*, ed. Carol H. Weiss 236–51. Newbury Park, CA: Sage.

CBO. 2016. "An Introduction to the Congressional Budget Office." Technical report, Congressional Budget Office.

Census, US 1975. *Historical Statistics of the United States: Colonial Times to 1970*. Washington, DC: US Department of Commerce.

Chiou, Fang-Yi, and Lawrence S. Rothenberg. 2014. "The Elusive Search for Presidential Power." *American Journal of Political Science* 58(3):653–68.

Chiou, Fang-Yi, and Lawrence S. Rothenberg. 2017. *The Enigma of Presidential Power: Parties, Policies, and Strategic Uses of Unilateral Action*. New York: Cambridge University Press.

Christenson, Dino P., and Douglas L. Kriner. 2017. "Constitutional Qualms or Politics as Usual? The Factors Shaping Public Support for Unilateral Action." *American Journal of Political Science* 61(2):335–49.

Christenson, Dino P., and Douglas L. Kriner. 2019. "Does Public Opinion Constrain Presidential Unilateralism?" *American Political Science Review* 113(4):1071–77.

Christenson, Dino P., and Douglas L. Kriner. 2020. *The Myth of the Imperial Presidency: How Public Opinion Checks the Unilateral Executive*. Chicago: University of Chicago Press.

Clarke, Andrew J. 2020. "Congressional Capacity and the Abolition of Legislative Service Organizations." *Journal of Public Policy* 40(2):1–22.

Clucas, Richard A. 2019. "Introduction: The Enduring Relevance of the State Assemblies." *PS: Political Science & Politics* 52(3):413–16.

Cockerham, Alexandra G., and Robert E. Crew Jr. 2017. "Factors Affecting Governors' Decisions to Issue Executive Orders." *State and Local Government Review* 49(1):6–14.

Cohen, Jeffrey E. 2012. *The President's Legislative Policy Agenda, 1789–2002*. New York: Cambridge University Press.

Conant, James K. 1988. "In the Shadow of Wilson and Brownlow: Executive Branch Reorganization in the States, 1965 to 1987." *Public Administration Review* 48(5):892–902.

Congressional Management Foundation. 2017. "State of the Congress: Staff Perspectives on Institutional Capacity in the House and Senate." http://www.congressfoundation.org /storage/documents/CMF_Pubs/cmf-state-of-the-congress.pdf.

Congressional Quarterly. 2012. *How Congress Works*. Washington, DC: Congressional Quarterly.

Cooper, Joseph. 2017. "The Balance of Power between the Congress and the President: Issues and Dilemmas." In *Congress Reconsidered*, ed. Lawrence C. Dodd and Bruce I. Oppenheimer, 357–98. Washington, DC: CQ.

Cooper, Phillip J. 2002. *By Order of the President: The Use and Abuse of Executive Direct Action*. Lawrence: University Press of Kansas.

Cox, Gary W., and Mathew D. McCubbins. 2005. *Setting the Agenda: Responsible Party Government in the US House of Representatives*. New York: Cambridge University Press.

Cox, Gary W., and Scott Morgenstern. 2001. "Latin America's Reactive Assemblies and Proactive Presidents." *Comparative Politics* 33(2):171–89.

Crook, T. Russell, James G. Combs, David J. Ketchen, Samuel Y. Todd, and David J. Woehr. 2011. "Does Human Capital Matter? A Meta-Analysis of the Relationship Between Human Capital and Firm Performance." *Journal of Applied Psychology* 96(3):443–56.

Curry, James M. 2015. *Legislating in the Dark: Information and Power in the House of Representatives*. Chicago: University of Chicago Press.

Cushman, Robert E. 1941. *The Independent Regulatory Commissions*. New York: Oxford University Press.

de Figueiredo, Rui J. P., Jr. 2003. "Budget Institutions and Political Insulation: Why States Adopt the Item Veto." *Journal of Public Economics* 87(12):2677–2701.

Deering, Christopher J., and Forrest Maltzman. 1999. "The Politics of Executive Orders: Legislative Constraints on Presidential Power." *Political Research Quarterly* 52(4): 767–83.

Derthick, Martha, and Paul J. Quirk. 1985. *The Politics of Deregulation*. Washington, DC: Brookings Institution.

Dickinson, Matthew J., and Jesse Gubb. 2016. "The Limits to Power without Persuasion." *Presidential Studies Quarterly* 46(1):48–72.

Dinan, John J. 2006. *The American State Constitutional Tradition*. Lawrence: University Press of Kansas.

Dodd, Lawrence C., and Richard L. Schott. 1979. *Congress and the Administrative State*. New York: John Wiley & Son.

Dodds, Graham G. 2013. *Take Up Your Pen: Unilateral Presidential Directives in American Politics*. Philadelphia: University of Pennsylvania Press.

Drutman, Lee, and Steven Teles. 2015. "A New Agenda for Political Reform." *Washington Monthly* March–May 2015, https://washingtonmonthly.com/magazine/maraprmay-2015/a-new-agenda-for-political-reform/.

Eisner, Marc Allen. 2000. *Regulatory Politics in Transition*. Baltimore: Johns Hopkins University Press.

Engstrom, Erik J., and Samuel Kernell. 2004. "Serving Competing Principals: The Budget Estimates of OMB and CBO in an Era of Divided Government." *Presidential Studies Quarterly* 29(4):820–30.

Epstein, David, and Sharyn O'Halloran. 1999. *Delegating Powers: A Transaction Cost Politics Approach to Policy Making under Separate Powers*. New York: Cambridge University Press.

Eskridge, William N, and John Ferejohn. 1992. "Making the Deal Stick: Enforcing the Original Constitutional Structure of Lawmaking in the Modern Regulatory State." *Journal of Law, Economics & Organization* 8(1):165–89.

Esterling, Kevin M. 2007. "Buying Expertise: Campaign Contributions and Attention to Policy Analysis in Congressional Committees." *American Political Science Review* 101(1):93–109.

Fairlie, John A. 1917. "The Veto Power of State Governors." *American Political Science Review* 11(3):473–93.

Feinstein, Brian D. 2017. "Congress in the Administrative State." Coase-Sandor Working Paper Series in Law and Economics 838.

Fenno, Richard F. 1966. *The Power of the Purse: Appropriations Politics in Congress*. New York: Little, Brown.

Ferejohn, John A., and Barry R Weingast. 1992. "A Positive Theory of Statutory Interpretation." *International Review of Law and Economics* 12(2):263–79.

Ferejohn, John, and Charles Shipan. 1990. "Congressional Influence on Bureaucracy." *Journal of Law, Economics & Organization* 6:1–20.

Ferguson, Margaret R., and Cynthia J Bowling. 2008. "Executive Orders and Administrative Control." *Public Administration Review* 68(s1):S20–S28.

Fine, Jeffrey A., and Adam L. Warber. 2012. "Circumventing Adversity: Executive Orders and Divided Government." *Presidential Studies Quarterly* 42(2):256–74.

Fiorina, Morris P. 1977. *Congress: Keystone of the Washington Establishment*. New Haven, CT: Yale University Press.

Fisher, Louis. 2005. Legislative Vetoes After Chadha (RS22132). Technical report, Congressional Research Service.

Fowler, Linda L. 2015. *Watchdogs on the Hill: The Decline of Conressional Oversight of U.S. Foreign Relations*. Princeton, NJ: Princeton University Press.

Fox, Harrison W., and Susan Webb Hammond. 1977. *Congressional Staffs: The Invisible Force in American Lawmaking*. New York: Free Press.

Gailmard, Sean, and John W., Patty. 2012. "Formal Models of Bureaucracy." *Annual Review of Political Science* 15:353–77.

Gailmard, Sean, and John W. Patty. 2013. *Learning While Governing: Expertise and Accountability in the Executive Branch*. Chicago: University of Chicago Press.

Galloway, George B. 1951. "Operation of the Legislative Reorganization Act of 1946." *American Political Science Review* 45(1):41–68.

Galloway, George B. 1955. *The Legislative Process in Congress*. New York: Thomas Y. Crowell.

Ginieczki, M. Boyce. 2010. "Are Appropriators Actually Authorizers in Sheep's Clothing? A Case Study of the Policymaking Role of the House and Senate Appropriations Subcommittees on Labor, Health and Human Services, Education, and Related Agencies." PhD diss., Virginia Polytechnic Institute and State University.

Ginsberg, Wendy, and Michael Greene. 2016. "Federal Inspectors General: History, Characteristics, and Recent Congressional Actions." Technical report, Congressional Research Service.

Gleiber, Dennis W., and Steven A. Shull. 1992. "Presidential Influence in the Policymaking Process." *Western Political Quarterly* 45(2):441–67.

Graves, W. Brooke. 1947. "Legislative Reference Service for the Congress of the United States." *American Political Science Review* 41(2):289–93.

Graves, Zach, and Kevin Kosar. 2018. "Bring in the Nerds: Reviving the Office of Technology Assessment." Technical Report 128, R Street Institute, Washington, DC.

Hall, Peter A., and Rosemary C. R. Taylor. 1996. "Political Science and the Three New Institutionalisms." *Political Studies* 44(5):936–57.

Hamilton, Alexander, James Madison, and John Jay. 2009. *The Federalist Papers*. New Haven, CT: Yale University Press.

Hanson, Peter. 2014. *Too Weak to Govern: Majority Party Power and Appropriations in the US Senate*. New York: Cambridge University Press.

Harris, Richard A., and Sidney M. Milkis. 1989. *The Politics of Regulatory Change: A Tale of Two Agencies*. Oxford: Oxford University Press.

Healy, Gene. 2008. *The Cult of the Presidency: America's Dangerous Devotion to Executive Power*. Washington, DC: Cato Institute.

Heard, Alexander. 1983. *State Legislatures in American Politics*. New York: American Assembly.

Howell, William G. 2003. *Power without Persuasion: The Politics of Direct Presidential Action*. Princeton, NJ: Princeton University Press.

Howell, William G. 2005. "Unilateral Powers: A Brief Overview." *Presidential Studies Quarterly* 35(3):417–39.

Howell, William G., and Jon C. Pevehouse. 2007. *While Dangers Gather: Congressional Checks on Presidential War Powers*. Princeton, NJ: Princeton University Press.

Howell, William G., and Saul P. Jackman. 2013. "Interbranch Negotiations over Policies with Multiple Outcomes." *American Journal of Political Science* 57(4):956–70.

Howell, William G., Saul P. Jackman, and Jon C. Rogowski. 2013. *The Wartime President: Executive Influence and the Nationalizing Politics of Threat*. Chicago: University of Chicago Press.

Howell, William, Scott Adler, Charles Cameron, and Charles Riemann. 2000. "Divided Government and the Legislative Productivity of Congress, 1945–94." *Legislative Studies Quarterly* 25(2):285–312.

Huber, John D., and Charles R. Shipan. 2002. *Deliberate Discretion? The Institutional Foundations of Bureaucratic Autonomy*. New York, New York: Cambridge University Press.

Huber, John D., Charles R. Shipan, and Madelaine Pfahler. 2001. "Legislatures and Statutory Control of Bureaucracy." *American Journal of Political Science* 45(2):330–345.

Hyneman, Charles S. 1938. "Tenure and Turnover of Legislative Personnel." *Annals of the American Academy of Political and Social Science* 195(1):21–31.

Jacob, Herbert. 1966. "Dimensions of State Politics." In *State Legislatures in American Politics*, ed. Alexander Heard. Englewood Cliffs, N.J: Prentice-Hall.

Johnson, Ronald N., and Gary D. Libecap. 1994. *The Federal Civil Service and the Problem of Bureaucracy: The Economics and Politics of Institutional Change*. Chicago: University of Chicago Press.

Jones, Bryan D., Sean M. Theriault, and Michelle Whyman. 2019. *The Great Broadening: How the Vast Expansion of the Policymaking Agenda Transformed American Politics*. Chicago: University of Chicago Press.

Jones, David R. 2001. *Political Parties and Policy Gridlock in American Government*. Lewiston, NY: Edwin Mellen.

Joyce, Philip G. 2011. *Honest Numbers: Honest Numbers, Power, and Policymaking*. Washington, DC: Georgetown University Press.

Kammerer, Gladys M. 1951. "The Record of Congress in Staffing." *American Political Science Review* 45(4):1126–36.

Keefe, William J. 1966. "The Functions and Powers of the State Legislatures." In *State Legislatures in American Politics*, ed. Alexander Heard, 37–69. Englewood Cliffs, NJ: Prentice-Hall.

Kennedy, Joshua B. 2015. "Do This! Do That! and Nothing Will Happen: Executive Orders and Bureaucratic Responsiveness." *American Politics Research* 43(1):59–82.

Kerwin, Cornelius M., and Scott R. Furlong. 2011. *Rulemaking: How Government Agencies Write Law and Make Policy*. Washington, DC: CQ.

Kiewiet, D. Roderick, and Mathew D. McCubbins. 1991. *The Logic of Delegation: Congressional Parties and the Appropriations Process*. Chicago: University of Chicago Press.

King, James D., and Jeffrey E. Cohen. 2005. "What Determines a Governor's Popularity?" *State Politics & Policy Quarterly* 5(3):225–47.

Kirkland, Patricia A., and Justin H. Phillips. 2018. "Is Divided Government a Cause of Legislative Delay?" *Quarterly Journal of Political Science* 13(2):173–206.

Korn, Jessica. 1996. *The Power of Separation*. Princeton, NJ: Princeton University Press.

Kousser, Thad. 2005. *Term Limits and the Dismantling of State Legislative Professionalism*. New York: Cambridge University Press.

Kousser, Thad, and Justin H. Phillips. 2012. *The Power of American Governors: Winning on Budgets and Losing on Policy*. New York: Cambridge University Press.

Krause, George A. 2007. "Separated Powers and Institutional Growth in the Presidential and Congressional Branches: Distinguishing between Short-Run and Long-Run Dynamics." *Political Research Quarterly* 55(1):27–57.

Krause, George A., and David B. Cohen. 1997. "Presidential Use of Executive Orders, 1953–1994." *American Politics Quarterly* 25(4):458–81.

Krause, George A., and Jeffrey E. Cohen. 2000. "Opportunity, Constraints, and the Development of the Institutional Presidency: The Issuance of Executive Orders, 1939–96." *Journal of Politics* 62(1):88–114.

Krehbiel, Keith. 1998. *Pivotal Politics: A Theory of US Lawmaking*. Chicago: University of Chicago Press.

Kriner, Douglas L., and Eric Schickler. 2014. "Investigating the President: Committee Probes and Presidential Approval, 1953–2006." *Journal of Politics* 76(2):521–34.

Kriner, Douglas L., and Eric Schickler. 2016. *Investigating the President: Congressional Checks on Presidential Power*. Princeton, NJ: Princeton University Press.

Kriner, Douglas L., and Eric Schickler. 2018. "The Resilience of Separation of Powers? Congress and the Russia Investigation." *Presidential Studies Quarterly* 48(3):436–55.

Kriner, Douglas, and Liam Schwartz. 2008. "Divided Government and Congressional Investigations." *Legislative Studies Quarterly* 33(2):295–321.

Krupnikov, Yanna, and Charles R. Shipan. 2012. "Measuring Gubernatorial Budgetary Power: A New Approach." *State Politics & Policy Quarterly* 12(4):438–55.

Kunkle, Gregory C. 1995. "New Challenge or the Past Revisited? The Office of Technology Assessment in Historical Context." *Technology in Society* 17(2):175–96.

LaFollette, Robert M., Jr. 1943. "A Senator Looks at Congress." *Atlantic Monthly* 172:91–97.

Lattimer, John N. 1985. "The Changing Role of Legislative Staff in the American State Legislatures." *State and Local Government Review* 17(3):244–50.

Lax, Jeffrey R., and Justin H. Phillips. 2009. "Gay Rights in the States: Public Opinion and Policy Responsiveness." *American Political Science Review* 103(3):367–86.

Lee, Mordecai. 2006. *Institutionalizing Congress and the President: The U.S. Bureau of Efficiency, 1916–1933*. College Station: Texas A&M University Press.

Levinson, Daryl J., and Richard H. Pildes. 2006. "Separation of Parties, Not Powers." *Harvard Law Review* 119(1):1–73.

Lewis, David. 2004. *Presidents and the Politics of Agency Design: Political Insulation in the United States Government Bureaucracy, 1946–1997.* Palo Alto, CA: Stanford University Press.

Lockard, Duane. 1966. "The State Legislator." In *State Legislatures in American Politics,* ed. Alexander Heard, 98–125. Englewood Cliffs, NJ: Prentice-Hall.

Lowande, Kenneth S. 2014. "After the Orders: Presidential Memoranda and Unilateral Action." *Presidential Studies Quarterly* 44(4):724–41.

Lowande, Kenneth. 2018. "Who Policies the Administrative State?" *American Political Science Review* 112(4):874–90.

Lowande, Kenneth, and Justin Peck. 2016. "Congressional Investigations and the Electoral Connection." *Journal of Law, Economics, and Organization* 33(1):1–27.

Lowi, Theodore J. 1969. *The End of Liberalism: The Second Republic of the United States.* New York: W. W. Norton.

MacDonald, Jason A., and Robert J McGrath. 2016. "Retrospective Congressional Oversight and the Dynamics of Legislative Influence over the Bureaucracy." *Legislative Studies Quarterly* 41(4):899–934.

Maestas, Cherie. 2003. "The Incentive to Listen: Progressive Ambition, Resources, and Opinion Monitoring Among State Legislators." *Journal of Politics* 65(2):439–56.

Marshall, Bryan W., and Richard L. Pacelle. 2005. "Revisiting the Two Presidencies: The Strategic Use of Executive Orders." *American Politics Research* 33(1):81–105.

Martin, Lisa L. 2000. *Democratic Commitments: Legislatures and International Cooperation.* Princeton, NJ: Princeton University Press.

Mashaw, Jerry L. 2012. *Creating the Administrative Constitution: The Lost One Hundred Years of American Administrative Law.* New Haven, CT: Yale University Press.

Mayer, Kenneth R. 1999. "Executive Orders and Presidential Power." *Journal of Politics* 61(2):445–66.

Mayer, Kenneth R. 2002. *With the Stroke of a Pen: Executive Orders and Presidential Power.* Princeton, NJ: Princeton University Press.

Mayer, Kenneth R. 2010. "Going Alone: The Presidential Power of Unilateral Action." In *The Oxford Handbook of the American Presidency,* ed. George C. Edwards III, and William G. Howell, 427–54. New York: Oxford University Press.

Mayer, Kenneth R., and Kevin Price. 2002. "Unilateral Presidential Powers: Significant Executive Orders, 1949–99." *Presidential Studies Quarterly* 32(2):367–386.

Mayhew, David R. 1974. *Congress: The Electoral Connection.* New Haven, CT: Yale University Press.

Mayhew, David R. 1991. *Divided We Govern.* New Haven, CT: Yale University.

McCarty, Nolan. 2004. "The Appointments Dilemma." *American Journal of Political Science* 48(3):413–28.

McCarty, Nolan. 2015. "The Decline of Regular Order in Appropriations." In *Congress and Policymaking in the 21st Century,* ed. Eric Patashnik and Jeffrey Jenkins 162–86. New York: Cambridge University Press.

McCrain, Joshua. 2020. "Legislative Resources, Staff, and Inequality in Representation." Unpublished manuscript.

McCubbins, Mathew D., Roger G. Noll, and Barry R. Weingast. 1987. "Administrative Procedures as Instruments of Political Control." *Journal of Law, Economics, & Organization* 3(2):243–77.

McCubbins, Mathew D., Roger G. Noll, and Barry R. Weingast. 1999. "The Political Origins of the Administrative Procedure Act." *Journal of Law, Economics, & Organization* 15(1): 180–217.

McCubbins, Mathew D., and Thomas Schwartz. 1984. "Congressional Oversight Overlooked: Police Patrols versus Fire Alarms." *American Journal of Political Science* 28(1): 165–79.

McGrath, Robert J. 2013. "Congressional Oversight Hearings and Policy Control." *Legislative Studies Quarterly* 38(3):349–76.

McGrath, Robert J., Jon C. Rogowski, and Josh M. Ryan. 2015. "Gubernatorial Veto Powers and the Size of Legislative Coalitions." *Legislative Studies Quarterly* 40(4):571–98.

Mezey, Michael L. 1979. *Comparative Legislatures*. Durham, NC: Duke University Press.

Miller, Gary J. 2005. "The Political Evolution of Principal-Agent Models." *Annual Review of Political Science* 8:203–25.

Miller, James Nathan. 1965. "Hamstrung Legislatures." *National Civic Review* 54(4):178–219.

Mills, Russell W., and Jennifer L. Selin. 2017. "Don't Sweat the Details! Enhancing Congressional Committee Expertise Through the Use of Detailees." *Legislative Studies Quarterly* 42(4):611–36.

Moe, Terry M. 1984. "The New Economics of Organization." *American Journal of Political Science* 28(4):739–77.

Moe, Terry M. 1985a. "Control and Feedback in Economic Regulation: The Case of the NLRB." *American Political Science Review* 79(4):1094–116.

Moe, Terry M. 1985b. "The Politicized Presidency." In *The New Direction in American Politics*, ed. John E. Chubb and Paul E. Peterson 235–71. Washington, DC: Brookings Institution.

Moe, Terry M., and William G. Howell. 1999. "The Presidential Power of Unilateral Action." *Journal of Law, Economics, and Organization* 15(1):132–79.

Moncrief, Gary F. 2019. "State Legislatures as Institutions." *PS: Political Science & Politics* 52(3):422–25.

Moncrief, Gary F., Richard G. Niemi, and Lynda W. Powell. 2004. "Time, Term Limits, and Turnover: Trends in Membership Stability in U.S. State Legislatures." *Legislative Studies Quarterly* 29(3):357–81.

Mooney, Chris. 2005. "Requiem for an Office." *Bulletin of the Atomic Scientists* (September–October):41–49.

Moore, Colin D. 2107. *American Imperialism and the State, 1893–1921*. New York: Cambridge University Press.

Nader, Ralph. 1965. *Unsafe at Any Speed: The Designed-In Dangers of the American Automobile*. New York, NY: Grossman.

Naughton, James R. 1998. "The Origin and Implementation of the Inspector General Act." *Government Accountants Journal* 47(3):12–19.

Neustadt, Richard. 1990 [1960]. *Presidential Power and the Modern Presidents: The Politics of Leadership from Roosevelt to Reagan*. New York: Free Press.

Novak, William J. 2008. "A State of Legislatures." *Polity* 40(3):340–47.

Parker, David C. W., and Matthew Dull. 2009. "Divided We Quarrel: The Politics of Congressional Investigations, 1947–2004." *Legislative Studies Quarterly* 34(3):319–45.

Perry, James L., and Lois Recascino Wise. 1990. "The Motivational Bases of Public Service." *Public Administration Review* 50(3):367–73.

Polsby, Nelson W. 1975. "Legislatures." In *Handbook of Political Science: Governmental Institutions and Processes*, ed. Fred I. Greenstein and Nelson W. Polsby 5:257–319. Reading, MA: Addison-Wesley.

Posner, Eric A., and Adrian Vermeule. 2010. *The Executive Unbound: After the Madisonian Republic*. New York: Oxford University Press.

Potter, Rachel Augustine, Andrew Rudalevige, Sharece Thrower, and Adam L. Warber. 2019. "Continuity Trumps Change: The First Year of Trump's Administrative Presidency." *PS: Political Science & Politics* 52(4):613–19.

Potter, Rachel Augustine, and Charles R. Shipan. 2019. "Agency Rulemaking in a Separation of Powers System." *Journal of Public Policy* 39(1): 89–113.

Presidential Task Force on Congressional Reform. 2020. *Congressional Reform Task Force Report*. Washington, DC: American Political Science Association.

Putnam, Herbert. 1915. "Legislative Reference for Congress." *American Political Science Review* 9(3):542–49.

Ray, David. 1974. "Membership Stability in Three State Legislatures: 1893–1969." *American Political Science Review* 68(1):106–12.

Reeves, Andrew, and Jon C. Rogowski. 2015. "Unilateral Powers, Public Opinion, and the Presidency." *Journal of Politics* 78(1):137–51.

Reeves, Andrew, and Jon C. Rogowski. 2018. "The Public Costs of Unilateral Action." *American Journal of Political Science* 62(2):424–40.

Reynolds, Molly E., and Philip A. Wallach. 2020. "Does the Executive Branch Control the Power of the Purse?" Technical report, American Enterprise Institute Washington, DC.

Ritchie, Melinda N. 2018. "Back-Channel Representation: A Study of the Strategic Communication of Senators with the US Department of Labor." *Journal of Politics* 80(1):240–253.

Rivers, Douglas, and Nancy L. Rose. 1985. "Passing the President's Program: Public Opinion and Presidential Influence in Congress." *American Journal of Political Science* 29(2):183–96.

Robinson, W. H. 1992. "The Congressional Research Service: Policy Consultant, Think Tank, and Information Factory." In *Organizations for Policy Analysis: Helping Government Think*, ed. Carol H. Weiss, 181–200. Newbury Park, CA: Sage.

Rockoff, Hugh. 2004. "Until It's Over, Over There: The U.S. Economy in World War I." NBER Working Paper 10580.

Rogers, Steven. 2016. "National Forces in State Legislative Elections." *Annals of the American Academy of Political and Social Science* 667(1):207–25.

Rosenthal, Alan. 1996. "State Legislative Development: Observations from Three Perspectives." *Legislative Studies Quarterly* 21(2):169–98.

Rothstein, Samuel. 1990. "The Origins of Legislative Reference Services in the United States." *Legislative Studies Quarterly* 15(3):401–11.

Rottinghaus, Brandon, and Adam L. Warber. 2015. "Unilateral Orders as Constituency Outreach: Executive Orders, Proclamations, and the Public Presidency." *Presidential Studies Quarterly* 45(2):289–309.

Rudalevige, Andrew. 2008. *The New Imperial Presidency: Renewing Presidential Power after Watergate*. Ann Arbor: University of Michigan Press.

Rudalevige, Andrew. 2012. "The Contemporary Presidency: Executive Orders and Presidential Unilateralism." *Presidential Studies Quarterly* 42(1):138–60.

Rudalevige, Andrew. 2018. "Beyond Structure and Process: The Early Institutionalization of Regulatory Review." *Journal of Policy History* 30(4):577–608.

Sadowski, Jathan. 2015. "Office of Technology Assessment: History, Implementation, and Participatory Critique." *Technology in Society* 42:9–20.

Saint-Martin, Denis. 2014. "Gradual Institutional Change in Congressional Ethics: Endogenous Pressures toward Third-Party Enforcement." *Studies in American Political Development* 28(1):161–74.

Savage, Charlie. 2012. "Shift on Executive Power Lets Obama Bypass Rivals." *New York Times*, April 23, 2012, A1.

Schick, Allen. 1975. "The Congressional Budget Act of 1974: Legislative History and Analysis." Technical report no.75–94, Congressional Research Service.

Schick, Allen. 1983. "Politics through Law: Congressional Limitations on Executive Discretion." In *Both Ends of the Avenue: The President, the Executive Branch, and Congress in the 1980s*, ed. Anthony King 154–84. Washington, DC: American Enterprise Institute.

Schick, Allen. 2008. *The Federal Budget: Politics, Policy, Process*. Washington, DC: Brookings Institution.

Schickler, Eric. 2001. *Disjointed Pluralism: Institutional Innovation and the Development of the U.S. Congress*. Princeton, NJ: Princeton University Press.

Schlesinger, Arthur M. 1973. *The Imperial Presidency*. New York: Houghton Mifflin.

Schwartz, Alan. 1999. "Comment on 'The Political Origins of the Administrative Procedure Act,' by McNollgast." *Journal of Law, Economics, and Organization* 15(1):218–21.

Sellers, Mitchell Daniel. 2017. "Gubernatorial Use of Executive Orders: Unilateral Action and Policy Adoption." *Journal of Public Policy* 37(3):315–39.

Shane, Peter M. 2009. *Madison's Nightmare: How Executive Power Threatens American Democracy*. Chicago: University of Chicago Press.

Shepherd, George B. 1996. "Fierce Compromise: The Administrative Procedure Act Emerges from New Deal Politics." *Northwestern University Law Review* 90(4):1557–683.

Shin, Kwang S., and John S. Jackson III. 1979. "Membership Turnover in U.S. State Legislatures: 1931–1976." *Legislative Studies Quarterly* 4(1):95–104.

Shull, Steven A. 2006. *Policy by Other Means: Alternative Adoption by Presidents*. College Station: Texas A&M University Press.

Sinclair, Barbara L. 2016. *Unorthodox Legislating: New Legislative Process in the U.S. Congress*. 5th ed. Washington, DC: CQ.

Sklar, Martin J. 1988. *The Corporate Reconstruction of American Capitalism, 1890–1916: The Market, the Law, and Politics*. New York: Cambridge University Press.

Skocpol, Theda. 1992. *Protecting Soldiers and Mothers: The Political Origins of Social Policy in the United States*. Cambridge, MA: Belknap Press of Harvard University Press.

Skowronek, Stephen. 1982. *Building a New American State: The Expansion of National Administrative Capacities, 1877–1920*. New York: Cambridge University Press.

Squire, Peverill. 1993. "Professionalization and Public Opinion of State Legislatures." *Journal of Politics* 55(2):479–91.

Squire, Peverill. 2007. "Measuring State Legislative Professionalism: The Squire Index Revisited." *State Politics & Policy Quarterly* 7(2):211–27.

Squire, Peverill. 2012. *The Evolution of American Legislatures: Colonies, Territories, and States, 1619–2009.* Ann Arbor: University of Michigan Press.

Stanton, Nile. 1974. "History and Practice of Executive Impoundment of Appropriated Funds." *Nebraska Law Review* 53(1):1–30.

Stathis, John W. 2014. *Landmark Legislation, 1774–2012: Major U.S. Acts and Treaties.* Washington, DC: CQ.

Strand, Mark, and Timothy Lang. 2019. "Lessons Learned from the 1993 Joint Committee on the Organization of Congress." Technical report, Congressional Institute.

Sundquist, James L. 1981. *The Decline and Resurgence of Congress.* Washington, DC: Brookings Institution.

Teaford, Jon C. 2002. *The Rise of the States: American State Government.* Baltimore: Johns Hopkins University Press.

Thrower, Sharece. 2017. "The President, the Court, and Policy Implementation." *Presidential Studies Quarterly* 47(1):122–45.

Ting, Michael M. 2001. "The 'Power of the Purse' and Its Implications for Bureaucratic Policy-Making." *Public Choice* 106(3–4):243–74.

Trask, Roger R. 2001. *Defender of the Public Interest: The General Accounting Office, 1921–1966.* Washington, DC: Government Reprints.

Wahlke, John C. 1966. "Organization and Procedure." In *State Legislatures in American Politics,* 126–53. Englewood Cliffs, NJ: Prentice-Hall.

Wallace, Jim. 2012. *A History of the West Virginia Capitol: The House of State.* Stroud: History Press.

Warber, Adam L. 2006. *Executive Orders and the Modern Presidency: Legislating from the Oval Office.* Boulder, CO: Lynne Rienner.

Watson, Richard A. 1987. "Origins and Early Development of the Veto Power." *Presidential Studies Quarterly* 17(2):401–12.

Weingast, Barry R., and Mark J. Moran. 1983. "Bureaucratic Discretion or Congressional Control? Regulatory Policymaking by the Federal Trade Commission." *Journal of Political Economy* 91(5):765–800.

White, Leonard D. 1948. *The Federalists: A Study in Administrative History.* Westport, CT: Greenwood.

White, Richard. 2003. "Information, Markets, and Corruption: Transcontinental Railroads in the Gilded Age." *Journal of American History* 90(1):19–43.

Wildavsky, Aaron. 1969. "The Two Presidencies." *Trans-Action* 4:7–14.

Williams, Robert F. 1989. "The State Constitutions of the Founding Decade: Pennsylvania's Radical 1776 Constitution and Its Influences on American Constitutionalism." *Temple Law Review* 62:541–85.

Wilmerding, Lucius. 1943. *The Spending Power: A History of the Efforts of Congress to Control Expenditures.* New Haven, CT: Yale University Press.

Wolfensberger, Donald R. 2013. "A Brief History of Congressional Reform Efforts." Technical report, Wilson Center.

Wood, Gordon S. 1993. "State Constitution-Making in the American Revolution." *Rutgers Law Journal* 24(4):911–26.

Woods, Neal D. 2004. "Political Influence on Agency Rule Making: Examining the Effects of Legislative and Gubernatorial Rule Review Powers." *State and Local Government Review* 36(3):174–85.

Yackee, David Webb, and Susan Webb Yackee. 2009. "Divided Government and US Federal Rulemaking." *Regulation and Governance* 3(2):128–44.

Young, Laura. 2013. "Unilateral Presidential Policy Making and the Impact of Crises." *Presidential Studies Quarterly* 43(2):328–52.

Zeller, Belle. 1954. *American State Legislatures: Report.* Springfield, OH: Crowell.

INDEX

Page numbers in italics refer to illustrations.

Princeton Studies in American Politics

Historical, International, and Comparative Perspectives

Suzanne Mettler, Eric Schickler, and Theda Skocpol, Series Editors
Ira Katznelson, Martin Shefter, Founding Series Editors (Emeritus)

A NOTE ON THE TYPE

This book has been composed in Arno, an Old-style serif typeface in the
classic Venetian tradition, designed by Robert Slimbach at Adobe.

GPSR Authorized Representative: Easy Access System Europe - Mustamäe tee
50, 10621 Tallinn, Estonia, gpsr.requests@easproject.com

www.ingramcontent.com/pod-product-compliance
Lightning Source LLC
Chambersburg PA
CBHW031126270326
41929CB00011B/1519